LOOMING BLACK
SHADOWS

SAWAD HADI

LOOMING BLACK
SHADOWS

THE RISE OF TERRORIST STATES AND
THE NEW GENERATION AL-QAEDA

PARTRIDGE

To order additional copies of this book, contact
Partridge India
000 800 10062 62
orders.india@partridgepublishing.com

www.partridgepublishing.com/india

CONTENTS

Dedicated to

my parents, who gave me strength and opportunity to be just, open, and critical

all those struggling hard to come out of terrorism after they fall prey to its traps

all parents desperately trying not to make their children extremists.

TIMELINE—A HISTORICAL BRIEF OF IDEOLOGY AND EVENTS OF TERRORISM

June 1967—Arab–Israeli War. The shameful military defeat for the combined Arab armies under Egypt, Jordan, and Syria with support from a host of Muslim nations against Israel cast a long-lasting shadow on the value of the popular Arab nationalist ideas, which later paved the way for Islamization of Muslims in Arab lands.

1 April 1979—Iranian Revolution. Successful removal of long-reigning Pahlavi dynasty under Mohammad Reza Shah Pahlavi, who was supported by the USA in February 1979. A mass popular movement followed by a national referendum on 1 April 1979 established the Islamic Republic of Iran under the Grand Ayatollah Ruhollah Khomeini. The Iranian Revolution was an inspiration for Islamists throughout the world and a role model for many Islamist groups trying to establish an Islamic state in their countries.

25 December 1979—the Soviet Union deployed its 40th Army into Afghanistan, attempting to suppress a growing Islamic rebellion in support of advisors it already had in Afghanistan to protect the ruling communist government. Though the Soviet army was deployed following a continued request from the ruling government, it was perceived as an invasion of Afghanistan, a Muslim country ruled by communist regime. Insurgency, followed by a prolonged war, started to fight against Soviet Union by a coalition of mujahideen fighters. It was backed by Pakistan and the CIA, which provided military training, arms, and money to fight against the Soviets in Afghanistan as part of the US covert operation code-named Operation Cyclone. Several other countries, including Saudi Arabia, United Kingdom, Egypt, China, and Iran played major role in the war against Russians.

1980—Tanzim al-Jihad, or Al-Jihad, split into two groups. The Cairo-based group became Egyptian Islamic Jihad (EIJ), and the Upper Egypt group formed al-G(J)ama'a al-Islamiyya, or Islamic Group. These groups had their origins in the Muslim Brotherhood and were deeply inspired by Hassan al-Banna. Both acted together on many occasions, and it was difficult to separate their activities. The spiritual leader of the Islamic group was Sheik Omar Abdel Rehman, who was placed in US custody in connection with the 1993 World Trade Center bombing.

1981—after finishing his career at King Abdul Aziz University in Jeddah, Osama Bin Laden reached Pakistan to see his mentor and a former faculty of his university, Abdulla Azzam, at Peshawar, Pakistan.

1983—Abdulla Azzam and Osama Bin Laden started Maktab al-Khadamat (MAK), meaning the Services Office to host, recruit, and train foreign jihadists reaching Pakistan for waging war in Afghanistan. MAK was the destination for most of Afghan Arab jihadists. It became the base and precursor of Al-Qaeda.

1983—following the June 1982 Israeli invasion of Lebanon, US marines reached Lebanon as a peacekeeping force, along with French troops. A suicide car bombing of the US embassy in Beirut, Lebanon, on 18 April 1983 killed sixty-three people. On 23 October 1983, the US marine barracks in Beirut was bombed by another suicide truck attack, killing 241 (220 marines and 21 service personnel) out of the 300 members living there. At the same time as the marine barracks was hit, another suicide bomber in a pickup truck bombed their barracks, killing fifty-eight French soldiers. Following these casualties, the US military departed Lebanon in February 1984. An unheard-of radical militant group, Islamic Jihad Organization, which is believed to be a front of Hizbullah, which was backed by Iran, claimed responsibility. This was the beginning of suicide attacks by Islamic militants, all initially carried out exclusively by Hizbullah. This became a major inspiration for Bin Laden and Al-Qaeda.

August 1988—Al-Qaeda was formed formally at a meeting at Peshawar, Pakistan, close to the border of Afghanistan. Osama bin Laden and Abdulla Azzam were founders with a host of members from Egyptian Islamic Jihad at the meetings in the wake of near-ending war between Afghan mujahideen and Soviet Union. The name and formation was a closely held secret.

February 1989—Soviet troops withdrew from Afghanistan following heavy casualties and increasing domestic and economic problems in USSR.

24 November 1989—Abdulla Azzam was assassinated in a mystery car bomb blast. Bin Laden became the top leader, and most of Azzam's followers joined the group of Bin Laden.

1990—Bin Laden returned to Saudi Arabia and was given a wide coverage as a Saudi jihad hero who had brought down a mighty superpower.

August 1990—Saddam Hussein's forces invaded Kuwait, put Saudi Arabia at risk of war, and was a threat to its monarchy. Bin Laden visited King Fahd and advised him not to invite non-Muslim assistance from the United States and others. His reason was once the US forces were given a chance to get based in the land of two holy mosques, Saudi Arabia, they would never leave. Instead he pledged his support and his legion. His offer was rejected, and Saudi invited US forces and went to war with Iraq. Bin Laden openly criticized the royal family.

1991—Egyptian Islamic Jihad broke its control with its mentor and imprisoned leader Abbud al-Zumar, and Ayman al-Zawahiri took control of its leadership. By this time, all its cadres were already exiled from their home country and set foot on many nations, mostly on Afghanistan and Sudan. They became a free transnational terrorist gang.

1992—due to his continued criticism of the country, Bin Laden was banished by Saudi Arabia and went to exile in Sudan.

29 December 1992—Al-Qaeda organized their first major terrorist attack at Movenpick Hotel and Goldmohur Hotel in Aden, Yemen, targeting US soldiers on the way to Somalia. No US soldiers were harmed as they were at another hotel. One Austrian tourist and a Yemeni staff were killed, seven more injured. It could have been dubbed as a failed attempt but gave confidence and strategic inputs to Al-Qaeda for future attacks. The killing of civilians was justified in a fatwa released by its ideologue.

26 February 1993, World Trade Center bombing—it killed six people and injured more than a thousand people. A truck loaded with about 600 kg explosives was detonated, intended to ground both towers of the twin tower. The destruction was not as massive as expected by its perpetrators, who had hoped for thousands of casualties. It was one of the first major Al-Qaeda attacks in the USA and was organized by Ramzi Yousef.

3–5 October 1993—the first battle of Mogadishu in Somalia between forces of the United States supported by UNOSOM II and Somali militiamen loyal to the self-proclaimed president Mohamed Farrah Aidid resulted in the death of nineteen US soldiers and injuries of seventy-three others. It was then the bloodiest US battle casualty after the Vietnam War. Al-Qaeda claimed they had been involved in the killing of American soldiers and they had provided training, weapons, and money to the militiamen.

8 August 1993—the first-ever suicide terrorist attack by any Sunni group was an assassination attempt on Hassan al-Alfi, Egyptian interior minister, by detonating a bomb-laden motorcycle to the minister's car, followed by firing with an automatic weapon at the busy heart of Cairo city close to Tahrir Square. Four persons were killed, and the minister was seriously injured. EIJ, or its closely related Al-J(G)ama'al-Islamiya, was believed to be behind the attack. Both groups followed similar ideology and had close tie-ups.

1994—following continued criticism of King Fahd, Saudi cancelled Laden's citizenship and forced his family to denounce ties with him. They stopped his seven million USD yearly family dividend.

19 November, 1995—a suicide bomb attack on the Egyptian embassy in Islamabad by EIJ, killing sixteen and injuring about sixty people. It was a prototype attack for many future attacks, as in the US embassy attacks in Africa. The attack was denounced by Bin Laden. But Zawahiri went ahead with the attack in Pakistan, in spite of Pakistan being the gateway to Afghanistan for Al-Qaeda members and one of their friendly countries where they had stayed for years and based their activities.

18 May 1996—Osama Bin Laden was forced to leave Sudan following widespread criticism from the USA and Arab countries for sponsoring terrorism. He went to Jalalabad, Afghanistan, from Sudan in a chartered flight and forged a close alliance with Mullah Mohammed Omar, the Taliban leader.

June 1996—a truck bombing at Khobar Towers barracks in Dhahran, Saudi Arabia, killed nineteen Americans.

August 1996—Bin Laden declared war against United States for its continued presence in Saudi Arabia, its support for Israel, and making Saudi Arabia 'an American colony'.

17 November 1997—Al-Qaeda funded the Luxor massacre, which killed sixty-two civilians, mostly international tourists. It shocked the world and outraged Egyptian public. Tourism industry was hit badly, which was the prime Egyptian industry and a source of foreign income. Government went for a heavy crackdown of Islamist groups in Egypt.

23 February 1998—Bin Laden and Ayman al-Zawahiri issued their first fatwa under the banner of World Islamic Front for Jihad Against Jews and Crusaders declaring the killing of Americans and their allies as the duty of every Muslim to liberate the Al-Aqsa Mosque (in Jerusalem) and the holy mosque (in Mecca) from their grip.

24 June 1998—an Al-Qaeda congress was organized by Bin Laden and Zawahiri.

7 August 1998—Al-Qaeda organized simultaneous truck bomb attacks in US embassies at Nairobi, Kenya, and Dar es Salaam, Tanzania, which killed more than 224 people and injured thousands. Most of them were local people. This placed Bin Laden on the Ten Most Wanted list of the US Federal Bureau of Investigation. Fazul Abdulla Mohammed, the alleged mastermind of the attack, was killed years later on 7 June 2011 by Somali forces following a routine security check in an unexpected counter-attack.

20 August, 1998—suspected Al-Qaeda bases in Sudan and Afghanistan were bombed by US forces in an operation code-named Operation Infinite Reach in retaliation for US embassy bombings in Africa. These attacks attracted worldwide condemnation against the USA, mainly from the Islamic world. The world was mostly unaware of Al-Qaeda and their activities at that time, and US actions were not convincing, especially the attack on the pharmaceutical plant in Sudan.

12 October 2000—bombing of the USS *Cole* in a port in Yemen by Al-Qaeda; seventeen US sailors were killed.

June 2001—Qaeda Al-Jihad was formed. Both groups were associates and acted together and sometimes independently. Egyptian Islamic Jihad merged with Al-Qaeda and formed an entity named Qaeda al-Jihad.

11 September 2001—World Trade Center attacks. Coordinated hijackings of four US commercial flights and hitting targets, including World Trade Center (WTC), caused the complete destruction of the twin towers of WTC and major damages on the Pentagon. It was done by Al-Qaeda trained hijackers under Khalid Sheik Muhammed and Osama Bin Laden. Including the nineteen hijackers, 2,996 people died and thousands were injured with an economic loss of $3 trillion. It became a game changer in world politics and for Taliban, Al-Qaeda, and USA.

7 October 2001—the American invasion of Afghanistan began for Taliban regime change and to capture or kill Al-Qaeda fighters, including Osama Bin Laden. US and British forces started aerial bombings targeting Taliban and al-Qaeda camps on October 7, followed by ground invasion. Taliban rule of Afghanistan ended on 9 December 2001.

12 October 2002—nightclub bombings in Kuta, Bali, Indonesia, killed 202, mostly Australian citizens. Al-Qaeda-affiliated Jemma Islamiyah, a Southeast Asian militant Islamist group indenting to establish an Islamic caliphate in the region, was behind the attack.

20 March 2003—US invasion of Iraq. The USA, under George Bush, started an invasion of Iraq to overthrow the regime of Saddam Hussein, who was alleged to be harbouring Al-Qaeda and weapons of mass destruction. In spite of complete invasion and capture of Saddam and many in his army, no nuclear or chemical weapons could be found. Iraq quickly descended into sectarian violence and insurgency. Al-Qaeda in Iraq came into prominence.

7 July 2005—several coordinated bomb explosions on three trains and a bus in London, England, killed fifty-two and injured seven hundred others. Al-Qaeda formally claimed responsibility.

20 November 2003—suicide car bombers simultaneously attacked two synagogues, the British Consulate, and HSBC Bank in Istanbul, Turkey, killing fifty-seven and injuring seven hundred.

October 2006—the leader of al-Qaeda in Iraq, Abu Ayyub al-Masri, announced the creation of the Islamic State of Iraq (ISI) and appointed Abu Omar al-Baghdadi as the leader of the group.

1 February 2008—ninety-eight people died and two hundred others were injured when two women suicide bombers who were mentally impaired attacked a crowded pet market in Shia-dominated eastern Baghdad. The US military claimed the Al-Qaeda in Iraq had been recruiting female patients at psychiatric hospitals to become suicide bombers.

April 2010—Abu Omar al-Baghdadi along with al-Masri were killed in a US–Iraqi operation. Abu Bakr al-Baghdadi became the new leader of ISI.

18 December 2010—Arab Spring. Democratic uprisings with riots and civil wars arose independently and spread across the Arab world during 2010–2012. The movement started in Tunisia on 18 December, 2010 and quickly turned into the Tunisian Revolution and spread throughout the countries of the Arab League and their neighbours. Rulers were forced out from power in Tunisia, Egypt, Libya, and Yemen. Civil uprisings had erupted in Bahrain and Syria. In Libya, a popular democratic movement was later turned into a major military campaign with widespread war aided by several countries. War ravaged Libya of its military and security apparatus. The long-term Libyan rule of Muammar Gaddafi came to a violent fatal end. Syria gradually descended into a major civil war with various factions controlling chunks of Syrian territory. Different jihadi outfits established camps, and a worldwide mobilization of jihadi fighters started flocking to Syria and Iraq. Though started initially as a secular civil upraising under the Free Syrian Army, later Al-Qaeda related Al-Nusra Front and the Islamic State of Iraq gained widespread territorial control amidst lawlessness.

2 May 2011 —Osama Bin Laden was killed by US Special Forces at his sprawling hideout in Abbottabad, Pakistan, less than a mile away from the Pakistan military academy. Ayman al-Zawahiri automatically became the acting amir of Al-Qaeda.

February 2012—Al-Shabab militants in Somalia were integrated into Al-Qaeda officially by accepting allegiance to Ayman Al-Zawahiri.

2012—over the summer of 2012, al-Qaeda in the Islamic Maghreb and Ansar Dine, another radical Islamist group, took advantage of the instability and an increasingly weak military in Mali and captured Timbuktu, Kidal, and Gao, cities in the north. They brutally enforced their version of sharia, or Islamic law. They also destroyed many ancient books and manuscripts and vandalized tombs, claiming that worshipping saints violated the tenets of Islam. The Islamists continued to stretch their area of control prompting concern. ECOWAS began a military action and reclaimed the territory from the Islamists.

11 September 2012—amidst a civil uprising in Libya, militants armed with anti-aircraft weapons and rocket-propelled grenades fired upon the American consulate in Benghazi, Libya. It killed US ambassador to Libya Christopher Stevens and three other embassy officials. It became a major embarrassment for the US military. Al-Qaeda groups like Ansar Al-Sharia and AQIM were behind the attack.

15 April 2013—multiple bombs exploded near the finishing line of the Boston Marathon. Three people were killed, and more than 170 people were injured. The two attackers were brothers. Evidence suggested they may have learned how to build the bombs online from an affiliate of Al-Qaeda in Yemen. One of them was killed by police; the other was captured and sentenced to death.

21 September, 2013—West Gate Mall in Nairobi, Kenya, an upmarket mall, was attacked by militants. Sixty-seven people were killed, including four attackers and nineteen foreign nationals. Around 150 persons were injured. The attack lasted for about three days, and Al-Shabab in Somalia claimed responsibility. The planning and sophistication of attack indicated outside support, more likely from Al-Qaeda.

22 September, 2013—two suicide bombers exploded at a crowd gathering of worshippers at All Saints' Church at Peshawar, Pakistan. About 127 people were killed and over 250 injured. It was the deadliest attack on the Christian minority in Pakistan. Jundullah, a group linked to Tehrik-e Taliban Pakistan (TTP), claimed responsibility for the attack.

February 2014—Al-Qaeda, under Zawahiri, denounced its ties to ISIS after months of fighting between ISIS and al-Nusra Front, the official al-Qaeda faction.

14–15 April 2014—Chibok schoolgirl kidnapping. All assembled for their examination, 276 female students were kidnapped from a school in Chibok in Borno State, Nigeria. Boko Haram, with ties to Al-Qaeda in the Islamic Maghreb (AQIM), an ISIL-affiliated group, was behind the attack. Its leader, Abubakar Shekau, claimed responsibility for the kidnappings and vowed to sell them as slaves. But most of the girls were married off to their fighters, and many were taken to neighbouring countries. Several similar episodes ensued in spite of worldwide outrage against the kidnappings.

9–10 June 2014—ISIS militants seized Mosul, the second-largest city in Iraq. They also freed up to one thousand prisoners; many of them had joined the group as fighters. They amassed large wealth by looting banks and a huge quantity of weapons.

29 June 2014—ISIS, now renamed Islamic State, announced that they had created a 'Caliphate (Islamic state)', and al-Baghdadi was self-proclaimed as the 'Caliph of World Muslims'.

July 2014—By then, ISIS had gained control of most of Syria's oilfields, including the fields of Homs and Al-Raqah. It became their prime source of funding for the group, ending their dependence on jihadi financiers, making it a self-sustaining criminal enterprise.

6–8 August 2014—ISIS militants stormed the Iraqi town of Sinjar, the bastion of Yazidis, a religious minority group. They killed, raped, and sold thousands of people as slaves. US President Obama authorized air strikes to protect against ISIS targets to protect the Yazidi people and promised all possible help to Iraq. US fighter jets started bombing ISIS sites.

16 December 2014—Peshawar school attack. Seven heavily armed gunmen, all foreign nationals affiliated with the Tehrik-e Taliban Pakistan (TTP) attacked the army public school at Peshawar, Pakistan. They entered the heavily guarded school in army uniform and opened fire on school staff and children, killing 141 people. A major military operation with targeted killing of militants using snipers was needed

to liberate more than nine hundred children taken hostage by the militants.

December 2014—ISIS fighters executed 150 Iraqi women in Al-Anbar province who refused jihad marriage to their fighters. Some of them were pregnant. A guideline was released by ISIL before these incidents on how to capture, keep, and sexually abuse enslaved females.

December 2014—death toll by Boko Haram attacks in Nigeria reached four thousand for the year. Bombings, looting, and massacres targeting mainly Christians and schoolchildren took a major toll. They captured a large area of land in Nigeria and neighbouring countries with a mass flood of people from their attacks and occupation.

7 January 2015—militants stormed the office of *Charlie Hebdo* in Paris and killed eleven staff members, creating insecurity among Jewish community in France. ISIS claimed responsibility.

26 June 2015—thirty-eight people were killed by a gunman at a hotel in Tunisia. The same day, a bomb explosion at the Shia Imam Sadiq Mosque in Kuwait City killed at least twenty-seven people. ISIS claimed to be behind both attacks.

10 October 2015—102 people were killed, and over 400 others injured in two bomb blasts at Ankara, capital of Turkey. ISIL was believed to be responsible.

31 October, 2015—a bomb on board a chartered Russian jet bound for St Petersburg. It was brought down at Sinai, killing all 224 Russian tourists on board. ISIS claimed responsibility.

13–14 November 2015—simultaneous coordinated terrorist attacks in Paris killed 136 and wounded more than 350. There were a series of attacks of mass shootings and suicide bombings. ISIS claimed responsibility. This incident was reminiscent of Mumbai attacks of November 2008, which killed 164 people.

PREFACE

The world first heard the word *"Al-Qaeda"* in August 1996 from inner-page column news as a jihadi terrorist outfit under Osama Bin Laden. On 7 August 1998, there was shock when Al-Qaeda bombed two US embassies in East Africa, killing hundreds of people. After three years, on 11 September 2001, the twin towers of World Trade Center were smashed to the ground, hit by two hijacked commercial flights, killing thousands of people. The world was horrified and in utter disbelief. The horror of terrorism descended to even the most unread people. It was not just the beginning of their terror campaign but was also only a chapter of the continuing saga of the terror story around the world, which started a decade back and continued further. Without any delay, the USA launched an attack on Afghanistan to expel Al-Qaeda and their host, Taliban, to kill Osama Bin Laden and Mullah Umer. Even after the end of the war, neither of them was caught nor killed. Taliban rule was rooted out, and democracy was installed, but they re-emerged in Pakistan in another form, Pakistani Taliban, as a threat to both the USA and Pakistan. Al-Qaeda resurfaced in Iraq in the deadly avatar of Al-Qaeda in Iraq. Its founder, Abu Musab al-Zarqawi, was much more bloodthirsty than all his mentors. He bombed US soldiers, beheaded foreigners, and massacred Shia worshippers. In fact, he targeted anyone in his way and on every possible enemy target around.

US drones killed the leader of Pakistani Taliban, Baitullah Mehsud. He was soon replaced by another leader but a more dreaded one, Hakimullah Mehsud, who orchestrated hundreds of attacks and thousands of killings. He too was eliminated, and their mountain hideouts were bombed. They struck back in urban areas of Pakistan, including their largest city, Karachi. The coexistence of Pakistani Taliban and their background support, Al-Qaeda, was like adding gasoline to a fire.

Osama was killed, both Mehsuds were killed, and Zarqawi was bombed out. Al-Qaeda should have been finished and Taliban wiped out. Strangely immediately after the death of Zarqawi, in October 2006, Al-Qaeda in Iraq declared their "Islamic State of Iraq"; made their top leader, Omar al-Baghdadi, the amir of their state and listed many of their leaders as ministers. Everybody laughed at them—an emirate without land and ministers without a parliament! After eight years, on 29 June 2014, the same group declared 'Islamic Caliphate' in Iraq and Syria. Their amir was renamed *Caliph*, and the world was in shock. By this time, many of the Iraqi cities, including the second largest city, Mosul, a major chunk of land of Iraq and part of Syria with a number of oilfields, were under their grip. Men in black fatigues wielding the black flags of Al-Qaeda paraded through the streets of Iraq in large convoys of hundreds of vehicles. Mosul, a city of two million people, promptly obeyed their new rulers; so did the neighbouring areas. The city was defended by national army units at least ten times more in number than the invading ISIL, but all were defeated to humiliation. Most of the army men simply fled their barracks, the rest were captured, and thousands were executed.

The terror of jihad is not only limited to Pakistan, Afghanistan, Syria, and Iraq. Black flags of Al-Qaeda are flown across many continents, and their ideology is cherished by thousands of people worldwide. Cities are descending into chaos from their vicious attacks as in Tripoli, Benghazi, Baghdad, Damascus, Aleppo, and Karachi. Day by day, new terror plots are filling the news headlines: the Russian aircraft sabotage at Sinai, the Paris attacks, the Mali capital attack, and so on.

If the past attacks of Al-Qaeda were like tornadoes striking specific Western and other enemy targets, the new-generation terrorist states are strengthening suddenly to cause the mayhem of superstorms. This book is about Al-Qaeda, the story of their masters, the origin of their deviant ideology, and the psychology of the attackers wearing suicide vests or beheading strangers. It goes deep into the world of their elusive supporters, financiers, weapon donors, and the tactics of extracting criminal money for 'holy war'. It is also about the plight of ordinary men in Syria who were struggling to get rid of the merciless regime of Assad and were doubly struck by the regime and the ruthless bloodbath of terrorists. I try to give an insight into the spread of anarchy, widening lawless lands, and the potential threat to the world recovering from the past horrors of jihadi blitzkriegs. This book, *Looming Black Shadows: The Rise of Terrorist States and the New-Generation Al-Qaeda*, invites the readers into the world of the most powerful terror outfit in the history, hoping to be more in depth, vivid, and simplified.

Sawad Hadi

CHAPTER 1

A Nightmare and the Sweet Dream

Terror is nothing other than justice, prompt, severe, inflexible.

Maximilien Robespierre, a notorious Jacobin Club leader of France, about their state sponsored violent campaigns during 1793–1794

Reign of terror—was first called *terrorisme* in French, which became *terrorism*.

Cheer and jubilation erupted across the world on 2 May 2011 when the news of death of Osama Bin Laden was released. He had killed by US Special Forces in Abbottabad, Pakistan, in an early-morning raid on that day. His death was major breaking news and cause for instant celebration across the world. This unusual celebration of his death and the number and spread of cheering people from across the continents tell the importance of his life story.

The rise and spread of Al-Qaeda under Osama Bin Laden was a phenomenon unprecedented in history. Probably some things close to this that have happened in history were the Crusades of the Middle Ages and the communist guerrilla movements of the last century. The death of Bin Laden marked the end of the first two generations of global Islamist inspiration and activism under the wide banner of Al-Qaeda. People from different nationalities, ethnicities, cultures, customs, languages, and opinions regarding their religious practices were organized under a banner with a uniform agenda, ideology, and world view. It was a unique assembly of people of many colours and traditions for a common cause: the spread of Islam and establishment of a global Islamic caliphate through struggles and jihad. Those who came under their banner were small in number with limited manpower, money, and material support.

1

But they believed that their ideological strength, determination, and possibly, help from God would make their venture possible.

The world had been rattling with horrible terrorist attacks, assassinations, unrest, and overall lack of security throughout the last three decades. One act of violence followed the other, more gruesome and reprehensible than what came before. Average Americans were not so bothered about issues in other countries—their internal security problems, violent movements, and insurgency. They had a sense of security and confidence that no world power was going to challenge the USA, especially on their soil. As a nation, it hardly faced any incidence of war or foreign aggression on its mainland after 1814, when the British troops burned down Washington City.

The USA and its military were involved in hundreds of conflicts across the globe. It seemed they believed these were trivial matters to be tackled by political leadership and the establishment. All of these world views of Americans changed overnight after the incident of 11 September 2001 morning in New York, the day when the twin towers of the World Trade Center were levelled to the ground by two commercial aircrafts of their own country that flew through the middle of the towers. The world had never seen a similar attack, and it was beyond the imagination of the general public, fantasy writers, security experts, and war specialists. The awe and ingenuity of the attack surprised everyone. The power of an ordinary aircraft used against one of the most protected civilian buildings in the world was shocking. Many attempts were made by terrorists before this to attack the World Trade Center but were mostly foiled or caused only minimal casualties. But this time, it was not only successful but was also coordinated with utmost precision and was followed by a similar attack on the Pentagon, the headquarters of the United States Department of Defense, one of the most secure locations in the USA. These attacks were unimaginable for general Americans, their intelligence agencies, and the US defence force supporting the world's only superpower. The World Trade Center represented the dominance of American economy over the world, the symbol of capitalism and American pride. On the other hand, the Pentagon

2

represented the American might and their authority over the world. It was a tactical and symbolic attack that was, perhaps stronger, effective, and damaging than an attack on any other target.

The modus operandi was unique—no heavy weapon, no large mobilization of fighters, no military fatigue, and no protective gears. It was done by people walking and chatting casually through the usual security apparatus of an airport and boarding aircraft just like any other passenger. Minutes after the beginning of their journey, they became martyrs for their masters, killing all their fellow passengers and many other thousands. They shattered the pride of a nation and their symbols for the world in flashes of seconds. The terror and insecurity that this attack caused on the Americans was unimaginable. The emotional shock to the average American viewing that horrific footage on their TV screens was unprecedented and was the beginning of a new era of fear, insecurity, suspicion, and xenophobia. Most people believed that any kind of action against those groups and their supporters was acceptable and necessary.

At the same time, in other parts of the world, there were mixed reactions. Almost all peace-loving people condemned the terror on humanity. But some even celebrated those events. Many got inspired. A section started to believe that many things that were impossible were now possible with dedication and determination. Even a small group of ordinary people could challenge any power or army with tactics and perseverance. That was the beginning of a new wave of militant activism around the globe. The perpetrators of those acts were revered among many circles, even among those who openly denounced violence and such attacks. Some highly inspired people started looking at those masterminds. Some openly, many more secretly, started supporting and some others dreaming to be part of the new shadow superpower called Al-Qaeda. It was not just those who were extremely religiously inclined but also those who wanted thrills, those who dreamed of revolutions and those aspired for power, heroism or adventure. They started their journey to the training camps in the remote lawless lands harbouring Al-Qaeda.

CHAPTER 2

A Will and Its Aftermath

The purpose of terrorism is to exploit the media in order to achieve maximum attainable publicity as an amplifying force multiplier in order to influence the targeted audience(s) in order to reach short- and midterm political goals and/or desired long-term end states.

Carsten Bockstette of George C. Marshall European Center for Security Studies

In spite of leading a fugitive life with isolation and secrecy for the last two decades of his life, Bin Laden made frequent and lengthy communications with his core activists. He remained the ringleader of all Al-Qaeda activities throughout the world till his death, as evident by numerous letters and documents captured by the US Special Forces who raided his Abbottabad safe house. In his internal communications to his cadres, Bin Laden used to refer to his organization often as Al-Qaeda or Qaeda al-Jihad. There was a growing frustration in the use of the name *Al-Qaeda*. Just before his death, he communicated this to his close followers. Bin Laden believed that the word *Al-Qaeda* was neutral and not associated with any religious overtones and hence their enemies could target them without it being perceived as an attack on Islam.

So the war against Al-Qaeda was just an assault on an organization, not against Islam or Muslims. He argued that if the name indicated Islamic ideology, it would have been difficult for the USA to project it that way. So he asked to suggest names for the organization that were not so short but represented Islamic identity and were close to the conscience of Muslim umma (nation/society). The need for the name change might have been due to the increasing frustration within Al-Qaeda. Constant war, attacks on civilians, brutal killings, and destruction by the group members caused widespread aversion to the organization. Even those in the organization seldom used the name, and many cadres almost forgot the name. There was a growing isolation of Al-Qaeda activists, even among Muslim circles. Though formed as a 'Jihadi outfit against crusaders and Jews', during their more than two decades of existence, most of the victims of Al-Qaeda were Muslims. The name did not carry any charm or enthusiasm among most Muslims any more. There was severe strain on terror financing under the Al-Qaeda banner. So he suggested to his followers to come up with new names that could put the ideology back into general Muslims under a new banner.

The Al-Qaeda group in Yemen and Maghreb responded to this call promptly. Al-Qaeda had a strong base in Yemen and was directly under the guidance of the Al-Qaeda core. They changed the name to Ansar Al-Sharia (Comrades for Islamic Sharia) in 2012, though some members still retained the old name, Al-Qaeda in the Arabian Peninsula (AQAP). In many other countries, like Libya, Tunisia, and Egypt, groups bearing the name Ansar al-Sharia were formed. They worked mostly independently with occasional mutual support. Al-Qaeda in Iraq was already known as Islamic State of Iraq, emphasizing their Islamic ideology, and in all their future name changes, they preserved the word *Islam* in the title. Other black-flag-bearing groups like Harkat al-Shabab al-Mujahideen (Movement of Youth on Jihad), better known as Al-Shabab in Somalia and Jama'atu Ahlu-Sunnah Lidda'awati Wal Jihad (People Committed to the Prophet's Teachings for Propagation and Jihad), better known as Boko Haram in Nigeria, were already with their unique Islamic names qualified for these criteria.

This idea of a name change can have some impact on terror fighting. The worrying reason—the logic for change in the name was not to separate Islam and the group but to make Islamic belief of general Muslims and the ideals of the organization synonymous. Bin Laden and his colleagues were aware that innocent Muslims not related to

Al-Qaeda were affected by the War on Terror' perpetrated by Western powers and other governments. There was a strong protest among the Muslims on the suffering of innocent Muslims from collateral damage on ordinary followers during the fight against Islamic terror. Since the word *Al-Qaeda* did not have any religious connotations, Bin Laden argued that a more religiously inclined name should be chosen so, he believed, when their enemies targeted them, it would be perceived by other Muslims as an attack on their religion, making the conflicts wider and deeper. Even in Muslim countries, targeting groups with strong Islamic identity in terms of their name and banner was difficult, as some may perceive it as an attack on the religion. Al-Qaeda wanted more conflicts. Al-Qaeda wanted ordinary Muslims to be targeted by their enemies, causing suffering and isolation of believers and labelling them as perpetrators of violence. More frustrated Muslims meant more men on their cadres and sufficient justification for their violent acts.

Among the several documents and letters collected by US Special Forces during their raid on Abbottabad which killed Bin Laden, many were written by Bin Laden, and others were communications to him. Some were available to the public and released by the Combating Terrorism Center. They gave insight into the activities of Al-Qaeda, their tactics, failures, and conflicts within the organization. Many of those letters showed frustration with Bin Laden for the increasingly violent sectarian actions of Al-Qaeda activists in Muslim countries and against Muslims.

Al-Shabaab in Somalia was not officially annexed with Al-Qaeda initially due to their notorious image as ruthless fighters and killers of Somalis. Bin Laden politely declined the request by the Al-Shabab leader for a merger. He advised them to be involved in continuing poverty in the country due to constant war and lack of security. He advised them to implement measures to improve the lives of ordinary people, which would be ultimately helpful to the organization, and expand their mission. This call was partly taken by Al-Shabab. They started concentrating on irrigation by making several canals for farmers. They instituted policies to encourage the use of local food and continued to prohibit the work of aid agencies in their areas. This created interest in farming, increased production, and improved life standards. It also meant more tax collection and increased support among the local population for Al-Shabab. Lower Shabelle, which used to be the bread basket of Somalia, improved a little with these efforts. The area is controlled by Al-Shabab. In 2011, there was severe famine in the area, which killed more than 250,000 people in Somalia. This was due to constant war and the resultant plight of farmers, coupled with severe draught.

But that does not mean that Al-Shabab now refrains from their habitual terror tactics of bombing and kidnapping or its suicide missions. The welfare measures were not due to ideological inclination or commitment to support ailing people but just measures to improve revenue and increase acceptance among local population. That allows them to equip more to attack the official government, the African forces, which provide security to the central government and against foreign countries. On 21 September 2013, an Al-Shabab attack on a famous shopping mall in the Kenyan capital, Nairobi, killed sixty-seven people. Al-Shabab was formally integrated into Al-Qaeda by Ayman al-Zawahiri in February 2012 after the death of Osama Bin Laden. Their focus was on gaining power and jihad. Al-Shabab attacked foreign-aid agencies and prohibited their activities in their strongholds. Famine re-emerged in Southern Somalia by late 2014 and is probably going to worsen further. In their efforts to block Somali and African Union troops, Al-Shabab sieged the access to many towns which they had lost control of, cutting them off from any supply, leaving the inhabitants to suffer from poverty without any outside help. Charity and welfare evolved as mere tactics of Al-Qaeda.

The name change in Al-Qaeda was also because of increasing disillusion among Muslims with the organization and their isolation. Their constant tendency for violence and armed action led to deterioration and recession. Many of their old activists were lost in missions or captured or killed by government forces. Not much new recruitment, which was essential for their progress and existence, was happening. So the new organization had to concentrate on grass-roots idealism, community reach (*dawa*), and social activities. Although a group by the name Ansar al-Sharia had been started long back by Abu Hamsa al-Masri in London in 1994 after his return from Afghanistan, it never got any prominence. The name change like Ansar al-Sharia was to guarantee a new face free from the stigma of old Al-Qaeda. They started working in social activities and *dawa*. This new banner, as a sociocultural and religious organization, made them acceptable in the society and protected them from the constant vigil of the world against any kind of Al-Qaeda activity. The core ideology and their central leaders remained the same. A group of people attracted to the religion and social activity were utilized in Libya and Tunisia as recruiting grounds for more serious missions and as a base for future fighters.

The biggest benefit of the name change among Al-Qaeda-related groups happened to the Islamic State of Iraq. They changed their name to Islamic State of Iraq and Levant (ISIL) or Islamic State of Iraq and Syria (ISIS) when they started their activity in Syria by the beginning of the Syrian Civil War, which expanded their influence and territory profoundly. Then they changed the name to Islamic State so as to project it as a pan-national or global outfit. More miraculous changes in their perception and reach occurred when they declared themselves an Islamic caliphate and renamed their leader as Amirul Mu'mineen Caliph Ibrahim to challenge the world's Muslims and their beliefs. This made all Muslims have to choose whether they were with them or against them, as *caliph* was traditionally to designate the global Islamic leader of all Muslims with obligations to follow. The name change instantly created confusion in the mind. Many of their heinous crimes and horrific bloodbaths in the past were forgotten by some people. Most Muslims were forced to reject this pseudo caliphate, which was not even an entity much people had bothered about before. They were worried that their religion had been hijacked by few criminals and lunatics. At the same time, some got more inspiration than before to sympathize with the group. In any case, the militants succeeded in their mission of making news, awareness, and unprecedented importance, whether they were labelled good or bad.

Al-Qaeda leaders were advised to be vigilant on local problems and needs of the local population to gain support for their activities. This was in contrast to their old strategy of selecting persons committed to jihad or suicide missions and aide them for their mission. Muslims who were locals where these groups acted were not cooperative and were indifferent to their activities. Bin Laden advised his cadres to assist people facing difficulties through social and charitable works in Muslim communities. This strategy was taken into consideration when Al-Qaeda fighters started their activity in Syria during the Arab Spring.

They started with community service activities like forming vigilante groups in communities which were facing law-and-order problems after losing the grip of government. Criminals used the opportunity to rob and intimidate people in liberated areas and in war zones. Al-Qaeda fighters also brought medicines and financial aid. They did general charity work and assisted the sick or injured. In fact, in the war-torn Syrian cities like Aleppo, the Al-Qaeda group ISIS operated the public transport system for a short while. They also provided security for basic infrastructures and hospitals. These tactics helped these groups establish their base in the community that was desperately looking for some reliable helpers, though these were part of propaganda!

But essentially, the core of all Al-Qaeda ideology is mentioned in his official will written for his family and comrades on 14 December 2001, after the events of 11 September 2001 while in Afghanistan. That time, he was expecting his death at any time by the hands of US or Allied forces.

He advised all Muslims to continue the fight against 'Crusaders and Jews' regardless of its cost and, ultimately, establish a government of the image of the Islamic Republic of Afghanistan, which he projected as the only country ruled by God's law. In his will, he asked the Muslim umma (nation/society) to (as per a translation of his will presented by the US Senate Foreign Relations Committee) 'strive to the death and dedicate your life and listen to the few scholars who maintain loyalty, and be hostile to those loyal to enemies of Nations' enemies who have taken the ideas, customs and quirks of Western ignorance such as borrowing from banks, usury laws, crimes and transactions, secularism and allowing the establishment of political parties, trade unions and women's associations.' His will ends finally as follows: 'My advice to all Mujahideen, where ever they are; recover your breath and the fight against the Jews and Crusaders; and to purge your ranks of defeatists and traitors and continue the Jihad of the Nation. Your brother Abu Abdulla Osama bin Muhammad bin Laden Friday, 28 Ramadan 1422.'

The world saw the response to his call in the next two decades, and his ideology still governs scores of organizations across the globe that promulgate jihadi spirit. The reciprocation for his call can be seen in areas where Al-Qaeda groups have established their rule, as in parts of Mali, Iraq, Syria, Libya, Yemen, Somalia, and tribal areas of Pakistan and Afghanistan. Apart from hundreds of terrorist attacks, bombing of a school in Nigeria by Boko Haram, destruction of Islamic libraries and gravesites in Mali by Islamic rebels, and enforcing crude sharia laws in impoverished lands like Somalia by Al-Shabab, all were just different extensions of this call.

A name carries attention. Attention creates strength. Terrorists use all tactics to be in the limelight. Some are very risky and ruthless. Some are very simple and cost not even a penny like a mere name change. The media and news value do the rest to give them free publicity and strength at a time when they are desperately looking for it.

CHAPTER 3

The Road to Aleppo—Transition from the Silk Route to the Trail of Warriors

What is at stake is nothing less than the survival and well being of a generation of innocents. Syria has become the great tragedy of this century.

Antonio Guterres,
United Nations High Commissioner for Refugees

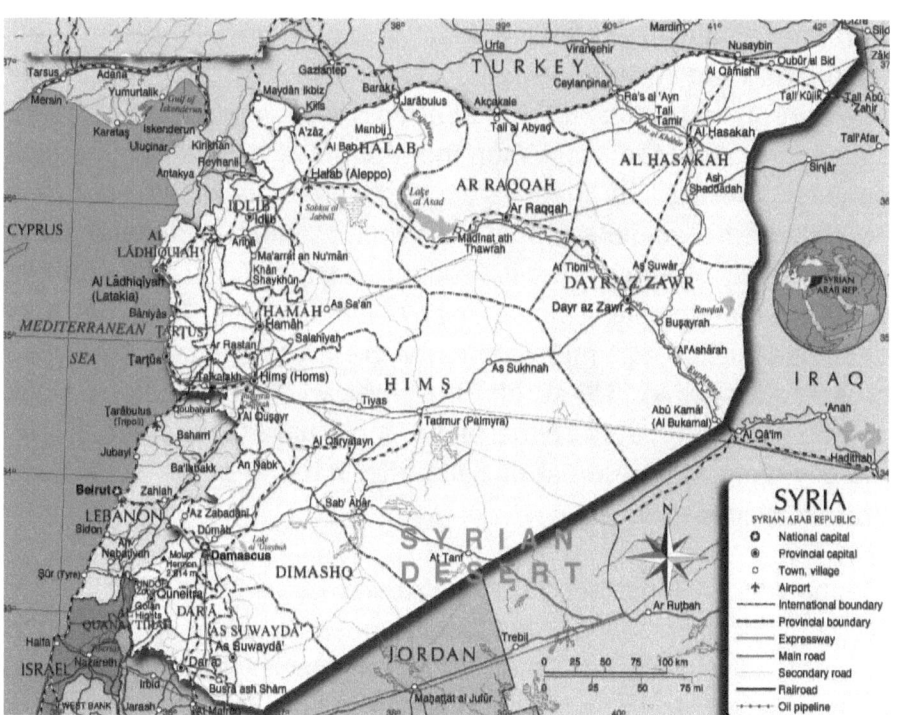

Syria—Political Map

When the new Arab nation of Syria was carved out of the old Ottoman Empire in 1923, the people in Aleppo were surprised and anguished that Damascus would be the capital of the new nation, not their dear city. Aleppo was a more ancient, important, and populated city than Damascus and was also much more prosperous. In reality, both of them held titles for being amongst the oldest continuously inhabited urban areas of the world. The ancient city of Aleppo is old as more than five thousand years before Christ. The city of Aleppo, a French name (Alep) with some Italian correction, is known in Arabic as *Halab*, a name since the Babylonian period. Jewish literature and the Bible refer to it as Zobah. There are several mentions of it in the Bible. It was not only the largest city in Syria but even in the entire Levant. During the Ottoman period, it was the third biggest city in the empire, next only to Istanbul and Cairo.

Its long history has witnessed many regimes like those of the Assyrian, Roman, Sassanian, Byzantine, Mamluk, and Umayyad rulers. Great conquerors like Alexander the Great and Saladin established their rule here. It had witnessed brutal atrocities by invaders like Hittites, Crusaders, and Mongols. When the Mongol army under Tamerlane captured the city, the inhabitants were ruthlessly massacred, and he ordered his soldiers to make a tower of twenty thousand skulls in the vicinity of Aleppo. Most people fled the city and only returned when the Mongols were thrown out by Mamluk rulers. After that, they defended the city from many more Mongol invasions. It became more prosperous after AD 1516, when it became part of the Ottoman Empire and continued to be so till the end of the empire. France controlled the city along with the rest of Syria after the end of the First World War until independence.

Aleppo was an important trade centre and was at the end of the Silk Route. Its position between the Mediterranean and Mesopotamia and its surrounding fertile farmlands made it an important business centre. It attracted traders, artists, craftsmen, and travellers from all across the world. Its rich and long history made the city an assembly of several cultures and traditions. The road to Aleppo has been coveted and famous from the ages of antiquity. It was a major crossroad in the

Silk Route on the way to Mesopotamia, Iran, Mediterranean, Turkey, Egypt, and far off to Europe, connecting India and China through Central Asia. Businessmen traded silk, cotton, spices, metals, and gems in its age-old markets. Settlers of all cultures, races, and religions embraced the city due to its business prosperity. This magnified its importance and enshrined a rich culture and heritage.

Aleppo was a city of continuity of the ages. New additions were made time to time. It survived many wars, invasions, natural calamities, and several devastating epidemics of plague and cholera. In spite of it all, the city continued to grow. Constant fear of invasion put the city in closed quarters for each community. Aleppo was a destination for travellers for several reasons. In the Ottoman period, it became an important railway junction connecting Istanbul and Damascus. The road connecting Damascus to Aleppo became the most important travel line in Syria, connecting cities like Homs and Hama. Iraqi cities like Mosul and Baghdad were connected by the road to Aleppo. Even after independence and in spite of the selection of Damascus as the capital, the city grew very fast. In fact, it was one of the fastest-growing cities in the historic areas of Levant (including Syria, Jordan, Palestine, Israel, the Mediterranean island of Cyprus, and parts of Turkey, all of which were part of former Aleppo Vilayet of the Ottoman Empire). Its importance as a trade route was considerably reduced after the opening of the Suez Canal. Political and economic preference given to Damascus by late Ottoman rulers and leaders of the Syrian Republic further weakened its dominance.

Aleppo was home to about 2.3 million people as of 2005 and about 3 million by 2011. It was a prominent cultural centre for Muslims, Christians, and Jews with numerous historical structures. Sunni Muslims are an overwhelming majority (80 per cent), followed by Kurds. About 250,000 Christians of several church orientations were living in the city, forming about 12 per cent of population. Many of them were Armenian in origin. The city maintained a unique blend of ancient, medieval, and modern structures. Souq al-Madina, stretching for a length of 13 kilometres, maintained a medieval ambience and architecture, selling cloths, spices, jewellery and crafts from across the world. It was the largest covered market in the world or the first supermarket in the world. Home to several impressive historic mosques, including the Grand Mosque of Aleppo with its impressive high tower and the famous Shia mosque of al-Nuqtah Mosque, the city has a great treasure of Islamic heritage. Grand Mosque of Aleppo, also called Umayyad Mosque, is one of the oldest mosques in the world. Its huge size, magnificent architecture, and imposing minarets with four facets, which stood the desert heat, wind, and several occupations for the last 1,400 years is declared as a World Heritage Site. Several medieval madrasas, museums, and hammams are dotted in the city. It was a thriving centre of traditional and classic Arabic music. Several musicians from the Arab world used to compete for approval by the knowledgeable Aleppine *samia*.

Aleppo was recognized as the Islamic cultural capital by the Islamic Educational Scientific and Cultural Organization (ISESCO) in 2006. UNESCO recognizes the old Aleppo city and its surrounding dead cities as World Heritage Sites. Several universities and educational institutions in Aleppo attracted students from all over Syria and from other Arab countries. Tourism was a thriving industry which accounted for about 12 per cent of Syrian economy. Various musical festivals, cultural events, historic structures, famed cuisine, entertainment places, and vibrant nightlife all attracted people from across the world to this magical city of a medieval and modern blend. Throughout history, the road to Aleppo was active and innovative. Maybe in modern times, many may fly straight to the international airport instead of the old caravans. But the destination, Aleppo, was thrilling and rewarding for many who wished to see and be part of this citadel city of beautiful men and women.

This picture changed a little after December 2010, when the Arab Spring brought political upheavals in most parts of the Middle East. When the people in Daara, on the outskirts of Damascus, started agitation against President Bashar al-Assad in March 2011, defying the long-existing orders against assembly of more than five people and ruthless suppression by the government forces, most people in Aleppo and Damascus were not bothered. Business was as usual, especially among the urban class and in both cities' merchant classes were strong supporters of Assad's regime.

Syria is a land of political paradox, just like many other countries in the Arab world. But unlike other places, here the president rules, not the usual king. He is the leader of Ba'ath Syrian Regional Branch, the only political party allowed in Syria. Ba'ath, a radical socialist ideology with pan-Arabism started by Michel Aflaq, an orthodox Christian, along with his Sunni Muslim colleague, Salah al-Din al-Bitar, had established its roots in Iraq and Syria, which eventually paved the way for the rule of Saddam Hussein in Iraq and the Assad family in Syria. General Hafez al-Assad, who was a Ba'ath party ideologue and defence minister of Syria, seized power in 1970 in a coup called Corrective Revolution. He continued his rule until his death in 2000.

The ascent of Hafiz to the presidency of Syria was a political miracle. Born in a poor Alawite family and having grown through the ranks of the Ba'ath party, Hafiz ultimately became a game master. Alawites were outcast Shia Muslims living in mountains and poor villages, fighting for their survival and religious identity. They constituted only about 12 per cent of the Syrian population and were suffering from poverty and religious and social persecution in a country dominated by politically and economically strong Sunni Muslims. An Alawite president in Syria was unimaginable. But the long French occupation of Syria changed the social order to a great extent. A large number of Alawites joined the Syrian army and were promoted. Socialist Ba'ath resurgence also gave opportunity for mostly shy and underprivileged Alawites coming to political and military prominence. The majority of the Sunni population of Syria could not digest this, mainly the more conservative rural Sunni Muslims. When Hafiz al-Assad gained presidency, he consolidated power to his core supporters. Most of them were his family members or from his own tribe. He heavily recruited Alawites and Shia Muslims into the military. His government was mostly secular but ruthlessly suppressed all political opponents. Political activists, human rights activists, and journalists opposing the regimes were suppressed, arrested, and tortured in prisons. In the late 1970 there was an Islamist uprising organized by the

Muslim Brotherhood (Al-Ikhwan ul-Muslimeen), which eventually led to the brutal Hama massacre of 1982, which resulted in the killing of ten thousand to forty thousand people, mostly innocent civilians by the army. This was one of the bloodiest massacres of the civilian population by any government force of their own country in modern history.

Political conflict between Ba'ath and the Muslim Brotherhood was a regular event in post-independent Syria. Immediately after the first Ba'ath coup in 1963, during which the party gained power in Syria, riots started at Hama in April 1964. Islamist insurgents blocked the roads, ransacked wine shops, and started stockpiling weapons and essential supply. The resultant conflict and death of an Ismaili Ba'ath militiaman triggered an overt riot, and all known Ba'ath establishments were destroyed. The army was called in. Tanks rolled through the streets. More than seventy members of the Muslim Brotherhood were killed. Several more were captured, and many went underground. Since then, Muslim Brotherhood activity in Syria has been controlled by a few people in the field and more underground.

The major reason for the conflict was the secular nature of Ba'athists, advocating nationalism and socialism with emphasis on radical socio-economic programmes by the government. Ba'ath supporters were mostly poor, and majority were Alawites. Brotherhood is a Sunni Islamist ideology rejecting secularism and advocating that politics and religion are inseparable. They emphasize on Islamism rather than nationalism. Their supporters were traditionally Sunnis, who were the dominant majority and included the powerful businessmen that owned souks and those controlling vast areas of land. They were not interested in reforms. Even those who were not interested in Islamism also supported the Brotherhood, since they formed the only significant opposition to Ba'ath ideology. Unfortunately, both these organizations were radical in their thoughts and violent in their means. Both were minorities trying to control the majority with the help of violent methods like targeted killings and assassinations.

After the incidents in Hama in 1964, the Brotherhood and various Islamist groups engaged in periodic clashes throughout the country, which became more violent after the Syrian occupation of Lebanon in 1976. Many Brotherhood leaders and activists were imprisoned. From 1979, the Brotherhood organized a guerrilla campaign targeting government officials and army officers in many Syrian cities. The result was many arrests, massacres, and summary executions by Syrian forces. On 16 June 1979, members of the Syrian Muslim Brotherhood led by Adnan Uqla with the help of a duty officer named Ibrahim Youssef massacred about fifty to eighty-three Alawite cadets at Aleppo Artillery School. Officially, the Brotherhood denied responsibility and alleged that on the regime forces. This incident was regarded as an open declaration of war by the Brotherhood on the Alawite Government. The government responded by sentencing to death about fifteen prisoners belonging to the Islamist resistance movement. Following these events, terrorist attacks became a regular event in Aleppo and several northern cities. The government attributed all these to the Brotherhood. By this time, several armed groups emerged with no clear linkage attributable to the Brotherhood.

Aleppo was not only the most populated city and important city after Damascus; it was also an active centre for secular, democratic activists and armed Islamist opposition. Islamist opposition was the biggest threat to the state due to their organizational integrity and arm strength. Secular opposition was also a threat to Ba'ath rule that had strong support among the middle class and minority groups opposing Islamists. Violence engulfed Aleppo in November 1979 following the arrest of Sheikh Zain al-Din Khairalla, the leading Islamist and imam of Friday prayers at Grand Mosque of Aleppo. Daily demonstrations, boycotts, and attacks on Ba'ath party offices became common. Syrian military and security forces opened fire on peaceful student protests and on other demonstrations, resulting in many casualties. On the other hand, armed Islamist cells attacked police patrols and Ba'ath offices. Government forces raided opposition centres and meeting places and enforced a heavy clampdown on all opposition activities using thousands of police and defence brigades. In spite of all this, a large section of Aleppo was outside the government's reach. In early March 1980, the Muslim Brotherhood paralyzed the business district of Aleppo with two weeks of strike. This strike evoked sympathy waves in other cities like Homs, Hama, Idlib, and Hasaka.

To comb the strike and growing opposition activity, the government deployed the army's Third Division to Aleppo. This was supported by Special Forces. An about twenty-thousand-strong army and Special Forces enclosed Aleppo. Hundreds of tanks and armoured vehicles criss-crossed the city streets and started firing indiscriminately at residential areas. Forces sealed off neighbourhoods and searched from house to house for suspected Islamists and weapons. Several hundreds were killed by April 1980. Many people were arrested and detained in detention centres and a special prison camp at the citadel of the city. Government forces could control the city by May, but the situation was tense with sporadic incidences.

The army committed several mass murders even upon slight provocation. On July 1, in retaliation to an attack on a patrol vehicle, Special Forces rounded up about two hundred males in the Souq al-Ahad. They were aged fifteen and above, and they fired on them, killing about 42 and injuring more than 150. A similar massacre occurred at al-Mashraqah, following an attack on a patrolling force. In the morning of the Eid ul-Fitr celebration, Special Forces commander Hashem Mualla ordered his troops to surround neighbourhood of Mashraqah and randomly collected people. They paraded them to a nearby cemetery and opened fire, killing about eighty-three to one hundred civilians, mostly children. Several hundred more were injured. They used bulldozers to bury the bodies even when many were still alive.

People were selected so randomly that a few of those killed were government workers, Ba'ath party members, or supporters of the regime. The next day, thirty-five citizens were taken from their homes by forces of the Third Division and shot dead. Those people who witnessed those days of horror in Aleppo remember the roar of the commander, General Shafiq Fayadh, shouting at the public on the street, standing on a tank on April 5, threatening to kill a thousand people a day to get rid of the Muslim Brother worms!

Many hit-and-run attacks and bomb explosions targeting Syrian army men were common in 1980 throughout Syria. A near-successful assassination attempt on President Hafiz al-Assad by Brotherhood workers in June 1980 during an official state reception for the president of Mali was a turning point. Hafiz al-Assad survived with minor injuries. The retaliation was brutal and merciless. Within hours of this incident, a large number of Islamist prisoners reported that more than 1,200 had been executed at Tadmor prison near Palmyra, orchestrated by units loyal to Rifaat al-Assad, the president's younger brother. Rifaat was a senior military officer and had his own wing of special forces called Defence Companies (Saraya al-Difaa). Tadmor, set in the desert of Palmyra, a cradle of civilization, was a notorious prison throughout its history, if not the most notorious in the world. The place was aptly called the Kingdom of Death and Madness. The victims were subjected to all forms of terror and torture irrespective of their crime. Controlled by military police, some victims could not even survive the initial reception with hundreds of lashes all over the body by whips. Inmates were regularly subjected to all forms of torture and isolation and denied judicial justice. Many victims were selected at random, beaten up to breaking their bones. Cutting into pieces by axes and gouging of eyes were not rare in the prison. Punishment was not only for any mistakes but just random to create an atmosphere of terror and subjugation. Inmates were tortured whenever they moved out, during meal or when taking a bath, or using the toilet. Most of the trials were done by field military courts, which were very liberal with execution orders, and there was no chance for appeal anywhere else. Escape from this prison was like a new birth. Amnesty International's reports on these prison conditions were chilling and elaborate. The prison was more terrific in the 1980s, relatively mild in the 1990s, closed in 2001, and opened back in June 2011, in tandem with the political atmosphere in Syria.

In July 1980, government declared capital punishment for being a member of Muslim Brotherhood. In 1981, a powerful explosion rocked the al-Azbakiyah neighbourhood of central Damascus, close to the Intelligence agency complex. It killed about two hundred people, including many army men, and destroyed several buildings. This was attributed to the Brotherhood.

Hama, a city close to Aleppo on the highway to Damascus, was a stronghold of the Brotherhood. It witnessed the bloodiest battle against the Muslim Brotherhood, called the Hama massacre, and exposed the brutality and terror of the Syrian Ba'ath regime. An army unit searching for Umar Jawad (Abu Bakr), the local guerrilla commander of Brotherhood was about to close in him but was attacked by about early morning of 3 February 1982. The rebels alerted other insurgent cells by radio, and snipers on the rooftops killed several soldiers. Army units called for reinforcements to capture Abu Bakr and those who gave orders for attack on the army units. Mosque loudspeakers called for jihad against the infidel Ba'ath regime. Hundreds of Islamist insurgents sieged the city, attacking Ba'ath party offices, their leaders, and homes of government officials. The large number of insurgents overran police posts and ransacked armouries. Islamist and opposition activists called Hama a liberated city and called all Syrians to rise up against the infidel regime of the country. By the end of the day, about seventy Ba'ath leaders were killed.

President Hafiz al-Assad sent a large column of Special Forces of Rifaat (Defense Companies) and several regular Syrian army units to Hama. The city was under siege by a twelve-thousand-strong army for about three weeks. Before the offensive, the government called for complete surrender of city, and anyone remaining in the city was declared as insurgent. People frantically left their homes and businesses with very little reserve food or water. They struggled to escape through the advancing tanks and army troops. Before a ring of fire started with artillery, the old city was bombed from the air to crush any active insurgents. The army took control of the city in one week, and in the next two weeks, they hunted for insurgents or anyone in the city. Every army men deployed to the city were instructed to crush the rebellion at any cost and with whatever means. Mass executions, torture, arrests, and killing ensued, resulting in the death of about ten thousand to forty thousand people by different sources. About one thousand soldiers were also killed. When the army commander expressed his difficulty to flush out all insurgents, Rifaat believed that many insurgents or fleeing people were inside the underground tunnels in the city. He gave order to pump diesel into the tunnels and set them to burn. In addition, they put tanks on the tunnel mouths to shell if anyone escaped from the tunnel!

The army crushed the rebellion with brutal force. Brotherhood claimed that about forty thousand citizens were killed, and Rifaat later claimed the credit to kill thirty-eight thousand people. About one hundred thousand people were expelled from the city, and fifteen thousand were missing. The defeat of Hama was crucial for the Brotherhood, the major opposition party in Syria. There was no support for them during the massacre of Hama from any other part of Syria or section of society. Brotherhood was fragmented into two groups; one denounced violence and migrated to European countries, where they established headquarters in London. A small guerrilla group was exiled to Iraq, where they got government support. But eventually, most of them merged with the London-based non-violent fraction. The events in Hama marked a near full stop for opposition activity in Syria. The horror of Hama shocked the world. But Ayatollah Khomeini of Iran made only a mild criticism, not to disturb the relation between the Syrian Shia regime and Shiate Iran.

In the 1990s, Hafiz started liberalization of the economy. Many got benefits, but mostly those in the corridors of power. Eventually, most people in the cities supported the regime for progress, stability, and modernism, especially the rich merchants in Damascus and Aleppo and those close to power centres. But liberalization started by Hafiz and continued by Bashar widened the rich–poor divide, and a large number of people in the villages and poor city neighbourhoods were disillusioned with the power of the Assad family regime.

Rifaat was commander of a special security force loyal to political members of Ba'ath and helped Hafiz for the coup of 1970. He was widely believed as the successor of Hafiz. When Hafiz was in sickbed in 1983, he formed a six-member core group composed of his loyal middle-level Sunni army officers to handle the administration sidelining Rifaat. This alienated Rifaat and many Alawite senior army officers who inclined with Rifaat. Rifaat tried to grab power with the help of forces loyal to him. At that time he was commandeering an army of fifty-five thousand troops equipped with tanks, helicopters, and artillery. He started asserting control over Damascus and put pressure on army units. But Hafiz recovered quickly and regained control. Then all officers rallied in his support. He wanted to retaliate against Rifaat but compromised for the sake of family prestige upon compulsion by his daughter Bushra. On a compromise deal, Rifaat was given the nominal post of vice president but was later forced to live in exile in France and Italy. In 1998, he was removed from all posts. He now lives in exile in France, completely isolated from all powers in Syria. His army unit was sidelined and, later, completely abolished. This made the succession of Bashar al-Assad smooth, without any political rival. Rifaat had a huge business empire in Syria and outside, most of which were controlled by his son, Sumer. From France, he claimed he was the only authority to succeed Hafiz as vice president and frequently issued statements against Bashar al-Assad and his rule. He tried to forge political parties but with little success.

After the death of Hafiz of a heart attack, his son Bashar al-Assad, who was thirty-five years, was elected as the president by the party and through an unopposed referendum. It was renewed from time to time. Bashar was originally uninterested in politics. He was trained as a doctor from Damascus University, later specialized in ophthalmology in Britain and worked as an army doctor. The unexpected death of his brother Bassel in a car accident, who was groomed and projected as the future president, turned attention on Bashar. He was elevated in ranks in the army to make the way for the future heir. He was put on important charge as in Lebanon affairs. Senior army officers and politicians were sidelined, accommodating young loyal officers supporting Bashar. He was appointed as political adviser to Hafiz al-Assad with sweeping powers. Bashar went ahead with an aggressive campaign against corruption. This gave him some popularity and also the opportunity to suppress all rivals who could challenge his future positions. When he became president and regional secretary of the Syrian branch of the Ba'ath party in 2000 after the death of his father, there was widespread activism on the grounds of urging for political reforms. Initially seeming supportive of political and economic reforms, he soon started crushing those leaders of Damascus Spring who were advocating for changes.

Immediately after becoming president, he married Asma Akhras, a British national born to Syrian parents. Their marriage brought some initial optimism, as she was modern and a Sunni Muslim. She got wide attention in social circles who thought she could influence her husband to be moderate and reformist. Later, she proved to be simply supportive of Bashar in all his political ruthlessness. Her private e-mails exposed her extravagant foreign shopping, flooding public money even during the financial crisis and war. She ridiculed the protesters. All these exposed her as just part of the brutal Assad regime. Once a fashion icon for Western magazines and projected as a liberal socialite, she is now being exposed as a supporter of a merciless regime. She faces travel sanctions in the European Union except Britain, where she is a citizen.

Bashar also inherited his family tradition of having a ruthless brother's support from his younger brother, Maher al-Assad. Unlike Bashar, who was a doctor by profession, Maher had military combat experience and was a commander of a tank battalion. Maher was ruthless just like Rifaat and played a similar role in Syria as Rifaat had done in the past during Hafiz regime. He was the commander of the Republican Guard, commander of the elite Fourth Armoured Division, and a member of the central committee of the Syrian Ba'ath Party. Bashar, Maher, and their brother-in-law, Assef Shawkat, formed the power trio of Syria. Shawkat was married to influential Bushra al-Assad, sister of Bashar. Shawkat was the head of military intelligence. Maher, naturally a hot-tempered man, was opposed to the marriage of her sister with Shawkat and imprisoned him several times to keep them separate. But later, they had a good relationship. Maher and Shawkat were believed to be involved in the assassination of Rafik Hariri, a popular Lebanese prime minister in 2005, as per the leaked version of a UN-sponsored Detlev Mehlis inquiry report.

Maher was believed to be responsible for advising Bashar to end the Damascus Spring of 2000 by force. When the Syrian uprising began in March 2011, Maher and his troops played a key role in suppressing the protests violently in the city of Daara, Homs, and Banias. *Los Angeles Times* reported that they got video evidence showing Maher personally shooting at unarmed protesters. Defected soldiers from his units claimed that they were given orders to use deadly force from the beginning. Snipers who worked for him and later defected, claiming that they had been given instructions by Maher to shoot at the head or heart and kill as many protesters as possible. Recep Tayyib Erdogan, prime minister of Turkey, condemned his action and he claimed to have pressured Bashar to send Maher to exile. The USA, European Union, and Arab League issued sanctions against him, froze his assets, and enforced a travel ban by December 2011.

A bomb explosion on 18 July 2012 at the National Security headquarters in Rawda Square, Damascus, killed several high-ranking military officers who were assembled for the military crisis group, a powerful body of eight top defence personnel created by Bashar al-Assad. Assef Shawkat, then the deputy defence minister, and the defence minister, Dawoud Rajiha, along with two other officers were confirmed dead, and other four were injured on the event. There were reports that Maher was injured badly and lost his one leg and the function of one arm and was in treatment in Moscow. There were rumours that he had been killed. He was not seen in public for years after the incident. The Free Syrian Army, and an Islamist group Liwa al-Islam (the Brigade of Islam) claimed responsibility for the incidence. It is believed that the bombs were placed in the hall several days before the meeting and were exploded using a remote control with the help of staff working in the facility when all the attendees were assembled there. Shawkat was given a state-level funeral on July 20, but it was not attended by Bashar and Maher.

In September 2012, Bushra, along with her five children and mother, Anisa Makhlouf, moved to the United Arab Emirates and started living in Dubai. This left Bashar al-Assad as the lone Assad family member active in Syrian politics facing the political turmoil in Syria waiting for his fate. He had another brother, Majid al-Assad. He was an electrical engineer and a low-profile person who died in 2009 following prolonged illness. All his family members now face sanctions and travel restrictions by the European Union. In June 2014, twitter photos of Maher were released by a Lebanese TV presenter, which he claimed had been taken a few days before. He was found to be healthy and happy in those pictures, contesting his death or serious disability.

By 2011, Aleppo was undergoing a rapid transformation. The economy was buzzing; new constructions were coming up every day. The old city looked vibrant with a major facelift. Many new boutique hotels came up in the city. Numerous factories, mainly textile and garment factories, dotted the city, which provided work for thousands of people from nearby villages. Less than fifty miles from the Turkish border the city attracted entrepreneurs from European Union on a renewed cooperation with Syria. Declining oil wealth prompted diversification of economy from too much reliance on oil and agriculture. Growing industry and increasing tourist revenue added a boost to the economy. The city focused on survival and progress more than the politics and democracy. The city, from the medieval period, had acquired a habit of quick recovery from political turmoil and showed great resilience to political activism. The city witnessed several attacks by radicals and sudden ruthless retaliation by security forces. But it moved on. Arab Spring made a halt on this progress. Slowly and steadily, the number of protests and its violent suppression started to affect the atmosphere of Aleppo. Aleppo, just like Damascus, was under the tight grip of military and police apparatus. People were initially not interested when small-scale protests started as early as January 2011 elsewhere in Syria and subsequent revolution.

The first mass protests started in the southern city of Daraa following the arrest and torture of some teenagers who painted revolutionary slogans on a school wall. Subsequent firing on the demonstrators killed several persons, triggering nationwide protests demanding the resignation of President Bashar al-Assad. Several policemen and Ba'ath party members were killed in the violence. By April 2011, protests became widespread, and an army was deployed to quell the agitation.

Hundreds of thousands were marching on the streets across Syria by July 2011. The killing, torture, and arrest of hundreds of activists did not suppress the movement. More and more people joined the protests. Opposition groups eventually started using weapons to defend from the heavily armed regime forces and later to expel forces from local areas. Heavy crackdown on civilian protests and indiscriminate killing of protesters caused several army men to defect from the army. The defected officers became a sizable number, and on 29 July 2011, they announced the formation of the Free Syrian Army (FSA) as an umbrella organization of opposition forces without a central command. FSA was composed of defected armed personal and civilian volunteers. They owed to remove Bashar al-Assad and his government from the power.

With the emergence of FSA, the movement formally became an armed resistance. By October 2011, FSA started to receive support from Turkey, and a rebel army headquarters was established in the Hatay governorate of Turkey, close to the Syrian border. The FSA could launch an attack on Syrian border towns while using the Turkish border as a safe hideout and supply route. Their number became twenty thousand by December 2011. They started to control several towns and villages. By early April 2012, the death toll reached ten thousand. Syria came to world attention. UN and the Arab League started to be involved actively in resolving the crisis. But the fight intensified, and the conflict was labelled a civil war by the UN in June 2012.

Many months after protests started elsewhere in Syria, on 12 August 2011, several small anti-government protest marches were held in different districts of Aleppo. The largest one, at Sakhour district, attracted about one thousand people. The next month, on 11 October 2011, a massive pro-Assad demonstration was held at Saadallah al-Jabiri Square. The local media claimed more than 1.5 million participation in a city of about 3 million. The government enjoyed a silent majority in both major cities of Syria—Damascus and Aleppo. These cities were tightly under their control. By early 2012, security forces were targeted by bombing on a small scale. A suicide attack on 10 February 2012 on two security establishments in Aleppo, including the Military Intelligence Directorate, killed about 28 people and injured around 230.

By July, major fights reached Damascus and Aleppo. Though Aleppo city was in the tight grip of the government, its countryside were gradually becoming rebel strongholds by early 2012. A large rebel group stormed the city on 19 July 2012 with the capture of Salaheddine District in the west part of Aleppo and then gradually spread to other areas. Following the initial surge of about six thousand to eight thousand fighters from several battalions with major contributions from FSA, composed of mainly defected army veterans, they gradually gained more areas. The major regime offensive started on 28 July on rebel-held areas with hours of artillery followed by tanks and ground troops. A fierce fight occurred in the city centre and on many commercial and historical centres. Both groups, rebels and regime forces, followed almost the same tactics. Both were of the mind that the attacking area was enemy land, and they confronted all with vengeance and brutality. Not much regard was given for not harming civilians and protecting national treasures or religious places. But both claimed that they were fighting for the welfare of their countrymen who were now their victims or enemies just because they happened to be on the other side. Extensive looting was the norm. Looting prospects attracted many into either side.

Ample reinforcements for both sides ensured a prolonged war. After many months of war, no one could win a decisive victory, which was expected by either side. Both sides used all possible weapons and all possible tactics. The continuous siege of an area was a common strategy of both groups. All exits would be closed, the power and water supply would be cut off, and people or enemies would be under fire and left to starve. With these tactics, both gained and regained territories. After many months, most of the western half of the city came under rebel control and east under the regime with a dangerous no man's land in between. Syrian air forces frequently bombed rebel-held areas. Artillery bombed buildings and apartments. Snipers were working on both sides, aiming at enemies on the other side. Not only combatants but also innocent civilians were also victims. In the contested areas on all open places and streets, people had to run till they got cover to avoid snipers. On several instances, small children were purposefully targeted and killed by snipers. Pregnant women were killed deliberately to kill the unborn baby and mother together.

A house-to-house fight ensued, and several people were thrown out of their windows from apartments, and many were set on fire alive. For civilians, the plight was terrible and were labelled as enemies based on which side of the territory they happened to be, no matter whether they supported any group or not. Those who could escape left the city, leaving their homes and belongings. When any new area was captured, looters stormed the area for anything valuable. Many rebel forces, including Islamists, were busy in looting than fighting, and one major reason of rivalry among fighters was on the looted goods. In the regime forces, the major skimming work of valuables were carried out by the militia, called shabiha, and a paramilitary force called NDF (National Defense Force). Regular army men also found looting prospects lucrative, from ordinary fighters to commanders. It is believed that more than one thousand different groups are active in the Syrian civil war. When the war broke out in the industrial area of Aleppo, thousands of factories were systematically looted, and the looted goods and valuables were transported to different warehouses. Syrian officials then claimed that they were all transported to the rebel hideouts in Turkey with direct knowledge of the Turkish authorities. In any case, it is commonly agreed that several factories and business places were looted out, big or small, and their owners became paupers overnight, looting alienated people from supporting rebels and regime forces. The regime controlled areas mostly maintaining an urban atmosphere. But in rebel-held areas, there was systemic dysfunction of food supply, sanitation, water, electricity, and transport, as the rebels were not equipped nor trained to do such services.

One of the major concerns for any fighting group was supply lines. Food, weapons, other supportive equipments, and money had to reach the fighters. They mainly came from foreign countries. The strength and reliability of supply and aid determined the strength of the rebel groups. Fighters may switch over their affiliation to another group if the prospects were better. Many groups recruited fighters with a fixed salary. In a war-torn country, a usual salary as low as thirty dollars a month was also a great thing. For government employees and soldiers also, the remunerations were very low for a decent living even before the war. After the beginning of the war, their salaries became erratic and less. On top of that, the skyrocketing of prices of essential goods made things go out of control, even for those living in peaceful areas and with a decent background. These created another group involved in trade and illegal export from other countries. Smuggling of goods in and out of the country became a lucrative business. These smugglers handled basic goods, medicines, weapons, illicit drugs, and even humans.

Import and export through the ports and the airport became limited due to security reasons, and very few international traders were interested to trade with Syria due to an inherent risk of loss of goods and payment. There was a sense of sanction in trade for the government also. This forced even the government to rely on smugglers for food and essential goods. So day by day, the war economy became big. These groups liked to prolong the war at any cost. The war was a catastrophe for the majority of people, but for a small group, it was a great opportunity to become super-rich and influential. Many small-scale Ba'ath members became influential leaders in the regime-aligned militia like Shabiha, the Popular Committee, and the Ba'ath Brigades due to their heroism, worth in war, and looting skill. So also, many rebel fighters and their leaders amassed money and weapons. It was a common practice to siphon off money by rebel leaders from donors, including governments and private donors. Looting of aid materials and money were also common among rebel groups. These are not only social problems but also future risks for ending the war. These new rich and powerful bandits would be the future warlords and influential politicians of post-war Syria.

A major offensive in the souk al-Medina caused fire in the world-famous heritage market. The grand mosque (Umayyad Mosque) of Aleppo, where a large number of people, including women and children, used to gather for prayer, was under rebel control as a base and refuge. A major offensive by regime forces on 24 April 2013 destroyed most parts of the sprawling building. Its 1,400-year-old minarets were destroyed in heavy artillery. After the conquest, the Syrian army allegedly did many atrocities, including killing many women and children and several instances of rape. But within two days, rebels could recapture the mosque and adjacent areas.

A sprawling city of millions became a ghost city. Numerous tall, empty buildings, fully or partly destroyed, dotted the city, and mountains of concrete heaps from levelled buildings and garbage piled up everywhere. Its parks, mosques, souks, and many roads were not recognizable from their surrounding dust and mud heaps. The intensity and tactical importance of the war in Aleppo made it the 'mother of all war' in the Syrian civil war. A large section of its population already left the city, most of them to Turkey, where they lived in primitive conditions. About 80 per cent of them were children and women. They are vulnerable for all sorts of exploitation, including human trafficking and organ trade. The war seemed far from over. The government reasserted their control over major cities. The rebels in Aleppo fought against each other and tried to establish their own territories.

Once an ambitious Islamist extremist group, the Islamic State of Iraq and Sham/Syria (ISIS) lost its entire patronage from global jihad leader Ayman al-Zawahiri and was pushed out from some of its strongholds in Aleppo. It was pushed back near to its traditional bastion in Iraq, in east Syria around Deir ez-Zor, and Raqqa by May 2014. Jabhat al-Nusra, the official Al-Qaeda flag bearer in Syria, had strengthened its position in the south, close to the Jordan border. Jordan was worried over the Al-Qaeda–linked Islamist bastion in their border and havens inside their territories, which acted as a supply base or even an extortion hideout. Jordan may shortly forge alliance with Damascus to keep rebel jihadis at bay.

Turkey continues to be open for foreign fighters, and their soil is a base for many rebel groups and supply lines. But the Recep Tayyip Erdogan government is not so enthusiastic about the Saudi style of rebel support and may influence the warring factions in Syria. Pressure is mounting on Turkey to control the flow of Western fighters. Governments in Tunisia, Morocco, Algeria, and to an extent, Libya are screening all new potential jihadi recruits exiting their country for jihad in Syria, which has already became a social problem and a potential future security threat.

Security in Iraq was deteriorating with more frequent attacks by insurgents and their conquering of large areas of land and cities. After a massive conquest of ISIS in Iraq and it's rebranding itself as Islamic State; US Air Force started bombing ISIS targets in Iraq. Following these attacks, these militants started strengthening their Syrian stronghold and captured more areas from Syrian forces, including the last army air strips in the Raqqa province under Syrian regime by August 2014. These groups may continue to support Syrian jihad to prevent from dying out with one-third of Syria under their control. After their unbelievable success in Iraq, it is believed that many fighters of FSA and Al-Nusra Front deserted their old bases with depleted stocks and money and joined Islamic State with pockets rich from looted money from Iraq and Syria. The declaration of a caliphate by Islamic State was also a boost to these fighters, who had lost morale after fighting a long battle.

Now the Syrian battlefield is gradually becoming a fight between the ultra-orthodox terror outfits of Islamic State versus the old brutal Assad regime. Any backer or opposition has to choose either of these two groups! Mass slaughtering of rival ethnic groups by Islamic State may continue to dominate the picture. Assad may escape from the war, at least for a while. That was the miracle he was expecting, and he is possibly planning not to concentrate on attacking them but to attack the moderate opposition like the Free Syrian Army, who are gaining international sympathy and support. His regime was at the verge of collapse. But with the emergence of Islamic State, their consolidation of power has become a major threat to the region and even the world. So all attention will be on Islamic State, since the extinction of Islamic State will have to be the priority as it poses a bigger threat to millions in the region. Their dramatic spread and potential to invade other neighbouring countries like Jordan and Lebanon poses a real threat to the world and peace. All international attention may fall on them, whether to support them or to finish them. Arab nations may have no choice; the international community will have few other options. The USA is coordinating with Britain, France, Turkey, and other powers in NATO for a broad coalition to crush Islamic State. Lately, Russia joined the group after a humiliating Russian airline crash orchestrated by Islamic State in Sinai by the ISIS. They are trying to gather support from Arab nations, mainly Sunni states who were mostly supporting these groups before. Otherwise, it is going to be a repetition of the story of the first Iraq invasion, which led to unimaginable bloodshed, anarchy and eventually turned the large nation of Iraq a terrorist pastureland. It eventually led to the so called caliphate of 'Islamic State'.

Both groups may continue to fight until a decisive victory. But what will be left at the end—a country which has lost most of its infrastructures like factories, establishments, homes, civic amenities, hospitals and schools? A country without proper police or army to protect their citizens! A country which can't afford to feed its population. Unlike Iraq, Syria is not an oil-rich country. It may take decades to build back its infrastructure spoiled in the past many years of war even if the war ends quickly. If the war is prolonged, it will become another Somalia, a threat to the entire world. Foreign countries supporting either side have to take some responsibility for the cost it has on Syrian people, economy, destruction of infrastructure, failing security, and integrity of an evolved nation. Regime change is inevitable, as is punishment for those who committed horrendous atrocities. But soldiers on both sides and citizens who support them are legitimate citizens of that country who deserve to live, exist, and have their family and society as any other society in the world. It is also shame to the world when people are dying without food or water. Orphans are created at every other moment; people are forced to flee their homes with no idea where to go and when they can come back.

Turbulence caused by the war will continue to haunt the peace of Syria for decades. In the new information technology era of mobile phones and social media, people will add more uploads to the already circulating millions of uploads in the first YouTube war in the history. Political pundits and defence analysts predict the war may go on for a decade or more. For more than half of the 23-million population of Syria who are displaced from their homes, the nightmare will continue indefinitely. Returning to their homes and going back to their normal work or school will remain a distant reality. The burgeoning war economy will try everything possible so that the war and anarchy will continue indefinitely. Rebel groups, criminal gangs, regime militia (Shabiha), and paramilitary NDF (National Defence Force) will struggle to make some money by looting, torture, or extortion. Many new criminals are created by the war either from compulsion of a brutal war or they just become opportunists for making some easy money or power.

Once a major trade route and trail for tourists, the roads to Aleppo are now frequented by a different group of travellers. For the inhabitants of Aleppo, these roads are now the exit routes from the hellfire and mayhem of a man-made misery. For rebels and the regime men, they are their supply line, a place to put their check posts, and locations to set siege, ambush, and loot. Another enthusiastic group coming and making this route as the way to their dream and paradise is a group of Islamist jihadis from more than eighty countries, including the neighbouring Arabian countries, Maghreb, Turkey, Pakistan, Balkan, and from Europe. They come from as far as America, Indonesia, and the Philippines. This was the city where the Al-Qaeda jihadis showed their strength for the first time in Syria and were concentrated. Later,

ISIS established their Syrian headquarters in Raqqa. This is also the way for Iranian fighters and their Quds force, Hisbullah fighters from Lebanon, and Shia volunteers from Iraq. Many veterans of Afghan jihad and the Iraq war and insurgency are finding this way with nostalgia for their old war and jihad. It is also the road for smugglers. Occasional foreigners are also crossing these roads to find some cheap donors of kidneys and other organs. Some come to buy a new wife or mistress or to recruit young girls from impoverished families or those that have become orphans to brothels. When will the tourists ride these roads to see the glory of the cradle of civilization, their beautiful historic buildings in their olden glory, their charming, cheerful children, men, and women?

CHAPTER 4

New Generation Al-Qaeda

Blood must flow. There must be widows. There must be orphans

Sheikh Abdulla Azzam, the mentor and founder of Al-Qaeda,
on jihad

Al-Qaeda was formed in August 1988 at a meeting of Afghan mujahideen under Osama Bin Laden at Peshawar, Pakistan, as an elite vanguard for global Islamic jihad. That was the time when Afghan jihad was near to an end, and Soviet forces started their withdrawal from their barracks in Afghanistan after occupation for about a decade. The leftover war equipment, money, men, and wealth of experience they gained from a long war in one of the most difficult terrains on earth were their initial capital. These mujahideen used to call their training camp *al-Qaeda*, the Arabic word for 'the base' and the name was carried forward for the new organization.

The victory of Islamist fighters who came from all over the world as volunteers to fight against a mighty empire USSR was not so small or easy. It was a country which had a land area of more than one sixth of the globe and had influence on about half of the land area of the world as the centre of the communist bloc. This unbelievable victory and subsequent crumbling of the Soviet Union itself had instilled in the group—a small group among hundreds of Afghan mujahideen groups—a profound optimism that many things once believed to be impossible could be feasible.

Bin Laden became a hero among the various political factions of Afghanistan, among Pakistani and Saudi establishments, especially

35

among intelligence circles who were the major architects of the Afghan war. He became a religious hero for Saudi people as their mujahideen prince who defeated communist Russia. So it also was an inspiration for Islamists across the world who heard about his story. His heroism, commitment to ideology, and dedication to the cause despite his rich background was inspiration and acceptance to a growing number of youngsters looking for an Islamic revivalism in the world. Bin Laden was going to get a heroic welcome in his home country, Saudi Arabia.

On the other hand, most of the Bin Laden's associates were from Egyptian Islamic Jihad (EIJ) and other similar banned organizations in their native countries who expected possible arrest and persecution if they return to their parent countries. They were just activists with not-so-good financial background or who were cut off from their families and their assistance. They saw a huge sum of personal money Bin Laden acquired and pledged for the cause along with his charisma to organize more funds from many potential donors. This led to the origin of Al-Qaeda. But the name was rarely used by their associates simply because not much importance was ascribed to the name or to a formal structure for the organization.

Charisma, knowledge, wealth, and respect made Bin Laden a formidable leader in the group without dispute. His brilliant knowledge in Islamic theology, history, and geopolitical structure of the Middle East and the world was unchallengeable in the group. His literary skill was exceptional. This gave him a clear lead against others, especially his potential challenger, Ayman al-Zawahiri. EIJ was holding the largest faction within the Al-Qaeda core, and it was structurally a separate entity under Zawahiri. Many were members of both Al-Qaeda and EIJ. In 2001, EIJ merged formally with Al-Qaeda, though both groups carried out operations together and were almost synonymous before. With this merger, Zawahiri became more prominent, second in command in Al-Qaeda, almost at par with Laden due to the fact that most of Shura-e-Majilis's highest decision-making body of Al-Qaeda members were from an EIJ background and the new entity was referred to as Qaeda al-Jihad.

During the years of the Afghan war against Russians, Bin Laden and his associates received indirect aid from the USA through cooperation with Central Intelligence Agency (CIA) and the Pakistan army. The USA supplied arms and money to the Pakistan army and its ISI (Inter-Services Intelligence), which in turn was used for waging war against Soviets by mujahideen forces. ISI armed and trained several mujahideen factions in various training grounds in Pakistan and Afghan territories. Peshawar, a city bordering Afghanistan on the road to Kabul, became the hub of all proxy war and mujahideen activities. But at the end of the war, Bin Laden and his group turned against their benevolent supporter, USA. What caused this shift of allegiance and the twist where a friend became a bitter foe was due to their ideological background.

Egyptian Islamic Jihad, a violent mutant of its parent, Muslim Brotherhood in Egypt, had long held America as their enemy for patronizing Israel and supporting dictatorial regimes in the Islamic world. The Muslim Brotherhood had the history of fighting against Israel in several conflicts, and they were highly spirited warriors fighting for victory or attainment of martyrdom. USA, throughout the history of Israel, had maintained an active supportive role for Israel. More than a friendly country, it was protecting it on all necessary occasions with arms and material and political support. They used their veto power in the UN to oppose sanctions or resolutions condemning Israel on several occasions. When one of their major ideological opponents, communism, which occupied the Muslim land of Afghanistan, was defeated in Afghanistan, the attention of Al-Qaeda leaders shifted to their long-time enemy, the United States and its allies.

Bin Laden also maintained the USA as a major enemy of Islam. His knowledge about US involvements in Arab affairs and constant support for Israel made the USA the number 1 enemy. This was amplified in August 1990 when Saddam Hussein invaded Kuwait, putting Saudi Arabia at risk, which led to assistance from the USA and allies. During the ensuing Gulf War, US forces landed in areas in Saudi Arabia, and in fact, their major bases were close to Jeddah near the holy place of Mecca. For Bin Laden, this was a nightmare, and he tried everything possible to avoid US involvement with his limited ability. He personally met King Fahd and advised him not to bring US forces or receive support from other non-Muslim countries and offered his and his group's support. His reason was once the US forces are allowed to have a base in the land of holy cities, they would never leave. His predictions were right; even after the Gulf War, US forces maintained bases in Saudi with the pretext of avoiding any future hostilities, and they continued to maintain their bases.

In Egypt, the USA was a major supporter of long-reigning dictator Hosni Mubarak, who ruthlessly suppressed Islamists, including the Brotherhood and its offshoots like EIJ. The USA was also against the regime in Sudan under Omar al-Bashir and his Islamist deputy, Hassan al-Turabi, who were inspiring Islamists all over the world. They were welcoming Muslims from anywhere in the world. They offered entry without a visa for any Muslim from any nationality to settle in their country. Many of Bin Laden's associates landed in Sudan. Bin Laden landed there after he was banished from Saudi Arabia following his criticism of the Saudi royal family in the aftermath of the Gulf War. The USA was against the Sudan regime. The CIA advised Saudi Arabia to extradite Bin Laden from Sudan and execute him if possible. But the Saudi government refused, and eventually, Laden had to abandon his base in Sudan and head to Afghanistan. Many of these developments further alienated the Al-Qaeda group against the USA.

Al-Qaeda like global jihadi vanguard was not the brainchild of Osama Bin Laden. When Bin Laden reached Pakistan and Afghanistan, he did not have much practical experience in any organization, insurgency, war, or in the military. He had grown in a strict religious background with sound understanding from Wahhabi teachers and Muslim Brotherhood ideologues. By this time, he was very religious and deeply convinced that a fight against Soviet infidels who were occupying the Muslim heartland of Afghanistan was a religious duty of utmost importance for all Muslims. Immediately finishing his course in King Abdul Aziz University, Jeddah, he headed to Peshawar, Pakistan, in 1981 at the age of thirty-four. Peshawar was the hub of all Afghan mujahideen activities and training camps for various fighting groups waging war against Soviet forces in Afghanistan. There he met Abdulla Azzam, who was a respected scholar, Islamist, and Brotherhood member originally from Palestine. Bin Laden might have known him from his university days.

Azzam worked with Islamist fighters from Arabian countries who came for Afghan jihad. He provided hostels for the new entrants, guided them, and later recruited to various mujahideen factions. Bin Laden joined with him. They together founded Maktab al-Khadamat (MAK), meaning Services Office, in 1984, with Peshawar as the headquarters. Osama pumped in large sums of money from his personal wealth, and he organized funds from Saudi governments, members of the royal family, and many wealthy petrodollar millionaires. He inherited a large sum of money from his father (about twenty-five to thirty million US dollars) and got a stipend of about seven million US dollars every year from his father's wealth. Bin Laden was trusted among Saudi circles due to his family background, his pleasant manners, and his deep commitment to his words.

Azzam was an academic scholar with masters in sharia and a PhD in Islamic jurisprudence (Usool ul-Fiqh) from Al-Azhar University, Cairo, Egypt. Immediately after the 1979 invasion of Afghanistan, he issued a fatwa, 'Defence of the Muslim Lands, the First Obligation after Faith'. He declared that Afghan and Palestinian struggles were jihad and killing occupants of their land (whatever their faith may be) was Fard al-Ayn (a compulsory obligation) for all Muslims. The fatwa was supported by Abd al-Aziz Bin Bazz, Saudi Arabia's grand mufti (highest religious position) at that time. From Saudi Arabia, Abdulla Azzam headed for Islamabad, where he joined the International Islamic University in Islamabad in 1980. Soon he shifted to Peshawar, close to Afghanistan, to concentrate on Afghan jihad. Later, he expanded his activities along with Bin Laden starting MAK.

Azzam was highly enthusiastic of jihad (alms struggle) and advocated both defensive and offensive jihad in Afghanistan and later to other areas where the Muslims are oppressed. He was an active founding member of Markaz-ud-Dawa-wal-Irshad (Center for Preaching and Guidance, or MDI) formed in 1986 from the parent Jama'at-ud-Dawa (JuD, an organization for preaching) a puritan missionary group dedicated to promoting the Ahl-e-Hadith version of Islam in Pakistan. The MDI was formed by the merging of JuD with an anti-Soviet jihadist group under Zaki-ur-Rehman Lakvi. The leader of JuD and MDI was Hafiz Mohammed Saeed. Zafar Iqbal was another founder. This organization became a major terrorist organization called Lashkar-e-Toyiba (LeT) in 1990, concentrating against anti-India activities, mainly in Kashmir. They eventually organized the Indian Parliament attack of 2001 and the 26 November 2008 Mumbai attack, killing 164 and wounding more than 300 people. LeT is a banned terrorist organization in the USA, UK, India, European Union, and many other countries. It is banned in Pakistan, but its politicians and Inter Services Intelligence (ISI) continue to provide protection and support. Hafiz Saeed and Zaki-ur-Rehman Lakvi were accused as the main masterminds of Mumbai attack and are wanted by India.

Following the Grand Mosque seizure in Mecca in November 1979 by an extremist armed group and ensuing clean-up against all possible dissidents and Islamist revivalists, Azzam was expelled from his lecturer position at King Abdul Aziz University in Jeddah, Saudi Arabia. Soon he joined the International Islamic University in Islamabad, Pakistan, to be involved in the Afghan war. He was a noted scholar and prominent academician. Though known among Islamist circles, he was not actively working with any organization. It is believed that while in Pakistan, he was convinced by Mohammed Atef to denounce his career and devote himself solely to preach jihad. Mohammed Atef was a former Egyptian Air Force officer who later became the military chief of Al-Qaeda.

Mohammed Atef al-Masri (alias Abu Hafs al-Masri) was born in Menoufya in Nile Delta, close to Cairo and the birthplace of two Egyptian presidents—Mubarak and Sadat. It was also the stronghold of Egyptian Islamic Jihad, and he became a member. After working in the Egyptian Air Force for two years as part of the compulsory military service, he became an agricultural engineer. When the Afghan war started, he headed to Pakistan to join the Afghan jihad. There he met Abdulla Azzam, who eventually sent him to an Afghan training camp, where he met Ayman al-Zawahiri, another Egyptian with an EIJ background. Zawahiri introduced Atef to Bin Laden. Shortly, he became a member of the inner circle of Bin Laden. He attended the founding meetings of Al-Qaeda. Apart from his military background, his determination, ambition to attain martyrdom, and loyalty to his chief, Bin Laden, and his group made Atef powerful in the central core of Al-Qaeda. He was a major planner and architect of many armed missions, including embassy bombings in Africa. Bin Laden put him on a regular monthly salary from his fund. After Al-Qaeda's first military commander, Ali al-Rashidi, commonly called Abu Obeida al-Bansheeri, died in a Lake Victoria boat mishap on a recruiting mission, Atef was selected to the post.

Atef was in charge of Bin Laden's security. He used to personally frisk journalists who wanted to meet Bin Laden. He appeared in the video with Bin Laden and Zawahiri in which Al-Qaeda formally accepted the responsibility for the September 11 attacks. But he never publicly spoke in those videos. One of the sons of Bin Laden was married to Atef's daughter. Atef directed the training camps in Afghanistan. Being a serious man, he seldom mingled with young jihadi recruits. He is believed to have written a 180-page Al-Qaeda military manual titled 'Military Studies in the Holy Struggle against Tyrants'. One of the early Al-Qaeda recruits, Paulo Jose de Almeida Santos, a newly converted Portuguese Muslim who became an Al-Qaeda member and had close contact with many early leaders of Al-Qaeda, remembered him thus: 'Abu Hafs was the real chief of al-Qaeda. Bin Laden was very humble, I could ask him for advice in particular circumstances and he would simply say: "Go and ask Abu Hafs, who is more intelligent than me."' He further stated in his interview, 'There wasn't a well-defined hierarchy, we were rather disorganized; you could give a try to whatever entered into your head. Bin Laden was the guy who gave money to keep the organization going, but he didn't give many orders.'

Atef closely followed Al-Qaeda activists during their Sudan years. When they were forced to leave Sudan, he settled in Afghanistan.

He was closely involved in the African missions of Al-Qaeda. He might have personally participated in the training of Aidid's men in Somalia, resulting in heavy casualties of US soldiers in the first Battle of Mogadishu. He was also the architect of embassy bombings in Kenya and Tanzania. Along with six others, he was killed in a drone strike in his compound near Kabul by US forces in November 2001.

But the major military trainer for Al-Qaeda was an Egyptian Islamic jihad ideologue called Ali Mohamed. Ali Abdul Saoud Mohamed was working as a major in the Egyptian army's military intelligence unit. It was not clear whether the army had officially sent Ali Mohamed to the Afghan war as the country was offering support in the war against Soviets or if he had voluntarily gone to be a part of the armed struggle like other jihadis. He was a mystery man with intelligence background throughout his activist life. In early 1980, he trained fighters en route to Afghanistan. He might have personally participated in some military activities in Afghanistan. During this time, he made contact with Ayman al-Zawahiri, who was working in the same field. Ali was an exceptionally fit man, an expert in martial arts, very intelligent, and was fluent in many languages, including English, Hebrew, Arabic, and French. When Zawahiri went to the USA to gain support and funds for the Afghan jihad, Ali accompanied him as his translator.

Zawahiri advised him to infiltrate the US establishments. Egypt dismissed him from his military job due to his fundamentalist activities in 1984. The same year, he reported to the CIA station in Cairo and wanted to meet the station chief to offer his service. The CIA initially thought that he was an Egyptian spy. Even then, he was recruited as a junior intelligence officer and was deputed to work in Hamburg, Germany. There he was asked to infiltrate a mosque with Hizbullah connections. He simply informed the leader of the group that he was an American spy trying to collect information on their activities. Another agent present there reported his strange behaviour to the CIA, who dismissed him and sought to ban him from entering the USA. But even before the procedure processing was complete, he landed up in California in September 1985 through a visa waiver programme sponsored by the CIA itself to shield valuable assets or those who performed important services for the country. On the way to America, he met an American woman, Linda Sanchez from Santa Clara, California, on the flight, and they became friends. After six weeks, they got married, and he shifted to her house. This enabled him to become a US citizen in 1989. He was picked up by Special Forces in the American army in 1986 and sent to John F. Kennedy Special Warfare Center and School at Fort Bragg, North Carolina, and was stationed there until 1989. It was his second coming to the centre; the first had been in 1981 when he was working in the Egyptian army on a training mission. Fort Bragg was regarded as the US military's top warfare planning centre. There, he was encouraged to pursue a doctorate in Islamic studies. He was noted as a highly accomplished performer. He used to teach courses on the Middle East and Arabic culture to armed personnel. He gave orientations to army personnel deputed to work in the Middle East about the culture and politics of Arabia.

In 1988, Ali took a leave from the army to fight Soviets in Afghanistan. Though his senior reported this to army intelligence, no one responded. One month later, he came back with souvenirs that he claimed were uniform belts of two Russian soldiers he killed in Afghanistan. His seniors were baffled by his bizarre behaviour. His commanding officer, Lt. Col. Robert Anderson, later revealed that he wrote a detailed report aimed at getting army intelligence to investigate Ali and have him court-martialled. To his big surprise, his reports were ignored. It was unthinkable for him that an American army officer would go unpunished after fighting an unauthorized foreign war. More surprising was a person of his background who was an active member of a banned extremist group in Egypt responsible for the assassination of its president (Anwar Sadat) being recruited by the CIA and later trained by the Special Forces of the US army. He believed that the only possible reason could be that he was sponsored by some intelligence agency, likely the CIA.

In the USA, Ali imparted training on clandestine military and sabotage activities to many jihadis associated with the al-Kifah Refugee Center in New York. His students, like El Sayyid Nosair and Mahmud

Abouhalima, were involved in the future assassination of Meir Kahane and assisted Ramzi Yousef for his 1993 World Trade Center attack. He photocopied many military documents of the US army and prepared many miniature charts and maps of the US military. In 1989, he honourably retired from the US army, and he was on army reserves for the next five years. The *New York Times* reported that commendations in his file included one for 'patriotism, valour, fidelity, and professional excellence'. At this time, he was showing secret official US military videos to the prospective terrorists at the al-Kifah Refugee Centre. Even during his army days, he used to visit the centre regularly on weekends to give training. The future jihadis were given shooting training in several shooting ranges around New York.

The al-Kifah Refugee Centre in Brooklyn, New York, was the headquarters for MAK in the USA, coordinating the activities of about thirty branches in major US cities. They recruited about two hundred people for Afghan jihad. After imparting training on various guns and basic military tactics, they would be sent to the MAK base in Peshawar, Pakistan. They were provided a visa, air tickets, contact details, and money from the large fund MAK had acquired over the years. All were provided only a one-way ticket symbolizing their willingness for jihad and martyrdom. They would be then recruited to the radical MAK-affiliated Afghan faction led by Abdul Rasul Sayyaf or the one led by Gulbuddin Hekmatyar. The MAK collected millions of dollars from US donors for the Afghan jihad. Azzam and Zawahiri visited the Kifah centre and other US cities.

After his retirement from the US army, Ali Mohamed went back to Afghanistan in 1990. He was introduced to Bin Laden by Zawahiri. There he indulged in training of Al-Qaeda members on intelligence tactics like surveillance, counter-surveillance, secret codes, and ciphering codes. His first batch of students included Bin Laden, Zawahiri and some top Al-Qaeda leaders. He prepared a multi volume Al-Qaeda military training manual with the help of documents acquired during his army service in USA. He introduced the 'cell structure' with groups within terrorist members making harder to destroy terrorism. Various terror tactics like kidnapping, assassinations and hijacking planes were taught to his jihadi students which he learned while working with Special Forces in USA. During these years he used to fly frequently to US to indulge in activities in California and New York.

In 1991, Al-Qaeda shifted their base to Sudan. It was a major operation involving crossing through many countries by at least two dozen Al-Qaeda members and their equipment. Ali coordinated these activities. His later activities included, as he told to a judge when he was caught, 'In the early 1990s, I assisted Al-Qaeda in creating a presence in Nairobi, Kenya, and worked with several others on this project. Abu Ubaidah was in charge of Al-Qaeda in Nairobi until he drowned. Khalid al-Fawwaz set up Al-Qaeda's office in Nairobi. A car business was set up to create income. Wadih el-Hage created a charity organization that would help provide Al-Qaeda members with identity documents.' Ali also told the court that he had been asked by bin Laden to identify possible targets and he conducted surveillance on the American embassy buildings in Africa.

Osama trusted Ali Mohamed to the core. Ali personally organized his journey to Sudan and in 1996 to Jalalabad, Afghanistan. But Mohammed Atef had doubts that he could be working with American authorities. Atef refused to allow Ali Mohamed to know which name and passport he would be travelling under. Following the 1998 embassy bombings in Kenya and Tanzania, the FBI raided the flat of Ali and found many Al-Qaeda documents and terrorist plots. He was later arrested and tried secretly. He cooperated with investigators and told his entire story and involvement to the trial judge. His verdict was postponed many times, and his whereabouts are still unknown.

Later on, his former association with CIA and FBI became more evident with many new reports trickling in. On 16 June 1993, he was detained by the Royal Canadian Mountain Police in Vancouver, Canada, while he was picking up Essam Marzouk to help him to infiltrate the USA. Marzouk was carrying numerous fake passports. They found him involved in a terror group. After several hours of questioning, Ali said that he was an FBI informant and he asked to contact his handler in the FBI, John Zent. Zent confirmed that he was their agent and asked them to release him. Marzouk was sent to jail.

Al-Qaeda financed for his bail, and after one year, Ali personally helped him to get released and was allowed to live in Canada. Marzouk was later involved in embassy bombings in Kenya and Tanzania in 1998.

After his release, Zent interviewed Ali at the FBI office in San Francisco. Ali was working as an FBI informant on smugglers of illegal migrants to USA from Mexico. Ali told Zent that Osama Bin Laden was running a group called Al-Qaeda. Ali claimed that he had met Bbin Laden and he was involved in the training of his group members in camps in Afghanistan and Sudan on intelligence and hijacking techniques. He said that Laden was building an army that could be used to overthrow Saudi's royal family regime. This was probably the first time FBI had heard the word *Al-Qaeda*, even though the CIA might have been aware of it as early as 1991 when Bin Laden shifted his base to Sudan. In 1991, the CIA was suspicious that Bin Laden had started an organization called Al-Qaeda and started spying on him. CIA assigned this job to Billy Waugh, a veteran army man and intelligence contractor. He later recalled in a book that he used to purposefully follow Bin Laden. He was an old man. Acting as a fitness freak, he used to jog in front of Laden's house. Once, they met face-to-face, and he was confident that Laden might have realised that the CIA was behind him. Waugh knew Laden from his Afghan years. But the state department publicly used the term *Al-Qaeda* only in August 1996.

But before the formal arrest of Ali Mohamed in 1998, the CIA made a major breakthrough on Al-Qaeda. In June 1996, Jamal al-Fadl, an operative from al-Qaeda's first meeting in 1988 to late 1995, walked to the US embassy in Eritrea after defecting from Al-Qaeda. He told the US everything he knew about al-Qaeda. He was present in the first planning meeting from 11–20 August *1988 along with Bin Laden, Abdulla Azzam, Al-Zawahiri, Mohamed Atef, Mamdouh Mahmud Salim, Wael Hamza Julaidan, and Mohammed Loay Bayazid and seven others to discuss the founding of Al-Qaeda. He was questioned by CIA and FBI for months. He continued to give inputs which led to the crackdown on* the Al-Qaeda network and activities. While in Al-Qaeda, he was actively involved in many financial transactions. He was aware of all training centres, business deals, and financial sources. He had access to all membership logs, leadership structure, ideologies, and many future plots. Though by this time the CIA had acquired a large amount of data about Al-Qaeda, he was a perfect guide to verify and fill all the gaps in their knowledge. A Sudanese citizen, he worked also in Sudan intelligence with the concurrence of Bin Laden. He helped to prepare the fact sheet on bin Laden released by the US sdepartment in August 1996, calling him 'one of the most significant financial sponsors of Islamic extremist activities in the world today . . . and responsible for killing of US soldiers in Somalia'. This document first reported the term *Al-Qaeda*, which was quoted by the media on the next day, for the first time ever. At the same time, another defector of Al-Qaeda joined US agencies. His identity was unknown. He also confirmed the inputs of al-Fadl.

While he was heading Maktab al-Khadamat (MAK), Azzam travelled throughout the Middle East, Europe, and several cities in the USA to gain support for Afghan jihad and raise money. He preached the need of jihad and inspired young Muslims with the heroism of Afghan fighters and many divine miracles in their battle. He used to quote stories of a handful of mujahideen fighters that defeated large columns of the Russian army, fighters who survived after having been run over by tanks, falling bombs from aircrafts intercepted by birds, and so on. A television documentary of Steven Emerson in 1994 showed video footage of Azzam advocating his audience to wage jihad in America, which he overtly explained as fighting only, fighting with swords. His cousin Fayiz Azzam recollected him saying, 'Blood must flow. There must be widows, there must be orphans.'

MAK became a prominent institution in Peshawar, and Azzam started his own militia. Bin Laden worked along with him. Though their main focus was on recruitment and training, they were also involved in some combat operations in Afghanistan. Azzam was an ideological figurehead among Afghan jihad leaders. He worked for unity among the groups. When the Soviet Union was getting defeated and started exiting from Afghanistan, Azzam and Bin Laden decided to make their jihadi organization permanent, and this led to the formation of Al-Qaeda al-Askariya, which can be translated as 'the military base', which was later shortened to Al-Qaeda, meaning 'the base'. By the creation of Al-Qaeda in August 1988 at Peshawar, Pakistan, MAK and its institutions became the de facto Al-Qaeda centres.

Azzam was constantly focused on jihad. His famous slogan was 'Jihad and the rifle alone: no negotiations, no conferences, and no dialogues.' His enthusiasm for jihad was compounded by his inspirational idea that 'one hour in the path of jihad is worth more than seventy years of praying at home'. In one of the several books he authored, *Join the Caravan*, released in 1987, he asked Muslims to rally in the fight to support Muslim victims of aggression, to bring back Muslim lands from foreign domination, and to uphold the Muslim faith. This later became the basic motive of Al-Qaeda. The idea of aggressive jihad of Azzam was at odds with Bin Laden, whose initial focus was trying to make political changes in the Arab world. Azzam insisted to continue the training camps in Afghanistan, while Laden fought with him to set up many training places throughout the world. A prominent Al-Qaeda leader, Zawahiri, had conflicts with Azzam. For Zawahiri and his EIJ activists, not only Jews, Christians, and Indian Hindus were their enemies but also the so-called Muslims in countries like Egypt, who were supporting the so-called oppressive regimes and their sympathizers. For them, they were all apostates, and even the secular Muslim governments too. But Azzam strongly opposed *takfir* (declaring apostate) of Muslims, including Muslim governments, as spreading fitna or disunity within the Muslim community. Towards the end of the Afghan war, Azzam's attention shifted to the struggle in Palestine, his home country. Many Hamas members were trained in his camps, and they participated in the Afghan war. They started returning to Palestine for the fight against Israeli occupation.

On 24 November 1989, while Muhammad Azzam was driving his two sons to his regular Friday prayer at the Arab mosque in Peshawar, his car was detonated in a bomb blast and thrown up into the air. His wife heard the voice from their home and immediately thought that it was him. She called up the mosque and asked whether it had been in the mosque or in his car; the replay came as his car. There had been several attempts on his life before in the past many months. The latest was one month before, when a bomb had been placed under the pulpit of the Arab mosque in Gulshan Iqbal Road in the university town neighbourhood of western Peshawar. He had regularly preached his sermon there during Friday prayers. It had been his jihad base. It had been a powerful bomb sufficient enough to kill all the people inside the mosque. But the bomb had been discovered before the beginning of the prayer and had been disposed of.

Time magazine reported, quoting Waheed Mazhda that he had noticed some crew on the road leading to the Arab mosque doing some work the day before. He had assumed it was routine roadwork, but that was strange in that area neglected by governments. The bomb was connected to a long cord, and his assassin had stood about fifty metres from the site near a sewage system. Azzam was buried near the grave of his mother who had died a year before at the Pabi Graveyard of the Shuhada (martyrs) in Peshawar. His assassins were never caught, and the mystery of his death was never solved.

At that time, he had many enemies, and he himself told one local journalist, Jamal Ismail, once, 'My destiny is already written. Nothing I can do to prevent what is meant to happen.' It is widely believed that Israeli Mossad was behind the assassination. Azzam was warned by an informer from Palestine Liberation Organization (PLO) that he was a target of Israel. Israel found many new Hamas fighters working in Israel were trained by camps run by Azzam in Afghanistan. Another suspect was the CIA, which was unhappy due to not disbanding mujahideen fighters after the Afghan war. Among the Islamist radicals, Gulbuddin Hekmatyar, a fearsome Pashtun warlord with close ties to Pakistan's intelligence agencies, was a strong possibility. He hated Azzam for backing Hekmatyar's great rival, Ahmad Shah Massoud. Massoud was an ethnic Tajik whom Azzam labelled 'the new hero of jihad', while Zawahiri was a supporter of Hekmatyar. Al-Qaeda later

49

sent a death squad to kill Massoud just two days before the 9/11 attacks. Any possible investigation on the murder should have been done by the ISI (Inter Services Intelligence) and would have acted to protect Hekmatyar if he was involved. Both Zawahiri and Osama Bin Laden were also suspected due to their differences with Azzam. Former FBI agent Ali Soufan, in his book *The Black Banners*, claimed that Ayman al-Zawahiri was behind the assassination. He was not happy with Azzam, as he felt him moderate and not cooperative with him on his wider plan for insurgency in Egypt, and if he would be eliminated, Bin Laden's fund would be directed to him. He used to call Azzam a CIA spy for his less aggressive stand. Critics claim that Zawahiri at that time was not prominent or influential enough to organize such an attack. But the situation in Peshawar at that time was so fluid that anyone with money could buy any weapon or hire fighters and assassins.

When Mohammed Saddiq Odeh was arrested in 1998 for his role in the African embassy bombings, he reportedly told the US interrogators that Bin Laden had personally ordered the killing of Azzam, as he suspected his former mentor had ties with the CIA. It is possible that he was just passing a rumour he had heard.

The assassination of Azzam did not become big news. No serious investigation was done in Pakistan as he was not their citizen. He was just an Arab fighting jihad on this foreign land. Moreover, not many people were seriously interested in a proper investigation, given the vast number of his enemies and political rivals. Another possible agency behind this was KGB or KHAD (the intelligence service of the communist government in Afghanistan), as he was a powerful leader in the Afghan jihad. Even the ruling prime minister, Benazir Bhutto, could have been implicated as Azzam was found to be behind one of the non-confidence motions against her government. Iran was also a suspect due to its anti-Shia stand. The killing of Azzam who was a major jihadi leader in Afghan war will remain a mystery like the death of the chief architect of Afghan war against Soviets, General Zia-ul-Haq, who was army chief and president of Pakistan. He was mysteriously killed along with many senior army officers and the US ambassador to Pakistan on 17 August 1988. The same possible conspirators, except those in Al-Qaeda, were suspected in his mysterious death in a deliberate aircraft accident. Some in the Pakistan army were also suspected. The Zia murder mystery was also never solved.

After the death of Azzam, most of his supporters joined Bin Laden, while some left. Bin Laden took full control of his recruitment and support network. MAK formally merged with Al-Qaeda. In the past, Bin Laden, Azzam, and Zawahiri had been working together in many spheres and supporting each other but maintained their own independent cells as well. Bin Laden and Azzam ran a magazine named *Al-Jihad* (the alms struggle).

The first branch of Maktab al-Khadamat (also called al-Kifah) to be established on US soil was in 1986 at the Islamic Center of Tucson, Tucson, Arizona. This Islamic Centre was, basically, the first cell of al-Qaeda in the United States, where all their US activities started. The organization's journal, *Al-Jihad* was first distributed in the USA from there. Many other branches sprouted up soon after. A number of important future Al-Qaeda figures were connected to the Tucson branch like Mohammed Loay Bayazid, one of the founders of Al-Qaeda. Wael Hamza Julaidan, another founder of Al-Qaeda and a Saudi multimillionaire, and Wadih El-Hage, who later became bin Laden's personal secretary and was convicted for his role in the 1998 US embassy bombings in Africa, also worked there. Hani Hanjour, a future 9/11 hijacker, moved to this centre around 1991 and spent the rest of the decade around there, but he was mostly elusive.

In December 1987, Mustafa Shalabi and others established the al-Kifah (Struggle) Refugee Center in Brooklyn, New York; it soon became the most important branch of MAK in USA. At first, it was located inside the al-Farouq mosque itself. But later, it got its own office space next to the mosque. Shalabi, who was a naturalized citizen from Egypt, ran the office with Mahmud Abouhalima. Jamal al-Fadl, who later went to Afghanistan and became a founding member of Al-Qaeda, was also recruited at the al-Kifah Refugee

Center in its early days. He later became a crucial FBI informant. The *Independent* news would later call the office 'a place of pivotal importance to Operation Cyclone, the American effort to support the Mujahideen. The Al-Kifah Refugee Center was raising funds and, crucially, providing recruits for the struggle, with active American assistance.'

Azzam, Bin Laden's mentor, frequently visited and made lectures in the area. In 1988, he told a crowd of several hundred in Jersey City, 'Blood and martyrdom are the only way to create a Muslim society. However, humanity won't allow us to achieve this objective, because humanity is the enemy of every Muslim.' Ayman al-Zawahiri was also associated with this centre and collected a considerable amount of money to take back to Pakistan. In July 1990, Omar Abdel Rahman, also called the Blind Sheikh, who was close to bin Laden, arrived in New York from Sudan on a controversial CIA-supported visa. Soon he took over the charge of the al-Kifah Refugee Center from Mustapha Shalabi. With his arrival, the centre for training, inspiration, and recruitment was suddenly transformed into a centre for activism.

Omar was the infamous spiritual leader of the outlawed Egyptian extremist organization Al-Gama'a al-Islamiyya. He worked in Afghanistan along with ISI and CIA on Afghan jihad. His sermons and videos were widely publicized in the USA and throughout the world where MAK had influence. Omar was widely known in the Arab world as the mastermind of the assassination of the Egyptian president, Anwar Sadat. Almost all known early Al-Qaeda militants in the USA had contact with him. Immediately after his entry into USA and taking over the affairs of the Al-Kifah centre, terrorist plots of Al-Qaeda in the USA started, one after the other.

The first-ever attack by Al-Qaeda can be regarded as the 5 November 1990 assassination of Meir Kahane, the founder of the Jewish Defense League (JDL), a New York–based Jewish extremist group and the founder of the Kach party in Manhattan. The purported motto of JDL was to 'protect Jews from anti-Semitism by whatever means necessary'. In FBI records, it was known as a violent extremist

Jewish organization with statistics from 1980–1985 showing their members were responsible for fifteen of the eighteen officially classified terrorist attacks in the USA committed by Jews. Most of their victims were Russians, Arab Americans, and on some occasions, even moderate Jews. They were involved in many bombings of business establishments and institutions and assassinations. Its sister organization with a similar ideology was the Kach party, which was banned in Israel as a terrorist organization. Several leaders of JDL faced violent death, including Meir Kahane. He was shot fatally following his speech to an audience of Orthodox Jews in a Manhattan hotel. El Sayyid Nosair was caught red-handed after the attack and was injured in the ensuing shooting attack by a police officer. He was initially acquitted by a jury and was later charged. None of his associates were implicated. The attempt was believed to be part of a larger plot to assassinate Ariel Sharon, a senior Israeli army officer who later became prime minister.

Bin Laden financed the legal expenses for Nosair through some Saudi businessmen. The initial lapse in the investigation against the murder of Kahane was controversial. It may be due to the fact that Kahane was a miscreant for the USA, or else the FBI and CIA were looking for some double agents among the Islamist extremists to track their future plots. It may also have been due to the fact that the CIA was well connected with the al-Kifah centre and was actively engaged with them for the war in Afghanistan. The cover-up was necessary to protect their interest, not to expose the association between criminal networks and the CIA or FBI.

Abdul Rahman firmly established his position at the al-Kifah centre and started exerting control over all operations, including financial dealings. By 1991, the centre became directly connected with the Pakistan office. Bin Laden and his team established total control over it through Abdul Rahman, in contrast to Shalabi, who was close to Abdulla Azzam. The first victim of this power change was Mustafa Shalabi himself, the founder and the official head of the centre. Shalabi's body was found dead on 1 March 1991. He had been murdered few days before. About one hundred thousand dollars in his possession had been stolen. He had been shot and stabbed several times. Investigators found two red hairs in Shalabi's hand, and FBI suspected Mahmud Abouhalima, who was red-headed, for the murder. It was also Abouhalima who first identified the body for the police, falsely claiming to be the brother of Shalabi.

Shalabi had an open dispute with Abdul Rahman over where to send about a million dollars the Kifah centre was raising annually. Shalabi wanted to send all to Afghanistan, and Abdul Rahman wanted some money to finance his operations in Egypt to sabotage the Egyptian government. The dispute intensified. Abdul Rahman used to call Shalabi a bad Muslim and posted posters to denounce dealing with him. Sensing trouble, Shalabi offered to quit, and he booked tickets to leave the USA. He sold his house and belongings and sent his wife to Egypt, his home country. He was killed brutally just three days before his planned exit to Afghanistan. The murder was never solved. Had they solved the murder initially, probably many major future terror plots in the USA could have been averted. The reason FBI did not show much interest in the murder could have been the same as that behind the laxity in Kahane's murder investigation. Some also allege that Mossad could have been behind his death as Shalabi was also following a 'Palestine next' approach. Following the death of Shalabi Abdul Wali Zindani, nephew of Sheikh Abdul Majeed al-Zindani, a radical imam in Yemen with close ties to bin Laden, took over as the formal head of al-Kifah. He apparently ran the office until it closed voluntarily shortly after the 1993 World Trade Center bombing. With the death of Abdulla Azzam, controlling Pakistan-Afghanistan fronts including global jihad headquarters followed by the death of Shalabi in the USA who was controlling the pivotal centre of US operations; Bin Laden took total control of the organization free from Azzam-era ideology and his principle-ridden jihad methodology.

The second known Al-Qaeda–related incident was a failed assassination attempt on the former king of Afghanistan Zahir Shah in his exiled home in Rome by a self-claimed early recruit of Al-Qaeda, Paulo Jose de Almeida Santos, on 4 November 1991. Santose was born in Angola and grew up as a devout Catholic and aspired to become a priest. Later, he was frustrated with Christianity as a religion. An English translation of the Quran which he bought from a second-hand bookstall led to his conversion to Islam. He adopted the name Abdulla Yusuf. He visited many Muslim countries. In Mecca, he met some Afghan pilgrim who invited him to join the war against the Soviets. He met Bin Laden many times. In one of their meetings, Bin Laden expressed his concern that Zahir Shah may return to Afghanistan. Afghanistan at that time was crippled under the civil war after the withdrawal of Soviet Union. Laden feared that Shah may lead a secular government there which was hostile to Bin Laden's interest. He claimed he didn't get specific permission but discussed with him his plan to kill Shah. Being a scholar in many languages and with a clean European passport, he could easily gain access anywhere. The Al-Qaeda core also trusted him. Posing as a journalist, he completed an interview with Zahir Shah in his heavily guarded house at Rome. At the end, he took out a Kandahari dagger which he had bought as a present to the king and said, 'And now I must kill you.' He stabbed his chest, targeting his heart. But the king was saved by the tin of Café Crème cigarillos in his pocket. Before overpowered by the king's guards, he stabbed him again many times on his neck. The king was taken to the hospital and recovered. Santos was sentenced to ten years in Italy for the crime.

The first major terrorist attack organized by Al-Qaeda which marked its planning and ideology was on 29 December 1992 at Aden, Yemen. Two bombs were detonated in Movenpick Hotel and at the parking lot of the Goldmohur Hotel. These bombings were an attempt to eliminate American soldiers supposed to be staying in these hotels who were on their way to Somalia to take part in the international famine relief effort, Operation Restore Hope. Though the attack was barely noticed in the USA, Al-Qaeda considered it a victory that scared the Americans. No Americans were killed, as the soldiers were staying in other hotels, and they travelled to Somalia as scheduled. One Austrian tourist and a Yemeni hotel worker were killed, and seven other Yemenis were injured. The incident was a game changer for Al-Qaeda, as they attacked civilian targets rather than fighting the army. To support such an attack, two fatwa were quoted by Mamdouh Mahmud Salim, the most theologically sound among al-Qaeda's members, to justify the killings according to Islamic law. Salim referred to an edict of thirteenth-century scholar Ibn-Taymiyyah, who sanctioned resistance by any means during the Mongol invasions. The fatwas were circulated among Al-Qaeda members alone, not to the general public. This attack marked the beginning of a wave of terrorist attacks with no mercy for killing civilians and innocents.

Terror reached the US people on Friday, 26 February 1993 at noon when a massive 600 kg bomb exploded at the base of the north tower of the World Trade Center in New York. The explosion instantly cut off the main electrical power line of the building, knocking out even the emergency lighting system and lifts. Four levels of the basement parking area were ripped off by the bomb blast, and thick smoke engulfed the building up to the ninety-third floor. The blast was indented to collapse the north tower to fall on the south tower, causing thousands of deaths. But its power was just short for that. Eyad Ismoil, a Jordanian, drove a yellow Ryder van filled with explosives along with Ramzi Yousef, the mastermind of the plot. They entered the building unchecked and parked their car on the underground B-2 level. Yousef, an expert bomb maker, ignited its twenty-foot fuse, and both of them left the building. Twelve minutes later, at 12.18 p.m., the bomb exploded in the underground garage, creating an initial suspicion that the main transformer might have blown out. Hundreds of people were trapped inside the lifts for hours. Several hundreds were suffocated in the thick smoke. The blast stopped all major television and radio transmissions in New York for a week. Telephone connections of most of the Manhattan region were also disrupted. Six persons were killed, fifteen people received a traumatic injury from the blast, and 1,042 people were injured most during the chaos and evacuation that followed. About fifty thousand people were evacuated, and WTC closed for about a month.

The World Trade Center (WTC) was a commercial office complex, covering sixteen acres, in downtown Manhattan, which was owed and maintained by the Port Authority of New York and New Jersey.

It adorned the New York skyline as its major landmark, with its impressive 110-story twin towers and multitude of offices, hotels, and restaurants. It was an easy target as it allowed transient parking and the parking lots were manned by only toll collectors. The obvious importance of the building and its lax security made it an easy target for a terrorist attack. It is believed that Yousef's original idea was to target the UN headquarters but he changed his plan to WTC due to heavy security there. Within hours of the attack, Yousef escaped to Pakistan. Immediately before the attack, Yousef mailed many New York news papers calling himself a member of 'Liberation Army, Fifth Battalion'. He made three demands in his letters: an end of all US aid to Israel, an end of US diplomatic relations with Israel, and a pledge by the US government not to interfere with the internal affairs of Middle Eastern countries. He threatened that it was a warning attack and more would come if his demands were not met.

From the debris of the blast, investigators collected the number plate of the van used in the plot, and it was traced to a New Jersey rental outlet. It was found that the van had been rented out by Mohammad Salameh, one of Yousef's co-conspirators. He had reported that the vehicle was stolen. When he turned up on 4 March 1993 to collect his deposit, he was arrested by the authorities. His arrest led the police to Abdul Rahman Yasin from a New Jersey apartment, the same building where Yousef lived. Yasin was questioned by the FBI and left. The next day, he flew to Iraq, the country where he had lived till 1992 though he was a US citizen. After that, he was never caught and his whereabouts were unknown. The investigators later claimed that there was not much evidence to implicate him and restrict his travel. But when the investigators raided his apartment, traces of bomb-making materials, a toolbox, and one of his jeans with an acid burn mark were found. During his questioning, investigators noted a burn injury on his thigh, indicating that he had helped Yousef in making the bomb. In spite of this, he was released. Iraqi Deputy Prime Minister Tariq Aziz in 2002 alleged that his release was a sting operation by the USA, purposefully done to falsely implicate Iraq for harbouring a WTC terrorist. In Iraqi official records, he was in jail waiting for punishment till the US invasion of Iraq, and after that, his whereabouts were unknown. Documents collected afterward by the USA revealed that Saddam Hussein did not trust Yasin and suspected him as a US agent. He was placed on the list of FBI's Most Wanted Terrorists in 2001, on which he still remains with a reward of five million dollars for his whereabouts.

When FBI raided the New Jersey city apartment of Ramzi Yousef, they found bomb-making materials and a business card of Mohammed Jamal Khalifa, the brother-in-law of Bin Laden, married to one of his sisters. Khalifa was known to Yousef, and they had worked together before. Khalifa was arrested on 14 December 1994 and was deported to Jordan, where he faced charges for bomb blasts. A Jordanian court acquitted him, and he lived as a free man in Saudi Arabia. He had a wife in the Philippines. Khalifa started Benevolence International Corporation in the Philippines in 1988 to recruit fighters for the Afghan war. It later became Benevolence International Foundation, which helped the funding of 1993 WTC bombing and terrorist plots in Philippines. He was arrested in Saudi Arabia shortly following the 11 September 2001 attacks. But he was released without charges. Later in that year, he publicly condemned Osama Bin Laden and Al-Qaeda.

Khalifa was assassinated on 31 January 2007 while visiting a gemstone mine he owned in Sakamilko, near Sakaraha town in southern Madagascar. Earlier, he had had to call the police to take back his mine from a gang who had occupied it. He could not go there due to travel restrictions outside Saudi Arabia after 2000. After midnight that day, around twenty-five to thirty armed men raided his residence and killed him. His body had many bullet wounds, stab wounds, and chop wounds by an axe. Money, computers, and other documents were stolen. Immediately following his death, the Madagascar police claimed that gang-related violence was the cause. His family members initially believed it but later suspected political killing, most likely from Joint Special Operations Command of the USA. They claimed that no serious efforts were made by the police there to investigate and find the perpetrators. His death still remains a mystery. It is believed that though he publicly denounced terrorism, he maintained many links and continued his support, which led to his unexplained death.

Muhammad Jamal Khalifa first met Osama bin Laden in 1976 while he was studying at university in Jeddah. In 1985, he travelled to Afghanistan to take part in the ongoing jihad against the Soviets and became a very close friend of Bin Laden. He married bin Laden's sister the following year. Back in Saudi Arabia after his overseas missions, he maintained a very low profile, especially after the 9/11 incident. He met a violent death on his first visit outside the country after several years. His body was taken to Saudi Arabia in a Chartered air craft send by Saudi government along with senior diplomats.

In March 1994 Mahmud Abouhalima, Ahmad Ajaj, Nidal A. Ayyad, and Mohammed Salameh, all connected to al-Kifah centre were convicted for the WTC bombing and sentenced to life in prison. Eyad Ismoil, who drove the van carrying the bomb, was convicted in November 1997.

Nidal Ayyad was a US citizen born in Kuwait to Palestinian parents. He was a chemical engineer working with Allied Signal Inc, Morristown, New Jersey. Hydrogen cylinders used in the bomb were procured by him through the company channel he was working. The letters delivered to the media in the name of Liberation Army Fifth Battalion were prepared by him from his office computer. He was implicated after finding his credit card with Mohammed Salameh, and Salameh phoned him many times the day before the WTC bombing. Salameh and Ayyad maintained a joint account into which money for the plot was transferred through a wire transfer from Germany. He was arrested on the same day as Salameh, on 4 March 1993.

Mahmud Abouhalima, nicknamed Mahmud the Red due to his red hair, was an Egyptian by birth and as an adolescent was inclined to al-Gama'a al-Islamiyya, whose spiritual leader was Omer Abdel Rahman (Blind Sheik). He had a troubled past, migrated to Germany, was involved in many illegal activities, and was denied asylum. But he married a German citizen and later migrated to the USA, where he got citizenship. While working as a taxi driver in New York, he worked with the Al-Kifah Center in his free time. He underwent arm training in shooting ranges around New York under guidance from Ali Mohamed. In 1988, he went to Pakistan to support the Afghan war, where he received combat training at Peshawar. When Nosair assassinated Meir Kahane in November 1990, Mahmud was driving his taxi for him, though Nosair got into another taxi accidentally after the murder. It was revealed that many eyewitnesses had seen him with Salameh at the Jersey City storage facility where they allegedly prepared the explosives. He escaped to Egypt following February 26, 1993 WTC bombing. He was arrested by Egyptian authorities, tortured and extradited to USA on March 24, 1993. In Egyptian custody he was confessed that he was a Member of al-Gama'a al-Islamiyya and it received money from Muslim Brotherhood office in Germany. There was corroborative evidence to suggest that the same source funded the WTC bombing by wire transfer.

Ahmed Ajaj had migrated from West Bank to Houston and was working as a pizza delivery man. On 24 April 1992, he abandoned his asylum claim and flew to Peshawar, Pakistan, along with a San Antonio cab driver, Ibrahim Ahmed, who was working with the Texas branch of al-Kifah Center. Ahmed was a courier for al-Kifah carrying a large sum of money in his suitcase to Pakistan on his frequent trips. While in Peshawar, Ajaj stayed many months at Abdulla Azzam House, a hostel and the headquarters of al-Kifah. Here he met Ramzi Yousef, who gave him explosives training at an Afghan training camp. He came back to the USA along with Ramzi Yousef from Pakistan on 1 September 1992. They booked first-class tickets to avoid hassle at the airport and did not mingle during the journey so that no connection between them would be noticed. At JFK Airport, both were subjected to secondary inspection. Yousef was carrying an Iraqi passport and claimed he was tortured in Iraq by the Saddam Hussein regime and needed political asylum. On another counter, Ajaj, carrying an original Swiss passport of another person with his photo simply pasted on it, was arguing with an immigration officer. He claimed he was a

Swiss journalist named Khurram Khan. He shouted at the officer upon questioning on the problems of his passport, 'My mother was Swedish! If you don't believe me, check your computer.'

On inspection of his baggage, they found many fake passports, a bomb-making manual, a manual in Arabic with the front cover as "al-Qaeda (which was read as 'the basic rule'), a stamping machine, and a cheat sheet showing how to lie to an immigration officer. In the ensuing chaos at the immigration counter and the realization that the detention centre was full, Yousef was allowed entry and asked for an asylum hearing. Ajaj was detained and charged for passport fraud. He was only released three days after the WTC bombing. Yousef went to the al-Kifah Centre, Brooklyn, to contact Abdel Rahman. He started living in a New Jersey apartment, the same building where Yasin, along with his mother and Mohammed Salameh, were living.

It is believed that Ajaj purposefully carried illicit materials and created a scene to distract attention from Yousef in the busy immigration counter. Both Ajaj and Yousef might have got assistance in Pakistan by ISI, as neither was carrying sufficient documents to travel to the USA. When he was in jail, Ajaj constantly maintained contact with Yousef indirectly and assisted him in the WTC plot. They were also allowed to talk on the phone, but their conversations were not translated before the WTC bombings. Ajaj was released after his six-month punishment for passport fraud three days after the WTC bombing, on 1 March 1993, and waited for his asylum application hearing. But he was rearrested on 9 March 1993 and was tried for WTC bombings. He was awarded a punishment for playing a role in 'the early stages of the conspiracy' with life in prison for 115 years and heavy fine.

In March 1993, an Israeli newsweekly, *Village Voice*, reported that Ajaj, a Palestinian, might have been a mole for the Israeli Mossad. It speculated that Ajaj might have 'advance knowledge of the World Trade Center bombing, which he shared with Mossad, and that Mossad, for whatever reason, kept the secret to itself'. When Ajaj was in Peshawar to recruit himself for training in Afghan camp, the camp manager was not satisfied with his credentials. He went to Saudi Arabia and came with a recommendation papers before commencing his arms training. A shrewd individual like Ajaj, who fought for his many rights even in prison and filed many lawsuits against the prison system while in prison, behaving silly and strange while going through a strict airport immigration procedure is hard to digest.

The FBI could solve the entire sequence of the WTC bombing through an informer, Emad Salem. From his contacts with Nosair, who was already in jail, and his associates, Salem realized that a group associated with Abdel Rahman was making a plan for bombing many New York City sites, including many Jewish temples and banks. He was on the payroll of FBI for about five hundred dollars a week and informed his handlers about the details of the plot. But they asked for more evidence and asked him to wear a wire to implicate them. He backed out and claimed it was too risky. Within many months, the plan was changed to a WTC attack after Yousef visited those sites. Emad Salem was a crucial witness on the WTC trial, and he was familiar with most of the accused.

The story of Ramzi Yousef is a mystery with activism, daredevil adventures, heroism, and unmatched ingenuity. Ramzi Yousef is probably an alias, as claimed by 9/11 commission, and his original name was Abdul Basit Mahmoud Abdul Karim. He was born in Kuwait to Pakistani parents. His father was Muhammed Abdul Karim from Baluchistan. His mother was the sister of Khalid Sheik Mohammed (KSM). After they settled in Pakistan, he was sent to England for higher studies. He did his electrical engineering in Swansea Institute in Wales from 1986 to 1990. It is speculated that he was recruited by CIA, like thousands of other recruits from the world over, for the Afghan war, as the author Richard Labeviere claimed in his book in 1999 and in a report in *Newsday* in 1995. Yousef probably worked with the Muslim Brotherhood in England. He went to Afghanistan in 1988 on a college break and was involved in months of training on bomb-making at Bin Laden's camps. At that time, Khalid's brother Zahid Sheikh Mohammed was working as the head of the Pakistani branch of the charity Mercy International, which had headquarters in

Switzerland and USA. CIA was funnelling money to Islamic fighters in Afghanistan and Bosnia through this charity. It is believed that in 1989, Yousef went to the Philippines on a Bin Laden mission to set up a new base there.

After finishing his courses in England, Yousef shifted to Afghanistan and joined his 'family enterprise of Islamic extremism' with his uncle KSM, Zahid, his own father, and two of his brothers who were already fighting along with bin Laden. He became an expert in bomb-making. He worked at a training camp at Khost in Afghanistan, connected to bin Laden, teaching bomb-making to militants. Yousef visited the Philippines several times afterwards and trained militants of the Abu Sayyaf group. He was introduced in the group as an emissary of Bin Laden and was known among its members as a major financier of their activities. Abdurajak Janjalani became a friend of bin Laden while they were fighting in Afghanistan in the late 1980s. He and many others from the Philippines were trained and paid by the CIA and Pakistan ISI. Immediately after establishing Al-Qaeda, Bin Laden asked Janjalani to establish a cell in Southeast Asia. Thus Abu Sayyaf was formed in Philippines and was led mainly by former Afghan jihad veterans. Many militants from the parent Moro National Liberation Front (MNLF), a larger rebel group, joined the newly formed Abu Sayyaf.

Some of the provinces of the Philippines became rebel strongholds and were restive during this time, which made these areas fertile ground for terrorist camps. Bin Laden was very keen on establishing a training centre and launching pad for Al-Qaeda terrorist activities around the world other than from Pakistan, Afghanistan, or a major Muslim country. This was evident from the fact that his top planners like Khalid Sheik Muhammed (KSM), Mohammed Jamal Khalifa (the brother-in-law of bin Laden), and Ramzi Yousef were all dispatched to the Philippines to set bases and coordinate activities. There, KSM proved his calibre in his Abu Sayyaf missions and gained confidence and operational freedom from Bin Laden. But Abu Sayyaf was deeply penetrated by government agents, and in fact, the second in command of the group, Edwin Angeles, was an undercover agent who frequently briefed the government about their activities. Soon KSM and Yousef had to run from there as they were exposed. Jamal Khalifa continued to liaison with Abu Sayyaf leaders, providing money, food, medicines, and ammunition and sometimes suggesting targets to attack till April 1993. The group engaged mainly in kidnapping and extortion, apart from occasional bomb attacks and killings. They were also involved in the bombing of Christian churches and markets and trying to sabotage the ongoing peace talks between the government and MNLF. Two American evangelists were killed by the group in April 1991. According to Philippine intelligence estimates from 1991 to 1995, Abu Sayyaf was responsible for 67 kidnappings and violent attacks, killing around 136 people and injuring more than a hundred. It is believed that Ramzi Yousef planned the idea of the WTC bombing in one of the Abu Sayyaf camps in early 1992.

Most of the time between 1992 to 1995, Yousef lived at the Bait ul-Shuhada (House of Martyrs) guesthouse in Peshawar, Pakistan, which was funded by Osama bin Laden. In Pakistan, Osama bin Laden had several friends in the high ranks of ISI who had funded him during the war in Afghanistan. The same contacts were nurtured by Yousef and his family members. They helped him to live safe with tip-offs and assisted him for his travel needs. When he reached the USA on 1 September 1992, he was carrying an Iraqi passport, which he had bought in Peshawar. During his interrogation at the airport for several hours, he admitted that he was a Pakistani citizen. After his release from airport, he went to the Pakistan embassy in New York. He obtained a temporary passport by which he escaped from the USA after the WTC bombing. When released from the airport in New York, Yousef went straight to the al-Kifah Centre and tried to meet Omer Abdel Rahman. Arrangements for his stay were made in a New Jersey apartment. It was Abdel Rahman who apparently selected the team for the future attack. Yousef, aided by Mohammed Salameh and Mahmud Abouhalima, assembled the urea nitrate fuel oil device at his apartment in Jersey City. Following the WTC blast, a massive investigation team was formed. Many of the old unnoticed links of the FBI and the CIA were reinvestigated, and the investigation team quickly reached the culprits. Now their old informant Emad Salem came to their help. He recollected that Abouhalima had called him to ask his help, apparently to make a bomb, to which he did not respond. On 21 April 1993, the FBI added Yousef on its Ten Most Wanted Fugitives list, and a massive worldwide manhunt for Yousef started.

Back in Pakistan after the WTC bombing, Yousef hid and lived with protection due to the connections he had developed and the influence his mentor, Bin Laden, had wielded at that time. In July 1993, Ramzi Yousef and his friend Abdul Hakim Murad planned to assassinate Benazir Bhutto, the opposition leader of Pakistan at that time, in front of her house. They were stopped by a police patrol. Yousef hid the bomb when the police approached, but it was detonated accidentally after the police left, injuring him. Khalid Sheik Muhammed (KSM) financed the operation. At that time, KSM was close to Nawas Sharif (a prominent Pakistani politician and many-time prime minister) or at least to his close associate. Benazir came to power later in October 1993 and was against most terrorist groups.

On 20 June 1994, a powerful bomb explosion at the prayer hall of the one of the most coveted Shia sites, shrine of the Imam Reza at Mashhad, Iran, killed twenty-six people and injured more than two hundred. It was the Day of Ashura, an important day for Shia, when a huge crowd was there at the shrine. Yousef maintained strong hatred for Shia. He was the mastermind of the attack, and he got assistance from a Pakistani Sunni fanatic, Abdul Shakoor from Karachi. It is believed that in this attack, Yousef also worked with his younger brother, Abdul Muneem, and his father, who were believed to have been arrested and detained in Iran. Iran cracked the Sunni terror plot but officially claimed Mehdi Nahvi, a supposed member of the People's Mujahedin of Iran (MKO), a dreaded terrorist group in Iran, as behind the attack to prevent sectarian violence. Though Yousef generally worked by orders from Bin Laden or his associates, this was a plot organized himself and against the interest of Bin Laden. It was a time when Bin Laden made an effort to work with Hizbullah, an Iranian-backed Shia militia group.

In August 1994, Yousef illegally entered the Philippines by boat in the southern island of Basilan, an Abu Sayyaf stronghold. Here he trained some members of the group on explosives. Terry Nichols, a white extremist from the USA whose wife was from Cebu, Philippines, met Yousef and Abu Sayyaf leaders, including Abdurajak Janjalani. He wanted to be trained in bombing buildings in USA. Janjalani and Yousef were overwhelmed by his interests and agreed to finance for the mission. On 19 April 1995, a truck bomb destroyed the Alfred P. Murrah Federal Building in Oklahoma City, killing 168 people and injuring 680 others. It caused damages in 324 buildings within a 16-block radius with an estimated economic loss of $652 million. The mastermind of the worst-ever domestic terrorist attack in USA was Timothy McVeigh, along with Terry Nichols. The cooperation of white supremacist and Islamic extremist was strange, but both were united in their enmity of Israel and Jews and deep hatred of the US government.

After a few weeks of arrival, Yousef went to Manila to procure materials for bomb and organize his next mission. Yousef conducted a trial of the ongoing plan on 11 December 1994 by boarding a Philippine Airlines Boeing 747 from Manila to Tokyo, Japan, with a short stopover in the Philippine city of Cebu. He boarded the plane as Armaldo Forlani, an Italian citizen. Yousef assembled the bomb in the toilet, set the time for the bomb after four hours, and put it in the life jacket pocket under seat 26K. He changed his seat many times so his possession of the seat would not be identified. A crew member noticed his strange behaviour of changing seats frequently on his short trip but did not bother to report. In Cebu, Yousef and several other passengers left the plane. New passengers, most of them Japanese, and a new set of cabin crew boarded for the trip to Tokyo with 273 passengers on board. Two hours before arrival at Tokyo, the bomb exploded in mid-air while the flight was cruising on autopilot. The explosion instantly killed and ripped off half of the body of twenty-four-year-old Haruki Ikegami, a Japanese businessman occupying seat 26K. Ten other passengers sitting in front and behind Ikegami were injured. The bomb tore out a two-square-foot portion of the cabin floor exposing what was underneath, but the fuselage of the plane was intact. With the heroic efforts of pilot captain Eduardo Reyes, the plane avoided a mid-air crash and made an emergency landing at the nearby Okinawa airport. Bomb fragments were discovered, which provided clues to the investigators in Manila. From Cebu, Yousef travelled to Manila. He had purposefully put a small quantity of explosive material in the bomb; a little stronger bomb would have resulted in a major aviation tragedy. He had calculated the strength of about one-tenth of the future bomb to be developed for the test attempt.

After the incidence, a man telephoned the *Associated Press* and claimed Abu Sayyaf's responsibility for the attack. Later, one captured Bojinka plotter confessed that the caller had been Yousef himself. Yousef had made the call as part of a long-term cooperation arrangement between the Abu Sayyaf group and Al-Qaeda. Yousef and his associate Wali Khan Shah had tested the potency of the bomb in a generator room of a mall in Cebu City and underneath a seat in a theatre during a show to test the effect of a blast underneath a seat in a plane before the actual trial inside the aircraft.

Immediately after this successful trial, Yousef returned to Manila and started making over a dozen bombs with larger weight of explosive material. Yousef rented a room in the six-story Doña Josefa Apartments in the Malate district of Manila, which was just two hundred metres from the embassy of the Holy See in the Philippines. Yousef personally chose room 603 with one window overlooking the path below, which was the proposed route of the pope's motorcade. When Yousef filled the registration form at the reception, by mistake, he filled in his original name and, upon noticing, tore the form and asked for a new form. The manager of the apartment, Edith Guerrera, laughed with his fellow receptionist, saying he even forgot his name. He booked the room under the name of Najy Awaita Haddad and claimed himself to be a Moroccan. His co-conspirator, a trained pilot named Abdul Hakim Murad, came to Manila and stayed with Yousef in the same apartment. To the apartment staff they looked like students. They collected many chemicals for the proposed bombs from Manila stores and personally transported the materials to the room without any help from the staff. They locked their room all the time and never called any room boy to clean up their room. Yousef and KSM had already brought enough nitroglycerine for their plot, which they made from a commonly available contact lens solution at that time.

It was just a week before his planned attacks on the evening of 6 January 1995. Yousef and Abdul Hakim Murad were preparing some chemicals in the apartment. Suddenly, thick fumes came out of the room, followed by fire. The fire made the apartment staff suspicious, and soon, firefighters and police, under Aida Fariscal, reached there. The fire was doused before their arrival. The Philippine intelligence agencies were aware of Yousef's presence in Manila and were closely monitoring his activities. There is also a belief that the police purposefully had set fire on Yousef's apartment to make a pretext to raid the place.

When the firefighters arrived, Yousef and Murad told the firefighters to stay away and fled, leaving everything behind. Murad turned back to collect the laptop of Yousef but was apprehended. Murad tried to run away but fell on the ground, hitting wood. He offered a bribe of Philippine pesos equal to two thousand US dollars to the policemen to let him go. It was much more than one month's salary of an officer, but the officers refused. In the precinct, Murad claimed he was Ahmed Saeed and signed a statement saying that he was an innocent tourist visiting his friend in his chemical import–export business. But when he murmured 'two Satans that must be destroyed: the pope and America', police got suspicious. The head of the Philippine National Police (PNP) team, Aida Fariscal, was fresh with her memory of recent bombings that had hit Metro Manila and Philippine Airlines Flight 434. She was determined for a thorough investigation.

She got a search warrant from a judge after contacting eleven other judges on that night. When they raided Yousef's flat on that night, they found a huge catch of materials including several chemical agents, wires, fuses, maps, finished pipe bombs, and two large Welch juice bottles filled with nitroglycerine. They got several Casio watches, which had been modified to use as timers. Another interesting find was a manual in Arabic on how to build liquid bombs. About twelve fake passports of different countries, including Afghanistan, Saudi Arabia, Pakistan, and Norway were found from the apartment. A business card of Mohammed Jamal Khalifa and his several phone numbers and the contact number of Rose Masquera, Khalifa's Filipino girlfriend, were also found. The huge catch needed three police vans to transport the materials.

The captured laptop of Yousef and four floppy discs showed the details of one of the largest failed terrorist plots in history, codenamed the Bojinka plot. The plot was also called Oplan Bojinka, Operation Bojinka, or 'forty-eight hours of terror' by the FBI. The strange name, *Bojinka*, was initially translated meaning 'loud bang' or 'explosion' in the Serbo-Croatian language. The word is more likely a shortened version of a Russian word meaning 'God'. Khalid Sheik Muhammed later disclosed that it was just a nonsense name he had heard in the war fronts in Afghanistan.

The first part of the plot was to kill Pope John Paul II when he would visit the Philippines during the World Youth Day celebrations of 1995. A suicide bomber would dress up as a priest and would go close to the pope and detonate the bomb. The plan was to be executed on 15 January 1995 in Makati City while John Paul II would pass during his motorcade on his way to the San Carlos Seminary. The assassination of the pope was intended to divert attention from the next phase of the operation. From Yousef's apartment, the police recovered street maps of Manila with routes plotting the papal motorcade, a photograph of the pope, bibles, crucifixes, and priest clothing, including robes and collars. A phone message from a tailor reminding the occupant that the cassock was ready to be tried on was also found from his room. This evidence was enough to expose the plot to assassinate the pope.

About twenty men had already been trained by Yousef for the second phase of the plan. The plot was to bomb eleven US-bound American flights from different airports in Asia starting on 21 January 1995 and ending on 22 January 1995 within a span of forty-eight hours, killing about four thousand passengers on board. Yousef's laptop had the detailed flight charts, timing of bombs, and coded information as who would carry the operations. The bombs would be placed inside life jacket pockets under seats as done by Yousef in his trial, and each bomber would then disembark during the first leg, leaving the preset time bomb to be exploded in mid-air over the Pacific Ocean. He would then board one or more flights and repeat the process. After completing their operation, each man would catch flights to Pakistan.

There was no need for US visas, as they would only travel on the US-bound flight during their first legs in Asia. Airlines from the USA were chosen instead of Asian airlines to maximize the shock in America. The proposed operatives were noted in the laptop with code names: Zyed, Majbos, Markoa, Mirqas, and Obaid. Zyed was Yousef himself, and Obaid was Abdul Hakim Murad. Immediately following the plot being unearthed, the concerned airlines were alerted. There were several contact details in Yousef's laptop and other documents. A massive hunt for all possible conspirators and financiers were started.

Known Al-Qaeda operative and close associate of Mohammed Jamal Khalifa, Wali Khan Amin Shah, an Afghan, also trained the Abu Sayyaf who participated in the plot. Khalid Sheik Mohammad also personally reached the Philippines and coordinated activities with Yousef.

Within hours of the arrest of Murad, Yousef escaped to Singapore and then to Pakistan. Khalid Sheik Muhammed also safely left the Philippines. On 11 January 1995, Wali Khan Amin Shah was arrested from an apartment. Police found a pager Yousef called was registered in the name of the girlfriend of Shah. But he escaped from custody shortly. Shah, who was the major on-ground financier, operated the financial dealings through his girlfriend and her contacts. He collected money originated from Bin Laden, Khalifa, and a company called Konsojaya, a front company that had been started by Riduan Isamuddin, better known as Hambali, the head of the group Jemaah Islamiyah, an Indonesian terror group. Wali Khan Shah was a board of director of the company. Shah was again arrested later by Malaysian authorities on suspicion. His identity was revealed upon fingerprinting.

He was extradited to the United States, and he cooperated with the authorities in the trial of the plot.

Aida Fariscal, a housewife, joined the Philippine National Police (PNP) after her husband was killed while working as a police officer. She gained wide reputation for her dedication. Her country awarded her a prize of 33,222 pesos (equivalent to $700) and a trip to Taiwan for her heroic work of exposing one of the largest terrorist plots of that time. She got a certificate from CIA citing 'in recognition of your personal outstanding efforts and cooperation'.

In custody, Ahmed Saeed turned out to be Abdul Hakim Murad upon interrogation. Murad was sent to Camp Crame, the headquarters of the Philippine National Police. He was tortured by Filipino investigators; the torture included beating him up with heavy objects like a chair and a wooden club, burning his genitals, and waterboarding. In spite of severe injuries in his body, he survived. He initially resisted interrogation. Towards the end, he started speaking up, apparently after a bogus Israeli Mossad agent was introduced who told him that he was to be handed over to Israel. He told his interrogators, 'This is my best thing. I enjoy it because the United States is the first country in this world making trouble for us, for Muslims and for our people.' Murad was extradited to the United States on 12 April 1995 after sixty-seven days of harsh interrogation. His testimony was crucial to convict Yousef later. Murad was convicted and was sentenced to life in prison.

Abdul Hakim Murad was born in Pakistan and lived in Kuwait. After his schooling in Kuwait, he joined pilot training at the Continental Flying School in the Philippines from 1990 to 1991 and later at Emirates Flying School in the United Arab Emirates in later 1991. He was further trained in four American flying schools and obtained his commercial flying license in 1992. After befriending Ramzi Yousef, he learned from him how to make bombs at Lahore, Pakistan. When Yousef reached Manila for the Bojinka plot, Murad also joined. Both were familiar with the Philippines by this time. He recalled that Yousef was not so religious, and along with Yousef, he went to karaoke bars in their leisure time.

Once, in their Manila apartment, Murad suggested to Yousef crashing an aeroplane into CIA headquarters, and Yousef said, 'OK, we will think about it.' That was possibly the origin of a future plot with a third phase of Bojinka. Murad suggested either to rent out, buy, or hijack a small aeroplane like a Cessna, fill it with explosives, and crash it into the Central Intelligence Agency headquarters at Langley, Virginia. Murad, already a trained pilot, was ready to be a suicide pilot. Later interrogation unearthed another large plan. Instead of small aircraft, multiple large aircrafts would be hijacked and then crashed into the World Trade Center, the Pentagon, the Capitol, the White House, Sears Tower in Chicago, and the US Bank Tower in Los Angeles. This plot was also averted as it was exposed. But after many years of waiting, it happened on 11 September 2001!

After the Bojinka plot was exposed, Philippine authorities informed the USA about the plot. An enhanced manhunt for Yousef started. But still Yousef travelled again from Pakistan to Thailand on 31 January 1995 to organize another plot to bomb a Delta airline flight and United Airlines flight to the USA with suitcase bombs. After two attempts to send the suitcase with Istaique Parker and a Qatari friend with diplomatic immunity did not materialize, he returned to Pakistan.

On 7 February 1995, Yousef was arrested in the Su-Casa guest house in Islamabad, one of Bin Laden's safe houses, on a combined ISI and Special Agents of the US Diplomatic Security Service raid, following a tip-off from Istaique Parker before he could escape to Peshawar. Parker was paid two million dollars for the information leading to Yousef's capture as part of the Reward for Justice Program of the FBI. Delta's and United Airlines's flight schedules and bomb components in children's toys were found when he was in custody. Yousef had chemical burns on his fingers. The next day, he was taken to the USA without due process of extradition. This was because the government of Pakistan did not want him to be there longer under custody, and they feared that any government involvement in his detention would be unpopular and problematic. Prior to his arrest, there had been a stand-off between the CIA and FBI, as CIA advocated continued monitoring of Yousef's activities. But with the president's involvement, the FBI was given an order to go ahead, and they coordinated the mission with the Special Agents.

While on a US Air Force rendition flight over New York City on his way to the prison cell, the FBI agent asked him, 'You see the trade centres down there, they're still standing, aren't they?' Yousef responded, 'They wouldn't be if I had enough money and enough explosives.' He was held in a prison in New York City until his trial was finished. He admitted his involvement to his interrogators but avoided hints about Bin Laden, Khalid Sheik Muhammed, and future plots like hijacking of commercial flights. While on trial when he was asked about his involvement in terrorism, he responded, 'Yes, I am a terrorist and proud of it as long as it is against the US government and against Israel because you are more than terrorists—you are the one who invented terrorism and using it every day. You are butchers, liars, and hypocrites.'

Yousef, Murad, and Shah were convicted on 5 September 1996 for their role in the Bojinka plot and were sentenced to life in prison without scope for parole. Yousef was convicted in 1998 to bomb the World Trade Center and sentenced for 240 years for the Trade Center attack and life in prison for the Flight 434 attack in 1994. Yousef and many other Al-Qaeda convicts were held at the high-security Supermax prison, ADX Florence in Florence, Colorado. His handlers at the jail revealed later that Yousef was an exceptionally different prisoner. In his initial years in jail, he almost spent his entire time in the prison cell praying every hour and refused to come out for recreation. He used to resist the mandatory strip-search on religious grounds. He was regarded as a dangerous man due to his imposing personality on prison staff. In later years, he claimed to have converted to Christianity, started showing Christian symbols, and started eating pork openly. His conversion and later behaviour were unbelievable for people who were familiar with him. Khalid Sheik Muhammed, who was third in command of Al-Qaeda, later said that Yousef was not a member of Al-Qaeda and he had never met Bin Laden. Bin Laden, in an interview, said that he did not personally know Yousef but he might have worked for his cause. Yousef was a phenomenon who, according to US district court judge Kevin Duffy who tried him, was 'an apostle of evil'; but for many others, he was a rootless global warrior against evil and oppression.

Even after being in jail, several confessions of associates and corroborative evidence on the story of Yousef continue, and he is still a mystery with many questions unanswered. So also are many other jihadis who were his fellow prison mates in Supermax ADX, Florence, like Mohammed Salameh, Mahmud Abouhalima, and Nidal Ayyad, who continued to write inspirational letters for future warriors. In one such letter, Salameh wrote, 'Oh, God, make us live with happiness. Make us die as martyrs. May we be united on the day of judgment,' and in another, he called Osama bin Laden 'the hero of my generation'. Their continued commitment to their cause is strange and unparalleled. Many of the unsolved stories and mysteries are partly due to the fact that some are secrets or classified information and may take decades to come out.

There were at least two assassination attempts on American president Bill Clinton in the Philippines with orders from Bin Laden. The first was on November 1994, planned by Khalid Sheikh Mohammed and operated by Ramzi Yousef. After exploring all options, Yousef quickly realised that it was a difficult mission with a huge risk and shifted his plan to Pope John Paul II. Again in 1996, Bin Laden personally engineered a plot to assassinate Clinton while he was in Manila for the meeting of Asia-Pacific Economic Cooperation. Only minutes before the motorcade was about to start, intelligence agents intercepted a message and alerted the US Secret Service. Later, a bomb planted under a bridge on his way was discovered.

Bin Laden, after his initial years in Afghanistan, returned to Saudi Arabia after the end of the Soviet invasion. He initially received a heroic welcome. He could establish close contacts with many high-ranking officials in the ruling regime. As a member of the Bin Laden family, the most influential family in Saudi Arabia after the royal family, he had no difficulty getting any audience, including the king. Bin Laden's family maintained very close relations with the royal family.

They ran a big construction company conglomerate, doing many of the most important developmental works in Saudi Arabia, including the renovation of the grand mosques of Mecca and Medina and the royal palace, and they were strong supporters of the administration. But his initial good relations soured shortly in the wake of the Kuwait invasion by Iraq and his continued open criticism of the royal family. He was not targeted by the regime but allowed to move out of the country.

He was looking for options. Bin Laden was just an Afghan war veteran, had no terrorist or criminal charges on his head at that time, and was still a friendly mujahideen for the USA. Though the Soviets had left, Afghanistan was still mostly ruled by a communist government, and various mujahideen factions were fighting each other to gain political control. It was not a good choice to move on to. So also was Pakistan after the Afghan war against the Soviets and the death of Zia-ul-Haq; it had lost interest for foreign mujahideen fighters in the country. America and Saudi Arabia were actively advising Pakistan to dismantle all mujahideen networks from Pakistan soil.

This time, Sudan was undergoing a rapid political change where President Omer al-Bashir, under the heavy influence of an enthusiastic Islamist, Hassan al-Turabi, opened his country for any Muslim without a visa. They were trying to build an Islamic society free from the grip of the International Monetary Fund (IMF) and America. Sudan at that time was very poor with a few industries and infrastructures and was just coming out of a long civil war which had ravaged the country. Bin Laden, a rich Saudi businessman with assets worth as much as two hundred million pounds, a large sum of which he recently inherited (though estimates vary in different accounts), was an obvious red-carpet guest. Some of his old friends from the Afghan war had already reached Sudan. He first went to Khartoum, probably by April 1991, and shifted almost completely by early 1992. As the government had expected, he invested heavily in the country. Among his several businesses, the biggest were al-Hijira, a construction company which took contracts for several roads, and Wadi al-Aqiq, a farming company which farmed hundreds of thousands of acres in the fertile lands of the central Gezira province cultivating sorghum, sunflower, gum Arabic, and sesame.

Though the government was sympathetic to his ideology, they were poor in payments of dues to Bin Laden's companies. On one occasion, the Sudan government, instead of paying his dues of about £20 million on a completed road segment, gave him a majority share in a government-owned tannery, worth £5 million. So many road projects his company undertook could not be completed due to heavy dues from the government. He transported many of the equipment and excavators which he used in Afghanistan to make mountain roads and trenches. Many of his employees in Sudan were his old comrades from the Afghan war field. He was generous with his workers. His employees, numbering about four hundred, received a monthly salary of $200 a month, which was very good earning in Sudanese standard of that time and lived in comfortable air conditioned apartments. But Bin Laden himself lived a modest life. He had a large three-story house in the affluent Riyadh neighbourhood of Khartoum. The second floor was used as an office. It was a heavily guarded house. He lived in a part of the house which had no modern home appliances like a refrigerator. He did not have any personal vehicle for transportation. More than in this house, he spent most of his time in a farmhouse at Soba, on the left bank of the Blue Nile River. It was a single-storied mud building with a wooden roof and a beaten mud floor and had no furniture. He lived there with his four wives and many children—in most accounts, four sons and a daughter. He had many horses at the farm.

Those who watched Bin Laden and his activities could not spot anything unusual other than that he was a rich Saudi businessman. He used to smile liberally at others and was very kind, and hardly anyone believed him as dangerous. In a small city like Khartoum at that time, any unusual activity would have been known to everyone in the city. American intelligence agencies were watching him but had no offences framed against him. The Sudan government defended Bin Laden and his group as a major business group helping their impoverished country and countrymen.

During his years in Sudan, Al-Qaeda organized the bombing of the Movenpick Hotel and Goldmohur Hotel in Aden on 29 December 1992, targeting US soldiers. It killed an Austrian tourist and a Yemeni hotel worker and injured seven persons; most were Yemeni hotel staff. None of them were targeted enemies. Following the blasts, two Yemeni Muslim militants, trained in Afghanistan and injured in the blast, were arrested. After this bombing, al-Qaeda developed their theological justification for killing innocent people. A fatwa issued by Mamdouh Mahmud Salim, the most scholarly among the cadres, reasoned that the killing of someone standing near the enemy was justified because any innocent bystander would find a proper reward in death, going to paradise (*janna*) if they were good Muslims and to hell (*jahannam*) if they were sinners or non-believers. The fatwa was circulated among al-Qaeda members only but not the general public. The same logic was modified later to justify suicide attacks.

Traditional Islamic laws forbid suicide for any reason. Killing of a single innocent human being is equal to the sin of killing all human beings, as per the undisputed Hadith of Prophet Muhammad. But takfiris, from whom Al-Qaeda have heavily borrowed their inspiration, have a different version on killing innocents and on suicide attackers. Many takfiris consider any political authority that does not abide by their interpretation of Islam as illegitimate and apostate. Violence against such regimes is considered legitimate. This view is close to the views of prominent Egyptian Muslim Brotherhood scholar Sayyid Qutb on *jahiliyyah* (pagan ignorance). Maulana Maududi, a notable scholar from the Indian subcontinent and the founder of Jamaat Islami, also maintained similar views. This allows takfiris to carry out their violent activities among the so-called Muslims and under Muslim rule.

Traditional Muslims follow that obeying the rules of a country as long as it does not contradict sharia is mandatory, as violation of rules is against the unity of any society, which creates anarchy. Takfiri views on suicide differ radically from orthodox Muslims. Takfiris believe that one who deliberately kills himself whilst attempting to kill an enemy is a shahid (martyr) and, therefore, goes straight to heaven. All sin will be washed away when a person is martyred. Such radical changes in the Islamic theology by scholars, starting from medieval Taqi al-Din Ibn Taymiyyah through eighteenth-century Islamic revivalist Muhammad Ibn Abd al-Wahhab, who started Wahhabism, to twentieth-century scholars like Maulana Maududi and Sayyid Qutb, were proponents of takfir to varying extents.

Ibn Taymiyyah issued his infamous fatwa, which was probably the theological beginning of Sunni extremism, declaring jihad against invading Mongols, not because they were invading but because they were takfir (apostates), and apostasy from Islam is punishable by death. At that time, Mongols had already converted to Islam, but for Taymiyyah, since they followed their traditional Yassa law, not the complete sharia law; they were not really Muslims but apostates.

Ibn Wahhab followers killed Arab Muslims and civilians mercilessly during invasions, as they were regarded as pagans or kafir. He called Shia, Sufi, and many Muslims practising other than his puritanical literary version of Islamic law *bida* (innovation in religion) and, hence, kafir (disbeliever). In his famous book *Milestones,* Sayyid Qutb argued that some Muslims should not be considered Muslims if they failed to obey sharia law and had hence fallen back to *jahiliyyah* (pagan ignorance). Towards his death, he called the entire Egyptian population followers of *jahiliyyah.* Maududi also maintained similar ideologies. Most of the Al-Qaeda leaders, including Bin Laden and Zawahiri, who had learned these ideologies from their childhood, developed their own takfiri versions which supported their ideology.

While Bin Laden and his group were based in Sudan, they concentrated their activities in Africa. Prolonged civil war and US involvement in Somalia as part of a humanitarian mission and UN-sponsored international mediation gave Al-Qaeda an opportunity to confront the US military in Somalia. With silent bases in Sudan, Al-Qaeda trained and armed rebel groups in Somalia linked to Mohamed Farrah Aidid. The ruling Somalian government under President Mohammed Siad Barre was overthrown in a civil war by a coalition of opposing clans in January 1991. The Somali National Army was disbanded, and some former soldiers reconstituted regional forces or formed clan militias. There were five major opposition groups who competed for political control.

In September 1991, severe fighting broke out in Mogadishu, which spread throughout the country, killing over twenty thousand people and injuring several thousands more. The prolonged wars ravaged Somalia's agriculture, which in turn led to starvation in a large part of the country. The international community responded to the famine and started sending a large supply of food. But almost 80 per cent of this was looted by local clan leaders, who exchanged it with other countries for weapons. This worsened starvation, and an estimated 300,000 people died and another 1.5 million people suffered prolonged starvation.

In July 1992, the UN brokered a ceasefire between the opposing clan factions and put observers in place. A massive humanitarian operation started supplying about 48,000 tons of food and medical supplies. They were airlifted to the various part of Somalia by US forces to avoid the regular looting of truck convoys. These major efforts proved to be a great help but inadequate by far, with continued death of about 500,000 and 1.5 million refugees and another 3 million struggling with starvation. The major obstacle to proper distribution and collapse of economy was the lawless situation in Somalia, where there was no national army, police, or government to maintain law and order. To meet this challenge, the UN Security Council authorized a mission, UNOSOM II, to establish a secure environment throughout Somalia, to achieve national reconciliation so as to create a democratic state in the near future. US forces took the leadership of the mission with assistance from Pakistan and Malaysian forces. In a unity Conference on National Reconciliation in Somalia held on 15 March 1993 at Addis Ababa, Ethiopia, all fifteen existing Somali parties agreed to restore peace and democracy.

Although a signatory to the March Agreement, by May 1993, Mohammed Farrah Aidid's faction was not cooperating. They started anti-UN propaganda through radio broadcasts and organized their clan. After proving a major obstacle to peace in Somalia and the humanitarian mission, the UN mission, under US forces who were authorized to use force, started targeting the activities of Aidid's faction. Aidid's men attacked a Pakistani unit on 5 June 1993 during an inspection of an arms cache at a radio station of Aidid. It resulted in the death of twenty-four Pakistani troops and the injury of fifty-seven soldiers. Three Americans and one Italian soldier were also injured. The UN Security Council passed a resolution for the arrest and prosecution of the persons responsible for the death and wounding of the peacekeepers.

A planned short raid on a safe house of Aidid on 3 October 1993 in Mogadishu finally resulted in a major war lasting two days. Though the house was conquered and secured by the forces, US forces suffered heavy casualties with the shooting down of two helicopters and damage to three others. The raid team and the shot-down helicopter team were stranded. They were overpowered by a large crowd of militia men and civilians. Their rescue team, though large, had to face several obstacles to reach the site due to a heavy dust storm, firing from all directions, and many roadblocks put up by the residents. Aidid's supporters called the residents on megaphones to come out and rescue their homes from invaders.

Thousands of people assembled on the street and outnumbered the stranded soldiers. Captured US soldiers were humiliated, and some were dragged through the streets of Mogadishu. It was broadcasted in US media. Finally the battle was won with a loss of 18 US soldiers and the injury of 73 others. One Malaysian and one Pakistani soldier were also killed. An estimate of Somali casualties varied from 300, as claimed by rebels, to 1,500 as per US estimates. More reliable estimates quote a death of 800–1000 militia men and civilians and thousands injured. A large crowd of civilians, including women and children, acted as human shields, and from behind them, militiamen fired on the army men from all sides. Many civilians also participated in the attacks.

This was one of the largest military casualties of US soldiers in combat after the Vietnam War. It caused a lengthy debate in US media and political circles, especially the humiliation of soldiers in Mogadishu streets. This ultimately led to complete US pull-out from the mission in March 1994 and acceptance of the UN mission as a failure. It ended on 24 April 1994 by UN secretary general Boutros-Ghali. For Aidid and his fighters, the fight was a victory as it had been a mission to capture Aidid and their top leaders who could escape. Inflicting heavy casualties of US soldiers and shooting down of military helicopters were a moral boost.

Later reports revealed Al-Qaeda had helped Aidid's men with weapons and training. Mohammed Atef had personally trained Aidid's men and another Al-Qaeda operative, Zachariah al-Tunisi, supposed to have fired the RPG that had downed one of the Black Hawk helicopters. Both of them were killed in Afghanistan in November 2001 during the US attack. It is believed that several trips were made by Al-Qaeda members from Sudan to Somalia through Kenya, sometimes using Osama's private jet for the journey. Osama bin Laden prized Somali fighters and ridiculed the US administration's decision to prematurely depart the region as 'weakness, feebleness and cowardliness of the US soldier'. Al-Qaeda's involvement in the battle and failure to effectively crush the rebellion later became a debate in the USA, though during that time, Al-Qaeda was not even known to US authorities. The failure of resolving the Somali conflict and the memory of the first battle of Mogadishu or 'Black Hawk Down' remained as a mind block for US military planners in interfering in future conflicts like the Rwandan Genocide of 1994.

Al-Qaeda's involvement in Africa was not restricted to Somalia. Bin Laden sent an emissary, Qari el-Said, with $40,000 to Algeria in 1992 or 1993 to aid the Islamists. He asked the militant faction GIA (Armed Islamic Group) to go ahead with war rather than negotiate with the government, unlike the ongoing compromise between the government and imprisoned leaders of Islamic Salvation Front (FIS). GIA went ahead with their advice. Initially started as a guerrilla group targeting army and police, they later started killing civilians, raiding villages and streets. They even fought with their former parent organization, FIS. GIA engaged in an attack on trains and an organized hijacking of a French aircraft that planned to hit the Eiffel Tower in Paris in December 1994 with assistance from Al-Qaeda.

French counterterrorism expert Roland Jacquard claimed that Bin Laden himself had travelled to Manchester and London in 1994 to meet associates of the GIA. He provided financial assistance to their overtly rebellious newsletter named *Al-Ansar*. The civil war that followed caused the deaths of 150,000–200,000 Algerians. It lasted for a decade and finally ended with the hunting down of Islamists and the surrender of the rest of the militants, thus effectively ending the conflict by 2002. During the Sudan years, Al-Qaeda developed cells in many African countries like Egypt, Tunisia, Kenya, and Tanzania. The other fronts of Al-Qaeda were also coordinated from their Sudan base by this time as in the USA, Philippines, Bosnia, and Croatia.

In 6 December 1993, British newspaper the *Independent* published the first ever interview of Bin Laden given to a Western journalist. In his article, the veteran journalist Robert Fist noted that the Western embassy circuit in Khartoum had suggested that some of the 'Afghans' whom this Saudi entrepreneur flew to Sudan were now busy training for further jihad wars in Algeria, Tunisia and Egypt. In the article, he maintained a sympathetic attitude towards Bin Laden as evident from his article headline 'Anti-Soviet Warrior Puts His Army on the Road to Peace'. When Bin Laden was asked about his name being recently mentioned by Muslim fighters in Bosnia, Bin Laden acknowledged his influence there but complained that it was difficult for his fighters to cross to Bosnia. In the interview, Bin Laden boasted about his role in recruiting thousands of fighters for the Afghan war.

Al-Qaeda organized their first major terrorist attack in the USA during their Sudan years on the 26 February 1993 World Trade Center bombing. The activities of the group further unfolded in the USA and in the Philippines later. Still in Sudan, Bin Laden and his group maintained their innocent image. Bin Laden married one of the nieces of Hassan al-Turabi, and in his family circles, he was known as a wealthy Saudi businessman and a family man. This popular image in Sudan was partly broken in 4 February 1994 when a group of Takfiris tried to kill Bin Laden in his compound in Khartoum.

Four activists from an ultra-extreme Egyptian militant group, Takfir wal-Hijra, attacked a mosque at Omdurman, where Bin Laden frequented, shooting sixteen people to death and injuring twenty others. The next day, they went hunting for Bin Laden, whom they judged to be offensively liberal. They came to Bin Laden's house and started firing indiscriminately. Shortly, shots were returned from the offices and from the roof of the house, killing three attackers and capturing the other one, whom they hanged. A Libyan named Mohammed Abdullah al-Khulayfi was the leader of the team, who was an Afghan war veteran who fought along with Bin Laden. Takfir wal-Hijra, which originated in Egypt, claimed the true followers of Sayyid Qutb considered current Islam so corrupt and all Muslims infidels.

After this attack, security in the house was beefed up with trenches all around the house and more guards. Ali Mohammed reached from the USA and trained Bin Laden's bodyguards further. It is believed that during this visit, Ali Mohammed arranged a meeting between Osama Bin Laden and Hizbullah leader Imad Mughniya, the mastermind of the 1983 Beirut US embassy and Marine barracks bombings which killed 304 people together, mostly American soldiers. It is also interesting to note that a similar urea nitrate bomb with hydrogen cylinders was used in Beirut bombings and, in 1993, the attempted World Trade Center bombing by Ramzi Yousef. After the meetings, some of the Al-Qaeda and Egyptian Islamic Jihad members went for explosives training in Lebanon.

On 3 July 1993, Omer Abdul Rahman (Blind Sheik) was arrested in the USA, and further investigations pointed to his relations with Bin Laden. Still, US authorities believed Bin Laden was just a financier and not directly involved in terrorism. He was put on a no-fly watch list prohibiting his travel to the USA. They were watching Bin Laden closely in Sudan from 1991. On 12 August 1993, the USA officially designated Sudan as a 'state sponsor of terrorism', subjecting it to a variety of US economic sanctions. While in Sudan, Bin Laden continued to criticize King Fahd of Saudi Arabia and tried to cause rebellion among ruling elites. On 9 April 1994, Fahd stripped bin Laden of his Saudi citizenship and froze his Saudi assets for supporting terrorist groups. He pressured Bin Laden's family to cut off his $7 million-per-year stipend. Shortly, his family followed him and officially disowned Bin Laden. But many believe that this was just a face-saving exercise, and Saudi continued to support Bin Laden as per the secret deal between Bin Laden and Saudi intelligence chief Prince Turki al-Faisal. There are reports that Prince Turki sent Bin Laden's mother, Hamida, and his brother Baker to Khartoum several times to convince Osama to abandon his terrorist activities.

On 26 June 1995, Egyptian president Hosni Mubarak arrived at Addis Ababa, Ethiopia, to attend the Organization of African Unity summit. His motorcade was attacked by militants on the way. Gunmen shot at his limousine and attempted to detonate a grenade, but it malfunctioned. A second ambush was already ahead, but the motorcade reversed the course and saved the president's life. Two of Mubarak's bodyguards were killed. Five assassins were killed by Ethiopian soldiers, and three were captured. Later investigations revealed Egypt-based militant groups Al-Gama'a al-Islamiyya and Egyptian Islamic Jihad (EIJ) had worked with al-Qaeda on the plot. Sudan was also involved as weapons had been smuggled into Ethiopia through the Sudanese embassy. Many of the conspirators were members of both Al-Qaeda and EIJ. Ayman al-Zawahiri personally inspected the ground and chose the spot for killing. When Egyptian authorities claimed to CIA agents that Osama had financed the operation, both groups agreed. The leader of the plot was Mustafa Hamza, a leader in both al-Qaeda and Al-Gama'a al-Islamiyya, who in 1998 became the head of Al-Gama'a al-Islamiyya while in exile. In 2005, he was extradited to Egypt from Iran for trial there. The United Nations Security Council placed sanctions on Sudan for harbouring terrorists, including Bin Laden, and assisting in the assassination plot of Mubarak. US authorities planned to attack Osama in Sudan, and the evolved plan was put on hold, as it was just like declaring a war on Sudan. Instead, US authorities started pressuring Sudan to dismantle Bin Laden's network and extradite Bin Laden. The relations between Sudan and Egypt deteriorated. There was a build-up of the Egyptian army on the Sudan border. Sudan expelled Egyptian Islamic Jihad activists from their soil. By this time, Hassan al-Turabi had lost his influence in the government.

In August 1995, Bin Laden wrote an open letter to King Fahd of Saudi Arabia calling him corrupt and asked for his resignation. He called for a guerrilla campaign to drive out US forces from Saudi Arabia, the land of two holy mosques. On 13 November 1995, two truck bombs killed five Americans and two Indians in the Saudi National Guard training centre in Riyadh, Saudi Arabia. Al-Qaeda was blamed for the attack. By this attack, US authorities changed their view of Bin Laden from financier to Al-Qaeda leader. The same day in Geneva, Switzerland, a senior Egyptian diplomat, Alaa al-Din Nazmi, was shot dead by EIJ workers. He had been working undercover on Islamist extremist groups and financial activities of Muslim Brotherhood. On 19 November 1995, a twin car explosion in the Egyptian embassy in Islamabad, Pakistan, killed sixteen people and the suicide bombers. This was organized by the Egyptian Islamic Jihad under Zawahiri, though Bin Laden was sceptical about attacking a friendly country.

During this time, four Yemeni gunmen attempted to assassinate Bin Laden; they attacked his house, killing two of his guards and three of the mercenaries. It was believed that Saudi Arabia was behind this attack. Bin Laden was now convinced that Saudi Arabia, Egypt, and the CIA were behind this assassination attempt. Ali Mohammed, then working in Sudan with Sudan intelligence, further increased his personal security. The violent incidents in Bin Laden's home and security build-up caused displeasure from neighbours in this posh neighbourhood of Khartoum, who also feared a missile attack by US forces on the area. The bullet marks in the house were still there even after Bin Laden left Sudan. Now Bin Laden feared his expulsion from Sudan, and he looked for options. Through an intermediary in London, Khalid al-Fawwaz, a Saudi businessman, he tried to get political asylum in Britain. After investigation on Bin Laden by Home Office, then British Home Secretary Michael Howard ordered a ban on him under British immigration laws.

Even after Russian withdrawal from Afghanistan, several mujahideen factions maintained numerous training camps. Thousands of fighters from around the world came to these camps and after their training returned to their home countries for their mercenary activities. Bin Laden also maintained camps in Afghanistan throughout these years, and he had also active cells in Pakistan. Towards the end of 1995, Saudi authorities negotiated with the Sudan government about Bin Laden. Sudan was keen to extradite Bin Laden to Saudi, and they asked them to give pardon for Bin Laden. Saudi authorities were not ready to extradite him, citing that he was no longer a Saudi citizen. US agents were also aware of these developments, and they planned to extradite him to the USA, but Sudan asked them to provide evidence or any convictions. At that time, there were no indictments against Bin Laden anywhere in the world.

The USA attempted to collect Bin Laden–related files from Sudan. But when they were ready to hand them over, the US agents increased their demands to hand over Bin Laden also. This stand-off caused valuable inputs. Sudan intelligence had been monitoring bin Laden since 1991 after he had arrived there. They had collected a vast intelligence database on Osama bin Laden and more than two hundred top members of his al-Qaeda network. An Egyptian intelligence officer with deep knowledge in Sudan later noted, 'they knew all about them: who they were, where they came from. They had copies of their passports, their tickets; they knew where they went. Of course that information could have helped enormously. It is the history of those people.' But the USA at that time was sceptical to bargain with Sudan, and many in the establishment believed their data might be unreliable. The 9/11 Commission report later noted, 'Ambassador Carney had instructions only to push the Sudanese to expel Bin Laden. Ambassador Carney had no legal basis to ask for more from the Sudanese since, at that time, there was no indictment outstanding against bin Laden in any country.' Finally, they all agreed to allow Bin Laden to leave Sudan to a country of his choice.

Bin Laden chose to shift to Jalalabad, Afghanistan, and boarded a chartered flight on 18 May 1996. Bin Laden's entourage flew in a large C-130 transport plane carrying about 150 men, women, and children. They stopped at Doha, Qatar for refuelling. In Qatar, government officials greeted them warmly. During this time, Bin Laden presumably met the influential royal family member Abdullah bin Khalid al-Thani, the country's religious minister who later became the interior minister. Bin Laden met him again at least once, likely in August 1996. The entire operation was coordinated by Ali Mohammed.

In Afghanistan, Bin Laden forged a close relationship with the Taliban leader, Mullah Mohammed Omar. The expulsion left bin Laden without an option other than becoming a full-time radical. Most of the three hundred Afghan Arabs who left with him eventually became dedicated terrorists. All Bin Laden's assets in Sudan and Sudanese banks were frozen. He had many million-dollar investments in Sudan and substantial dues from the government of Sudan. However, he left Sudan with many Al-Qaeda members, leaving much of his money and resources. Sudan maintained a stand that they were watching Bin Laden and that he was under control in Sudan. In a later interview with the *Washington Post*, then defence minister of Sudan, Elfatih Erwa, claimed, 'We warned US. In Sudan, bin Laden and his money were under our control. But we knew that if he goes to Afghanistan no one could control him. The US didn't care; they just didn't want him in Somalia. It's crazy.'

Many believed Bin Laden became totally broken. It may have been partly true financially, but his activities continued. Immediately after his forced migration from Sudan on 25 June 1996, a large truck bomb devastated the Khobar Towers in a high-security area in the city of Khobar, Saudi Arabia. The eight-storied building was housing United States Air Force personnel. Nineteen US servicemen died and 498 persons from many nationalities were injured. It was a powerful blast that destroyed almost the entire building. But a service person residing there noted the suspicious truck, and a prompt evacuation of the building was started, which averted a much more major casualty. An unknown group called Hizbullah al-Hejaz officially claimed responsibility. But it was found to be the handiwork of Al-Qaeda, which was later accepted by Bin Laden.

Immediately following the 13 November 1995 Riyadh bombing, US officials received threat from a group that Khobar Towers would be attacked if US troops did not begin withdrawal immediately. Accordingly, security in the Khobar Towers was increased but could not avert this attack. The explosives were smuggled from Lebanon. Most of the assailants were Saudi citizens. This was a major embarrassment for Saudi Arabia to admit their home-grown terrorists were making major attacks and exposing the presence of US soldiers in Saudi Arabia. So they tried to implicate Iran in the attack. During the interview with Abdel-Bari Atwan, editor-in-chief of the British-based pan-Arab daily *al-Quds al-Arabi* in the mountains of Tora Bora on 23 November, 1996 Bin Laden claimed the responsibility for the attack on Khobar Towers and Black Hawk Down. At that time, Atwan stayed with Bin Laden in a small cave. Bin Laden told him that he felt cheated by Sudanese who did not pay for the funds he invested there, but he still controlled a large part of his money.

Just after the end of Al-Qaeda's Sudan years, a close lieutenant and finance manager of Bin Laden, Jamal Ahmed al-Fadl, defected from Al-Qaeda. He first reached the USA in the 1980s and worked in some supermarkets and deli stores in New York. He was recruited by al-Kifah Center there. He worked with Bin Laden and most of the initial Al-Qaeda leaders from late 1980 in Afghanistan during the Afghan jihad era. He was present at the formation of Al-Qaeda. Later he moved to Sudan, his home country, where he brought properties for Bin Laden before the arrival of Bin Laden in Sudan.

While Bin Laden was in Sudan, Fadl managed his finances and was familiar with all the major transactions and activities of Al-Qaeda. He was not a very devout Muslim like most other Al-Qaeda members and was unhappy over his small salary of about US $500 compared to

US $1,200 for many top Al-Qaeda leaders of Egyptian background. Towards the end of the Sudan years, he siphoned out more than $100,000 from Bin Laden's assets. Fearing that Bin Laden would find his fraud and kill him, he walked into the US embassy of Eretria in June 1996 to claim that he was an Al-Qaeda agent. There he was questioned for many months by the CIA, and later, he was taken to Germany and handed over to FBI agents.

Al-Fadl became a crucial lead to expose Bin Laden and Al-Qaeda. He was enrolled into the Witness Protection Program of FBI and was provided security and financial assistance by FBI agents. The FBI worked with him for months and years and entered into a mutually beneficial relationship with him, which helped the first conviction against Bin Laden in 1998. He was a crucial witness to all Al-Qaeda activities which filled the gap in the vast amount of data collected by the CIA and FBI over the years. During his testimony, al-Fadl gave valuable details to the court. According to a report in the *New Yorker*, al-Fadl 'provided a surprisingly full picture of al-Qaeda, depicting it as an international criminal network intent on attacking the United States'. Al-Fadl told that he had handled many of al-Qaeda's financial transactions after bin Laden had left Afghanistan and moved the hub of his operations to Sudan in 1992. In this role, al-Fadl had access to bin Laden's payroll and knew the details of al-Qaeda's global banking networks, its secret membership lists, and its paramilitary training camps in Afghanistan, including the one which he had attended in the late eighties. His exposition changed the US authorities understanding of Al-Qaeda and Bin Laden from an organization sponsoring terror activities to the largest terrorist group in the world threatening to attack the USA at home and its interests worldwide. Two years before the African embassy bombings, al-Fadl warned of a possible attack in the USA or US establishments in other countries. He provided details about the Al-Qaeda cell in Kenya under Wadih El-Hage.

During the 1990s, Afghanistan was a land of chaos with crime, drugs, and arms. Its condition was described by a moderate warlord, Abdul Haq, in an interview with the *New York Times*: "For us, Afghanistan is destroyed. It is turning to poison, and not only for us but for all others in the world. If you are a terrorist, you can have shelter here, no matter who you are. Day by day, there is the increase of drugs. Maybe one day the US will have to send hundreds of thousands of troops to deal with that. And if they step in, they will be stuck. We have a British grave in Afghanistan. We have a Soviet grave. And then we will have an American grave.' His assessments were accurate, and his predictions were exact in the later history of Afghanistan.

Back in Afghanistan, Bin Laden soon established his old contacts. He could also raise money from donors from the days of Afghan jihad against Russians and from the Pakistan ISI. Bin Laden practically took over the Ariana Afghan Airlines, which shuttled Islamic militants, arms, cash, and opium through Pakistan and United Arab Emirates. False identities were given to travellers to avoid legal hassles. An arms smuggler, Victor Bout, helped him to run the airlines, maintaining planes and passenger and freight handling.

In August 1996, bin Laden issued his first public fatwa declaring war against the United States in the Arabian Peninsula titled 'Declaration of War against the Americans Occupying the Land of the Two Holy Places'. It was first published by the London-based newspaper *Al-Quds al-Arabi* and faxed to supporters worldwide. US president George H. W. Bush assured King Fahd of Saudi Arabia in 1990 in the wake of the arrival of US forces to expel Saddam's forces from Kuwait that all US forces based in Saudi Arabia would be withdrawn once the Iraqi threat had been eliminated. But by 1996, the Americans were still there, citing the necessity to deal with the remnants of Saddam's regime. For Bin Laden, the 'evils' of the Middle East had arisen from America's attempt to take over the region and from its support for Israel. Saudi Arabia had been turned into 'an American colony'. During this period, Bin Laden gave many interviews to Western media in which he claimed to be waging war against the USA.

Osama bin Laden and Ayman al-Zawahiri released another fatwa signed by them and three others in February 1998 under the name of the World Islamic Front for Jihad Against Jews and Crusaders, which declared that killing of Americans and their allies anywhere in the world an individual duty for every Muslim to liberate the al-Aqsa Mosque (in Jerusalem) and the holy mosque (in Mecca) from their grip. This fatwa was also signed by representatives from militant groups in Afghanistan, Pakistan, Saudi Arabia, Sudan, Somalia, Yemen, Eritrea, Djibouti, Kenya, Bosnia, Croatia, Algeria, Tunisia, Lebanon, the Philippines, Tajikistan, Chechnya, Bangladesh, Kashmir, Azerbaijan, and Palestine. Following the initial fatwa, a group of clerics in Afghanistan and another group in Pakistan issued a similar fatwa to legitimize Bin Laden. At the public announcement of the fatwa, bin Laden told the attending journalists that North Americans were 'very easy targets' and 'You will see the results of this in a very short time.' On 6 August 1998, Egyptian Islamic Jihad sent a warning that they would soon deliver a message to Americans 'in a language they will understand'. On 7 August 1998, two simultaneous explosions rocked US embassies in Nairobi, Kenya, and Dar-es-Salaam in Tanzania. The bomb in Nairobi killed 213 people, including 12 US nationals, and injured more than 4,500. The bomb in Dar-es-Salaam killed 11 and injured 85; no Americans died here. This made a major change in the mindset of the American establishment and the public against Al-Qaeda and threats from them. Though enormous intelligence data and confessions were proof of Al-Qaeda activities and potential threats, many had not been convinced till then.

On 12 August 1998, a small group of presidential advisors met Clinton reportedly with an intercepted mobile phone conversation between two of bin Laden's lieutenants that implicated them in the embassy bombings and evidence that bin Laden was looking to obtain weapons of mass destruction and chemical weapons to use against US installations. US agencies were taping the phones of Al-Qaeda activists, including the satellite phone of Bin Laden, collecting intelligence data coordinated through Alec Station, the CIA's bin Laden unit. On 20 August 1998, the USA retaliated with about 70 cruise missiles on Bin Laden's training camps, including Khost, Afghanistan, anticipating that he would be there. It killed 24 people. Thirteen cruise missiles were fired at the Al-Shifa pharmaceutical plant in Khartoum, killing the night guard. US intelligence claimed the plant was making chemical weapons for Bin Laden, which Sudan vehemently denied.

Bin Laden apparently changed his plan to visit Khost at the last moment as he discussed in the CIA-taped phone call the day before just by chance or due to a warning from Pakistan. The USA ordered seizure of funds of Bin Laden by the US Treasury, and Bin Laden was put on FBI's Ten Most Wanted terrorist list. On 8 June 1998, a grand jury in the USA issued a sealed indictment against Bin Laden for terrorism, which was initiated in 1996. It was superseded on 4 November 1998 with an open indictment against Bin Laden, Muhammed Atef, and other Al-Qaeda operatives for embassy bombings in Africa and other terrorist activities. Bin Laden and Atef were put on a $5 million reward. By now the hunt for Bin Laden became an official legal matter.

In Afghanistan, Bin Laden forged a deep alliance with the Taliban. He helped Taliban financially and provided Arab fighters who helped Taliban in many raids and wars. His vast contacts in the Arab world, Pakistan, and elsewhere were used to support the Taliban financially, militarily, and in administration. Taliban, with its strong tribal tradition of Pashtun loyalty, which treated and defended their guests and refugees as their family members, was a great support for Bin Laden and Al-Qaeda to continue their mission and secure the support against any possible aggression. Taliban quickly gained political control over the entire Afghanistan, including Kabul and Kandahar. For Bin Laden, Afghanistan under the leadership of Mullah Omer was the 'only legitimate Muslim country in the world'. In spite of a worldwide crackdown on Al-Qaeda, its financial dealings, and coordination of several intelligence agencies from a host of friendly countries, Al-Qaeda struck in the heart of the USA on 11 September, 2001 in an unprecedented coordinated suicide hijacking of four commercial US aircrafts hitting both towers of World Trade Center, separately grounding them to level. Also, a similar attack was orchestrated at the Pentagon in Arlington, Virginia, damaging the building substantially. Another attack intended for a target in Washington DC was foiled, but the aircraft crashed. A total of 2,973 people and 19 hijackers were killed, all of which were US citizens except 102 persons of different nationalities. The terror descended on the minds of even the most unlearned or uninformed American and the threat of terrorists anywhere became clear to the world.

The CIA and FBI quickly reached the conclusion that the culprits were Osama Bin Laden and Al-Qaeda, and their evidence was shared with Britain. Shortly, the United States launched the War on Terror, and many of its allies soon followed it to overthrow the Taliban regime in Afghanistan and capture al-Qaeda operatives. Several countries strengthened their anti-terrorism legislations to preclude future attacks. The Special Activities Division of CIA was given the lead in tracking down, killing, or capturing bin Laden. Much evidence trickled from several intelligence agencies about the plot and hijackers. Several inputs had been there before about an imminent airborne attack and training for an important mission happening in Al-Qaeda training camps in Afghanistan. But nothing prevented the mayhem of 11 September 2001. Two valuable informants in US custody, Jamal al-Fadl and Ali Muhammed, were totally unaware of the plots and the new breed of terrorist hijackers. The spread of terrorists during the Afghan years of Bin Laden was like a chain reaction with several scattered cells operating independently for a common cause but with varying targets.

Bin Laden and Khalid Sheik Muhammed (KSM) personally chose the nineteen hijackers at their Afghan training camp. KSM was responsible for the entire planning and execution of 9/11 attacks. He was arrested on 1 March 2003 from Rawalpindi, Pakistan, by Pakistani security officials working along with the CIA. He was then transported to Guantanamo Bay in Cuba. In March 2007, he confessed his responsibility in the court at Guantanamo Bay as he was 'responsible for the 9/11 operation from A to Z'.

Bin Laden initially denied his involvement. In a videotape first aired in the Al Jazeera channel based in Qatar on September 16. But after three years, in another videotape aired by Al Jazeera just four days before the American presidential election, Bin Laden abandoned his denial and said that he had personally directed the nineteen hijackers. He accused US president George W. Bush of negligence in the hijacking of the planes. He said in the videotape:

> God knows it did not cross our minds to attack the Towers, but after the situation became unbearable—and we witnessed the injustice and tyranny of the American-Israeli alliance against our people in Palestine and Lebanon—I thought about it. And the events that affected me directly were that of 1982 and the events that followed—when America allowed the Israelis to invade Lebanon, helped by the U.S. Sixth Fleet. As I watched the destroyed towers in Lebanon, it occurred to me punish the unjust the same way: to destroy towers in America so it could taste some of what we are tasting and to stop killing our children and women.

At the time of the September 11 attacks, Bin Laden had several indictments in US courts. An Interpol arrest warrant for the murder of a German intelligence agent and his wife in Libya was existing from 16 March 1998, which was his first indictment. Several pieces of evidence against Bin Laden and Al-Qaeda in the 9/11 attack were provided to Taliban. In spite of many requests, the Taliban regime in Afghanistan refused to extradite Bin Laden. Eight days after bombing began in Afghanistan by US and allied forces, which started on 7 October 2011, Taliban offered to turn over Bin Laden to a third country for trial in return for an end of US bombing. The offer was quickly rejected, and President George Bush stated that this was no longer negotiable and 'There is no need to discuss innocence or guilt. We know he is guilty.' He was confident that the Taliban would surrender quickly and Osama would be killed or captured soon. After the war and invasion of Afghanistan, US authorities captured many documents and videotapes about Al-Qaeda and Bin Laden. In spite of war, prolonged US invasion, cooperation with Pakistan, and establishment of a friendly government in Afghanistan, Bin Laden, Ayman al-Zawahiri, and Mullah Omer escaped unharmed. During the course, George Bush almost lost interest in Bin Laden, and he shut up the special operations paramilitary group of the CIA dedicated to capturing Bin Laden in 2005. For him, 'I don't know where bin Laden is. I have no idea and really don't care. It's not that important. It's not our priority.' But his successor, then presidential candidate Barack Obama, on 7 October 2008 in his presidential debate on foreign policy pledged, 'We will kill bin Laden. We will crush al-Qaeda. That has to be our biggest national security priority.' During his tenure, he revived the effort on the fight against Al-Qaeda.

After a decade of wait, a prolonged search, constant US presence in Afghanistan, continued war, spending so much money, worldwide raids, huge intelligence gathering, and opening of Americans' graves in many parts of Afghanistan as envisioned by Abdul Haq, the Afghan warlord well versed in Afghan history and psyche, the day finally came. One day in America but early morning (one o' clock) in Pakistan under the direct supervision of President Barack Obama, Bin Laden was killed by a well-planned, precisely executed raid at his Abbottabad (in Pakistan) safe house by Special Forces on 2 May 2011. The operation, codenamed Operation Neptune Spear of the US Central Intelligence Agency (CIA), was carried out by United States Navy SEAL Team Six. At the time of death, Bin Laden was carrying a reward of $25 million by the US government and another $2 million by the Pilots Association and the Air Transport Association for his head. On 15 June 2011, US federal prosecutors officially dropped all criminal charges against Osama bin Laden following his death.

But with the constant chasing and capturing of Al-Qaeda members and their associates, seizure of their financial sources, a worldwide alert and new rules on terror financing, and now with the death of Bin Laden, the leader, the mentor, and its commander, it could not be claimed that Al-Qaeda was finished. Later history of the world reveals that the seeds that Bin Laden and his early comrades had sowed have grown in many parts of the world, creating large swaths of land under the black banners of Al-Qaeda by 2014.

The main reason that Al-Qaeda as a group ideology cannot be easily destroyed is its structure. As portrayed by one of its defectors, Jamal al-Fadl, it works like a corporate company. In reality, Al-Qaeda is like a multinational corporate house running with a central director board, many divisions, and several financial sources and operational heads. It's Shura-e-Majilis working like a director board; the amir its CEO and chairman, and several leaders managing operations of different natures with independent cells. One member or leader may not be aware of the working of another cell, and operational details are rarely shared. The amir had overall control on the entire network, coordinating varied activities.

With history of its work for more than two decades, Al-Qaeda now may have hundreds of leading activists and thousands of sympathizers working in varying levels of involvement, spreading and executing the global jihad. Many names, many fronts, and many local involvements but with a core ideology and, often, an overall approval from a global leader! With the death of Bin Laden, the second in command, Ayman al-Zawahiri, automatically became the acting amir, and he later became the amir after his endorsement by Shura members.

Even during a worldwide alert against terrorism following the 1998 African embassy bombings, Al-Qaeda organized a meeting of hundreds of Islamists with extremist ideas in January 2000 at Beirut, Lebanon, which was dubbed as the First Conference on Jerusalem. Participants included those from Al-Qaeda, Islamic jihad, Hamas, Hizbullah, and from several countries, including Egypt, Pakistan, Jordan, Sudan, Algeria, Qatar, Yemen, and the USA. The participants created a new organization called the Jerusalem Project, intended to liberate Jerusalem. They called for a boycott of US and Israeli products, and one of the resolutions passed claimed, 'The only decisive option to achieve this strategy [to regain Jerusalem] is the option of jihad [holy war] in all its forms and resistance . . . America today is a second Israel.' Notable participants include Ahmed Huber, a director of Al-Qaeda–affiliated Al-Taqwa Bank, which had been shut down after 9/11. Huber is known for his connections to both neo-Nazi and radical Muslim groups. He later claimed that he met some al-Qaeda leaders there who were 'very discreet, well-educated, and very intelligent people'. Among the four participants from the USA;

one of them was Abdurahman Alamoudi, a prominent US Muslim and lobbyist for Islamic causes.

Even after the Russians left Afghanistan, Islamists from all over the world flocked into Afghanistan and were arms-trained in training camps there. Most of those camps collected money from the trainees, making it a profitable business. Bin Laden also maintained many camps there. Several people were trained there; some of them later became Al-Qaeda operatives, and others went back to their native countries or other war arenas. Several recruits came to Al-Qaeda training camps from different parts of the world. One such recruit was Abu Musab al-Zarqawi, originally Ahmad Fadhil Nazzal al-Khalaylah, a Bedouin from the Bani Hassan tribe of Zarqa, Jordan.

He came to Afghanistan when he was just twenty-three years old to fight against the pro-Soviet government there and was trained at an Al-Qaeda training camp. In 1993, he returned to Jordan, and shortly, he was arrested for possessing grenades and sentenced to fifteen years in prison. Inside the prison, he came in contact with a Jordanian militant network and gained many followers. When Abdulla II became the new king of Jordan in 1999, he was released from prison on a general amnesty for prisoners. Following his release in late 1999, he was involved in a failed major bombing offensive, called the Millennium Plot, indented to blow up Radisson SAS Hotel in Amman, Jordan, and many other sites on 1 January 2000, organized by Al-Qaeda. His fellow conspirators were caught on November 30, but Zarqawi escaped and was tried in absentia. By the end of 1999, he reached Afghanistan and met Bin Laden.

Bin Laden strongly disliked taking Zarqawi along with him, as he found him too hard-line, overambitious, and overbearing, and they had different ideological views. But Saif al-Adel, another Al-Qaeda leader and close aide of Bin Laden, found his potential and persuaded Bin Laden to give him a token of $5,000 to set his own training camp. Zarqawi started his training camp near Herat, close to the Iran border, by early 2000. Starting with a dozen people, it soon swelled into several thousand recruits. Most of his recruits were from Jordan and Syria due to his close links with Muslim Brotherhood there. Bin Laden repeatedly asked Zarqawi to come to him and take the oath of allegiance, but he denied. That was a time of constant war between the Taliban backed by Al-Qaeda and the Northern Alliance, and by any chance he did not want to get involved in it. He also did not find Bin Laden or Al-Qaeda serious enough about jihad. When America started bombing in Afghanistan against Taliban and Bin Laden after 9/11, his camp was also targeted. Though he was injured, he managed to escape to Iran with many of his followers, where he reorganized there, maintaining his militant group, al-Tawhid wal-Jihad. By mid 2002, he aligned with Ansar al-Islam, a Kurdish rebel-controlled Islamist group based in Northern Iraq opposed to Saddam Hussein. He established a training camp there for training on explosives. That was exactly an area of Kurdistan, protected by US forces, establishing the 'no-fly' zone imposed on Saddam Hussein's regime. Ironically, the USA later alleged Saddam Hussein's regime protected and supported this top Al-Qaeda leader.

If the waning power of Saddam's regime in Iraq following prolonged sanctions after the Kuwait War gave Zarqawi an opportunity to establish a few training camps in a weakened Iraq, the end of Saddam's regime and invasion by America in 2003 dramatically changed his stature with a flood of money, arms, and recruits willing to do anything at his order. The war and invasion catalysed his status from a small, unknown militant to the most wanted man in Iraq with a bounty of $25 million on his head. His dramatic change in profile enabled him to carry out some of the most dreaded attacks against US forces, UN headquarters, police stations, a multitude of Shia sites, and business places. Thousands of people died in those attacks, and his hands were practically washed with blood on several occasions with brutal beheadings and massacres of enemies and captured civilians. Not many early Al-Qaeda leaders can compete with his hands-on experience in brutality. Osama Bin Laden warned him many times and expressed his shock on the horror and ease with which Zarqawi and his group killed civilians in Iraq. A US invasion started with a claim that Saddam was amassing and harbouring weapons of mass destruction and senior al-Qaeda leaders like Zarqawi and were later shocked to realize that the warehouses of Saddam was unusually empty of weapons and there was hardly any trace of nuclear or chemical weapons in Iraq. Zarqawi was very dreaded to have a membership in the 'original Al-Qaeda'.

Ultimately, after several claims of his death in the past, Zarqawi, at the age of thirty-nine, was killed by a massive 500-pound bomb dropped on his safe house while he was holding a meeting with other leaders and his spiritual guide, Sheik Abdul Rahman. All died in the attack. Following this significant triumph for the US-led military coalition in Iraq since the 2003 capture of Saddam Hussein, the Iraqi prime minister, Nouri al-Maliki, declared in a press conference, 'Today Zarqawi was defeated,' and a few hours after in the USA, President George Bush commented, 'Through his every action, he sought to defeat America and our coalition partners and turn Iraq into a safe haven from which al-Qaeda could wage its war . . . Now Zarqawi has met his end, and this violent man will never murder again.'

The next day after his death, a poster appeared on a mosque in Ramadi, a militant stronghold, claiming to be from Al-Qaeda in Iraq and that the organization would be led by a new prince. He had been named by Zarqawi to succeed him and he would be a copy of Zarqawi. The claim was not totally wrong. His successors were also dreaded and more influential than Zarqawi himself, who could carve out a large piece of Iraqi land under his rule and even extend to neighbouring Syria.

The power of Al-Qaeda is such that in numerous mutations and forms, it continues to spread to a large part of the world and is a concern for virtually every country in the world. A classical Al-Qaeda is evolving into the new-generation terrorists and activists, some more brutal and violent than their parents, some more mature and calculative than the original. Its spread is there in every continent and in all major populated countries as extremists, activists, supporters, or sympathizers. Bin Laden died, but his ideology continues to inspire some highly spirited or deviated people. At the same time provoke several questions and thoughts on others. How to tackle this? How to stop the violent journey? Is Bin Laden becoming another Karl Marx?

CHAPTER 5

The Psyche of a Terrorist

Publicity is the oxygen of terrorism.

Margaret Thatcher, former British prime minister

The idea of jihad, holy war, or alms struggle, though fundamental to the political Islam, was projected in the political area of Islamic governance not so often. Twentieth-century Muslim revivalists like Hassan al-Banna, who founded the Muslim Brotherhood in Egypt, and his ideological colleague Sayyid Qutb promoted and refined the concepts of jihad, which later became the fundamental basis of many modern Islamist ideologies. In the Indian subcontinent, Sayyid A'la Maududi almost simultaneously promulgated a similar ideology by starting his Jamaat-e-Islami, which later paved the way for many terrorist-related organizations in the Indian subcontinent and adjacent areas. The ideology of Banna, Sayyid Qutb, and Maududi influenced almost all Islamist revivalist thinkers and organizations in the current world. They were not just thinkers but prolific writers with more than a hundred books to their credit, which are the most read Islamic works of literature throughout the Muslim world after the basic texts in Islam. Their reach in the Muslim world is indisputable. They created next many levels of scholars who promoted and explained their ideologies, which were after some time expanded and corrected over time.

More than just scholars, preachers, and writers, they created powerful organizations among Muslims. The Muslim Brotherhood in reality is a truly pan-national organization with independent regional branches in Egypt, Syria, Tunisia, Jordan, Bahrain, Iraq, Iran, and Palestine. Its influence reaches almost all Muslim countries and populations with presence possibly in around seventy countries. It is fundamentally a sociocultural organization. But in many countries, the affiliated organization is named different and may have a different political party or wing. From the very beginning, the Brotherhood maintained a dual face; one face was of a socio-religious organization canvassing people into religion, then to their version of religion and interfering with social issues positively. At the same time, another group concentrated on arms training and violent militant activities. This duplicity was a survival tactic, as many might see only one face and would be biased towards the idea, whether it was a revivalist religious movement or a violent political movement. It also needed a platform of social activism to mask the real intention of political control even if it needed violence, intimidation, and killings. Formed in 1928 in Ismailia, Egypt, it became an influential movement with about five hundred thousand followers during the time of Second World War.

In the 1940s, it mounted many violent attacks in Egypt, including bombings and the assassination of Egyptian prime minister Mahmud Fahmi al-Nuqrashi in December 1948 in retaliation for dissolving Brotherhood activities. Al-Banna himself was assassinated soon afterwards, apparently at the behest of the establishment. After the death of Hassan al-Banna, the ideology became more virulent with prominence of Sayyid Qutb. In the first Arab-Israeli war of 1948, the Brotherhood actively trained their cadres, and they participated in combats and were a formidable force. Many of their cadres fought to cause maximum damage to the enemy with strong intentions for martyrdom, close to suicide missions. Those who were arms-trained and were war veterans became a law-and-order problem for Egypt. Sayyid Qutb was a strong anti-Semitist. His book *"Our Struggle against the Jews*, released in 1950, later became a central argument of current Islamic anti-Semitism.

When the new revolutionary government under Gamal Abdel Nasser gained power in July 1952 through the Free Officers Movement, both Qutb and the Muslim Brotherhood welcomed the coup against the pro-Western monarchist government. They had cooperated with the movement before and just after the coup. Abdel Nasser was close to Sayyid Qutb, and they met regularly. Nasser sought Qutb's views on many matters. He offered Qutb any ministerial post in the government, but Qutb declined. Nasser and his movement realized that their secular ideology was not compatible with the islamism of the Brotherhood. Qutb also realized that his dream of making an Islamic state in Egypt through Nasser was not going to materialize. This led to an attempt to assassinate President Nasser in Alexandria on 26 October 1954, resulting in aggressive suppression of the Muslim Brotherhood and the arrest of Qutb. He was tortured in the prison. But towards the end of jail life, his condition improved, and he was able to communicate and write. During this time, he wrote his manifesto of political Islam, *Ma'alim fi al-Tariq* (*Milestones*), which became the handbook of Islamists and jihadists. Qutb was released in the later part of 1964 but was rearrested in August 1965, accused of plotting to overthrow the government. In that short trial, most of the evidence against him was derived from his book *Ma'alim fi al-Tariq*. He did not change his stand from his writing. On 29 August 1966, he was executed by hanging.

Qutb radically differed from many modern Muslims. Qutb viewed Islam as a complete system of justice, governance, and morality— Sharia laws and principles should be the sole basis of governance and everything else in life. For him, anything not Islamic was evil and corrupt, as explained in *Ma'alim fi al-Tariq*. Most Muslims believe that democracy is Islamic because the Quranic institution of Shura (consultation body) supported democracy and elections. But as per Qutb, Shura chapter of the Quran was revealed during the early Meccan period, so it did not deal with government. For him, Islam did not ask for elections and calls only for the ruler to consult some as part of Shura. As per him, a truly Islamic polity would have no rulers, not even religious ones, since Muslims would need neither judges nor police to obey divine law; a situation could be called Islamic anarchy. The way to attain such an Islamic society was to fight against jahiliyyah (ignorance) with preaching and jihad. Once an Islamic community was formed, it had to be extended to all of humanity, taking the leadership. More dangerously, Qutb called the entire Egyptian population *jahiliyyah*, thus making them liable for jihad and killing. For him, true jihad was not defensive (protecting Islam) but offensive (arms struggle to establish Islam). Thus he offered a complete justification for modern terrorist ideology.

Creating social disorder and disobedience of rules and existing leaders there by spreading anarchy are the deterrents for modern society and liberal Muslims against supporting terrorism. But for Qutb and terrorists, it is just the way and the end. Both do not accept people's wishes or democracy, but the ruler can decide. He also can decide whom to consult as per his wish. No one needs to be bothered, not even the so-called Islamic scholars, if the ruler does not find him ideologically sound. Thus mass murderers and anarchists like Zarqawi and Abu Bakr Baghdadi were not ideologically alone; they had strong support from the one so-called most prominent Islamic revivalist of the twentieth century, Sayyid Qutb. Qutb was not an ordinary scholar but the author of one of the most coveted Quran explanations, *Fi Zilal al-Qur'an* (*In the Shade of the Qur'an*)—a thirty-volume book translated into several languages, a versatile reference book among Muslims, and twenty-five other notable books.

The Muslim Brotherhood under Hassan al-Hudaybi, who was the general guide after Hassan al-Banna, officially denounced many of the radical views of Qutb, especially labelling the whole Egyptian society *jahiliyyah*, worth calling them non-Muslims (kafir). After the death of Qutb, in late 1960 and in the 1970s, the Brotherhood remained a clandestine organization but was revived in the 1980s. Qutb's philosophy (Qutubism for non-followers) still remains the major basis of the Muslim Brotherhood. Their famous slogan is 'Allah is our objective. The Prophet is our leader. The Qur'an is our law. Jihad is our way. Dying in the way of Allah is our highest hope. Allahu Akbar!' Qutb's followers advocating violent jihad had always existed in the Brotherhood, and they maintained their cells in the organization. Some others came out of it and opened new organizations with more militant ideology. These breakaway groups include Al-Gama'a al-Islamiyya, Egyptian Islamic Jihad, and al-Takfir Wal-Hijira; all are associated with violence. Al-Takfir wal-Hijira claimed true followers of Qutb and went into a society of hiding away from the outside world to strengthen to regain power to wage jihad. Later, the Brotherhood in Palestine evolved into Hamas, a radical Islamic group with a strong base in Gaza.

Osama bin Laden was acquainted with Qutb's brother, Muhammad Qutb. Muhammed Qutb reached Saudi Arabia following his release from an Egyptian prison and worked as a professor of Islamic studies. He edited and promoted Qutb's books and was his major advocate. Bin Laden and his close friend Mohammed Jamal Khalifa used to regularly attend weekly public lectures by Muhammad Qutb at King Abdul-Aziz University. Both used to read works of Sayyid Qutb and were deeply influenced by his ideas. Another great fan of Qutb was American jihadist and Yemeni al-Qaeda leader Anwar al-Awlaki. He used to regularly read Qutb's works almost every day while in jail and commented that he was 'so immersed with the author I would feel Sayyid was with me in my cell speaking to me directly'. Ayman al-Zawahiri was an Egyptian with a strong family background from the Muslim Brotherhood. Muhammed Qutb was one of his Islamist teachers in Egypt. His uncle was close to Muhammed Qutb and introduced Zawahiri to Muhammed. Young Zawahiri was deeply touched by the purity and suffering of Sayyid Qutb in jail. It is highly unlikely that any serious learner of modern Islamist ideology might have missed the major works of Qutb or at least their reviews.

Another notable scholar originally from India, who later migrated to Pakistan, Sayyid Abul A'la Maududi was an influential Muslim scholar in the Indian subcontinent and also among a large circle of Islamic readers around the world. He founded Jamaat-e-Islami, a religious movement similar to the Brotherhood which has a huge follower base in Pakistan, Bangladesh, and among many Muslims in India and Sri Lanka. Some of his ideas are modified by his followers who follow separate organisations in different countries with violent overtones in Bangladesh and Pakistan and a peaceful democratic path in India and Sri Lanka. Maududi was the author of over 120 books or pamphlets and made over 1,000 speeches. His magnum opus was an Urdu translation of the Quran, *Tafhim ul-Qur'an* (*The Meaning of the Qur'an*), widely read throughout the subcontinent and translated into several languages. In his book *The Islamic Law and Constitution*, released in 1941, Maududi coined and later popularized the term *Islamic state*. Thus, the modern concept of the Islamic state is his brainchild. He also coined and popularized the term *Islamic revolution* in the 1940s, even though 1979 Iranian Revolution later endorsed the word Islamic revolution. His concept of sharia and jihad were close to that of Qutb. In fact, he was the first to claim that Islamic society which failed to establish sharia did not hold the right to be called Islamic, long before Qutb. Both Banna and Qutb read Maududi's book, and Qutb heavily borrowed from Maududi for his infamous concept of jahiliyyah. Abdulla Azzam was profoundly influenced by Maududi. Another major Islamic activist of the modern era, Ayatollah Ruhollah Khomeini, met Maududi around 1963 and later translated his works into Persian. His concept of Islamic state was close to the ideals of Maududi.

The puritanical Islamist ideology of Wahhabism was started by eighteenth-century theologician Muhammad Ibn Abd al-Wahhab. He was from Najd, the homeland of the House of Muhammad ibn Saud, the founder of the current Saudi royal family who endorsed Wahhab's ideas to create the kingdom. Wahhabism has deep roots in Saudi Arabia. Historically, the movement is associated with political activism, violence, and narrow perception of Muslims with the segregation of Muslims to kafir based on practices. Apart from Saudi Arabia, it has a large follower base in Qatar, United Arab Emirates, and to an extent, in Bahrain and Kuwait. Wahhabism calls for the literal meaning of Quran and Hadith, rejecting dogmatic ideas and resisting changes in Islam. Ibn Saud destroyed the tomb of Hussein bin Ali (grandson of the prophet) and many of the historical structures of Mecca and Medina. They were fearsome worriers. Osama and most of Saudi-born Al-Qaeda ideologues were grown in a strong Wahhabi background.

Salafism, a little more refined version of Wahhabism, emerged later, though often both terms are used interchangeably. Derived from *salaf*, the early believers of Islam, it aims to maintain the same beliefs and ways of ancient, first-generation Muslims. The idea originated with the thoughts of Mohammed Abduh, an Egyptian, and was later perfected by Rashid Rida. Rida, originally from Ottoman Syria, later joined with Abduh, and both founded the leading *al-Manar* magazine and weekly comprising Quranic commentary. Rida's ideas evolved into the concept of the Islamic state by other scholars like Maududi. He called for an independent interpretation of Islam, not to blindly follow it as a tradition. Salafism is now called by many modern followers as Ahl as Sunna (people of Sunna—path of Muhammed) and in the Indian subcontinent as Ahl al-Hadith (people of Hadith—the tradition of prophet), mainly in Pakistan. The puritanical Ahl-al-Hadith segment later formed Jama'at-ud-Da'wah and Lashkar-e Taiba by Hafiz Said. They have close ties with Al-Qaeda, the Taliban, and Pakistan ISI. Main opponents of Lashkar are Indians. They worked mostly in Indian Kashmir and were responsible for the Mumbai attack of 26 November 2008. It was a death squad attack by 10 heavily armed terrorists in many popular landmarks of Mumbai, India, on 26 November 2008, killing 164 people and wounding at least 308, unleashing a spree of random shooting and hostage taking.

Another orthodox school of thought which paved the theological basis of Taliban and many Pakistani and Afghan terrorists' group was Deobandism. It originated from an orthodox madrasa, and its teachers were originally from Darul Uloom Deoband, India. Though the parent institution officially did not support terrorism, the ideology later became crucial in Pakistan, which established Darul Uloom Haqqania in Peshawar. It can be dubbed as a terrorist factory which trained several Afghan mujahideen and Taliban leaders. Jalaluddin Haqqani of the Haqqani Network was an alumnus, and Mullah Omer of the Taliban was closely associated with it.

The fundamental theological ideology of Al-Qaeda had been in existence long before. Its initial leaders just had to learn about it, modify it, and form an action plan to make an organization not answerable to anyone on earth but to Allah, the God. Abdulla Azzam, Osama Bin Laden, and Ayman al-Zawahiri were well versed in Islamic literature and were well trained in Islamist philosophy from their very young ages. For Osama, jihad became the central spirit of his life.

106

He read again and again, night after night, about its lessons and was convinced about his goals. In spite of having a large family, being father of many children, and wielding enormous wealth with access to any kind of education, nothing deterred him from a choosing a difficult path, on which he was sure to get a violent death in the near future. This was true for Azzam and Zawahiri.

Ayman al-Zawahiri was born in an upper-class family of doctors and professionals. He was a studious child and trained as a doctor. Immediately following his masters in surgery from Cairo University, he reached Peshawar, Pakistan, to participate in the Afghan war, where he met Osama bin Laden. He became Laden's personal doctor and close associate. With a background of working with the Egyptian Islamic Jihad in his country, when he reached the Pakistan–Afghanistan front, he met many associates of EIJ and took their leadership. As a young boy, Zawahiri joined the Muslim Brotherhood at the age of fourteen years. The next year, Qutb was executed. He, along with a few of his schoolmates, started a secret cell aimed to overthrow the government and to make the vision of Qutb a reality. Later on, this cell merged others, forming the Egyptian Islamic Jihad. Likewise, while Osama Bin Laden was in Peshawar working along with Abdulla Azzam, they ran a recruitment centre and sent new recruits to different training centres run by various mujahideen leaders. Osama went ahead with a plan to start his own training camp for Arab fighters in Jaji, a village in eastern Afghanistan close to the Pakistan border. Azzam was against the idea of a separate camp for Arabs for financial reasons. But Osama went ahead with more enthusiasm than his mentor cum guide. His first camp, named Maasada (lion's den) was within 3 km from a Russian army camp and vulnerable to attacks. He found a way to protect it; using construction equipment, he made seven large hidden caverns facing the main supply route from Pakistan, making it difficult to spot and attack.

Not any single character defines a member of Al-Qaeda or that of any other extremist organization. Some were extremely charged up with their attitude to be a jihadist. They just wanted an outlet for their inner inspiration to fight for the cause of God and attainment of martyrdom.

One such example was Abu Musa al-Zarqawi. He was so excited about jihad that Osama bin Laden thought that he was not fit to be in Al-Qaeda. But the mindset of the society from which the person comes will have profound influence on a youngster to become an extremist. It is unbelievable for a Western person or a person from politically silent localities to believe the social and family support some people get to become an extremist. For example, almost the entire family of Ramzi Yousef and his uncle Khalid Sheik Mohammed were active in jihadi activities of Al-Qaeda and other extremist groups. Yousef's father and his brother were believed to be working for Bin Laden in Afghanistan and other fronts. The same is true for Abdulla Azzam; he did not deter his sons to follow his violent path but encouraged them and took them to wage war in Afghanistan in their mid-teens. Osama, on the other hand, discouraged his children to be part of Al-Qaeda. But he also allowed his son to work in his organization, and his daughter is married to son of one of his associates, his friend and Al-Qaeda military wing chief, Muhammed Atef.

Al Jazeera reported a story of an elderly lady from Lebanon in 2013. When she was informed that her only son was killed in jihad under Hizbullah, she was excited. She waited for the arrival of his dead body along with family in celebration just like the traditional ritual welcome for a newly married son coming first to the home with his bride. Death for the cause of God is not a taboo in certain communities, especially for Shia, but a prestige in the family and acceptance that their child did something great for the society. The same is true for support for war or jihadi activities. This social support was echoed when Qadriya (mother of Khaled al-Islambouli, an Egyptian Islamic Jihad ideologue who murdered Egyptian president Anwar Sadat) spoke to Iranian media, Fars News Agency, in 2012 about her son. She said in the interview, 'I am very proud that my son killed Anwar al-Sadat . . . The government called him (Khaled) a terrorist, a criminal, and a murderer, but they didn't say that he was defending Islam. They didn't say anything about the oppressed people in Palestine, about Camp David, or how Sadat sold out the country to the Jews and violated the honour of the Islamic nation.' Her other son, Mohamed al-Islambouli, was sentenced to death in 1992 in Egypt for terrorist activities working with the Islamic group. The same sentiments were echoed in many Islamic societies to fighters and supporters who were waging war in Afghanistan, Iraq, Palestine, and Syria. Families, societies, social circles, mosques, and charities supported and encouraged willing volunteers.

Death is celebrated in parts of poverty-stricken Pakistani villages and towns where organizations like Lashkar e-Taiba arrange huge weddings like celebrations with gifts and praises for parents of kids who died during their militant activities. This money may not be anything great in other parts but may be great relief for impoverished members of overcrowded families living in small huts and shanty towns. In all communities which are war-ridden and poverty-stricken, anyone with few thousand dollars can recruit dozens of people willing for whatever activity they want, including killing or suicide missions. This was true in Pakistan, Afghanistan, Sudan, Somalia, and now in Syria. Not only enthusiasts but also a little money can buy fighters for any group. On top of that, if the cause is justified in the name of religion, all deterrents can be solved. Economic breakdown, lawlessness, and poverty can make an entire community amenable to be bought with money. When criminal can use them as in raids, blackmailing, and kidnapping for ransom, money simply follows; so do recruits. Warlords in Pakistan tribal areas, Afghanistan, and Chechnya survive and flourish on this business. They may be involved in the far more lucrative business of drug trade. More money also means more arms, equipment, and strength and also their ability to sustain in the society, changing the social order by bribing and influencing authorities.

Any group who becomes fearsome and dangerous, who can inflict a major assault on the general population or a security force, usually gets more bargain power. The Pakistani Taliban worked on this principle. A small group of Pakistani Taliban under Baitullah Mehsud, due to his terror attacks on the general public and army, gained strong bargain power. Initially just a bandit, he became a peace negotiator sitting on the other side of table with senior military commanders. The disputes were settled by the government paying huge money to the militants in order to buy peace and a ceasefire. In front of the general population witnessing these, a terrorist leader becomes a hero and power broker at par with senior army commanders representing the government of a nation. These demoralized societies who were fighting against such groups felt there was no difference between the government and militants, and the government itself legitimized these groups. On the other hand, militants might buy more arms and recruits, more people to restart the attack in a larger scale. The next bargain would be much more substantial. By this time, they would also buy some brokers from political leaders and the establishment by money, tribal loyalty, or political power or due to fear factor. Of course, militants had more fear power among people than the governments whose dictates were seldom ignored unlike the advice of governments. The spectacular rise of Boko Haram in Nigeria, in spite of several heinous atrocities by the group was due to similar tactics; they used to collect government money and collusion with the establishment. The major Pakistani terrorist group, Pakistani Taliban (Tehrik-e Taliban Pakistan [TTP]) was on the verge of taking over a large army and establishment over a large part of country under their control. Unlike the Afghan Taliban, for the TTP Pakistan army and the government was their enemy. Their growth was also due to a collusion of the group with Pakistan ISI, which promoted them just like Taliban in Afghanistan. But TTP later turned against the government and the Pakistan army, following their involvement in FATA (Federally Administered Tribal Area), a lawless tribal area close to Afghanistan, which is a TTP stronghold.

Al-Qaeda supported Pakistani Taliban groups since they offered them sanctuaries and fighters. Al-Qaeda provided them training, advice, money, and sometimes, arms. Zawahiri was believed to be living in tribal areas of Pakistan (FATA) under protection from the Pakistani Taliban. So also were the many Arab fighters of Al-Qaeda who had escaped from Afghanistan. TTP became a substantial force with about 30,000–35,000 fighters which could rival all Arab or Al-Qaeda fighters in the region, who were just a few hundred or, at the most, a thousand. Over a period of years, these groups established their cells in all major cities of Pakistan capable of attacking any major Pakistani institution. In region like FATA, who had Pashtun tribal tradition, anyone under their protection would get their support, even if that meant war with anyone, including the government. So these areas become like terrorist factories and havens for terrorists from other areas like Al-Qaeda fighters from Arabia, Chechnya, or Uzbekistan.

Most of the early Al-Qaeda leaders were good scholars in history, especially Arab and Israel history. This gave them new ideas and strategic deaths. Osama bin Laden was deeply impressed by the 1983 Beirut bombings, and he realised the power of a suicide attack from these events. Following the 1982 Israel invasion of Lebanon, America sent US Marines as a peacekeeping force. For most Lebanese people, this was just support for an Israeli invasion. On 18 April 1983, a large suicide truck bomb attack on the US embassy in Beirut, Lebanon, killed 63 people. Another similar attack on 23 October 1983 on a Marine barracks in Beirut devastated the area, killing 241 marines. Following these attacks, the US military departed Lebanon in February 1984. An unknown group called Islamic Jihad claimed the responsibility, but later, it was found that it was a front of Hizbullah. That was the beginning of suicide terrorist attacks. The following years witnessed several such attacks perpetrated by Hizbullah, a Lebanese militia group with close ties to Shiite Iran. In 1994, bin Laden arranged a meeting with a top Hizbullah leader, Imad Mughniya, and arranged for some of his operatives to be trained in the truck bombing techniques that had been used in Beirut. Zawahiri went a step further. He organized training of his members, likely with support from Iran, to carry out the first-ever Sunni suicide terrorist attack in history. Before this attack, suicide terrorism was the domain of only Shia groups, mostly Hizbullah.

On 8 August 1993 the motorcades of Hassan al-Alfi, the Egyptian interior minister was attacked by suicide attacker by detonating a bomb-laden motorcycle to the minister's car, followed by firing with an automatic weapon at the busy heart of Cairo city, close to Tahrir Square. Four persons were killed and the minister seriously injured. This was followed by another similar attack to assassinate Egyptian prime minister Atef Sidqi three months later. About 21 Egyptians were injured and killed a small schoolgirl, Shayma Abdel-Halim. This backfired against the EIJ. People with fresh memory of mass killings of over 200 people by al-Gama'a al-Islamiyya in recent times responded promptly. Her funeral became a massive parade across Cairo, carrying her coffin across the streets and crowds shouting, 'Terrorism is the enemy of God!' The police promptly arrested about 280 members of al-Jihad and executed six of them later after trials.

This effectively stopped all terrorist activities in Egypt for a few years. Many sympathizers became moderate, and some active workers denounced violence. By 1997, their activities were almost paralyzed. A major wing of the groups officially brokered a peace deal with the government and denounced violence and endorsed a non-violence initiative. That was frustrating for al-Zawahiri and his militant jihadi colleagues in EIJ and al-Gama'a al-Islamiyya (Islamic group), who were in exile. They felt it was 'surrender' and tried to break the peace with aggression, organising a major terror attack to provoke the government to restart their repressive activities promoting extremism.

On 17 November 1997, six men dressed in police uniforms went into a killing spree in the famous tourist place of Temple of Hatshepsut in Luxor by firing indiscriminately at and chopping with a knife everyone around. It went on for about forty-five minutes, filling the floors with blood. Fifty-eight foreign tourists, including a five-year-old British child, four honeymoon couples from Japan, and four Egyptians were killed. One of the attackers was killed, and others apparently committed suicide. Al-Qaeda financed the plot. This event also backfired badly against terrorist ideology, and Egyptians were stunned at the cruelty of Islamists. People organized massive protests asking for a crackdown of terrorists. Egypt's vital tourist industry virtually shut down. Thousands lost their jobs, including those who supported these groups before. The backlash was so strong.

Initially intending to claim responsibility proudly, the mastermind of the attack and leader of Islamic group, Refai Ahmed Taha, claimed that the only intention of the mission was to kidnap tourists. But it was clear the plan was just manslaughter and horror. Zawahiri blamed the Egyptian police for attack and blamed tourists for coming to Egypt. He claimed that people hated them to come for such picnics. The spiritual leader of the Islamic group, Blind Sheik Omer Abdul Rahman, who was already in jail in the USA for his involvement in a host of terrorist activities there, claimed Israel was behind the attack. The tactics of violence and then lying or denial were developed by Al-Qaeda groups with experience from such debacles. But terrorists and their sympathizers seldom lost focus in protecting their interests and supporters. In a victory rally, Mohamed Morsi of the Muslim Brotherhood, after being elected as president of Egypt following the Arab Spring, praised Omer Abdul Rahman and asked for his release. Later his government officially asked the government for his release from prison. Later, Morsi appointed El-Khayat, a member of the Building and Development Party, the political arm of al-Gama'a al-Islamiyya, as the governor of Luxor, the same province where his party organized the reprehensible massacre of innocent people. But he was forced to resign within a week due to public outcry.

Though political crime may be acceptable in activism and Islamic terrorism, other petty crimes are not generally welcome for Islamists. But some of Al-Qaeda leaders were caught for petty crimes and were punished. Many times these were human mistakes but, on occasion, formed strong impressions on the activities of such people later. Anwar al-Awlaki, a well known orator and inspiration for many Islamists who later spent his life in Yemen leading the local branch of Al-Qaeda there, was caught in the USA for soliciting prostitutes and was punished two times while he was living and preaching in California. The founder of Al-Qaeda in Iraq, Abu Musab al-Zarqawi, was a notorious criminal in his home town Zarqa in Jordan. As a teenager he was a thug, a heavy drinker, and a bootlegger. When he was fifteen years old, Zarqawi, with others, was involved in a house robbery of his relative in which his relative was killed. He dropped out of his school before graduation. At the age of twenty-three years, he had thirty-seven criminal cases against him, including sexual assault. But three months before he went to Afghanistan to participate in the

Afghan war, he changed into a religious man and wanted to clean himself. That time, he was influenced by Tablighi Jamaat, which brought these changes to him. But while in Afghanistan, he became a jihadi and a radical. His flirtation with violence and crime made him a different man throughout, unlike most Al-Qaeda leaders. He personally went on gruesome executions, assassinations, extortions, and bomb blasts in civilian areas, which others in Al-Qaeda found odd to accept. Al-Qaeda central leadership was sceptical on endorsing him publicly due to his involvement in reprehensible mass murders of Iraqis on his way to create his 'ideological paradise' of Islamic State.

Razor-sharp focus on their mission was a major factor that contributed to the survival and success of Al-Qaeda members. That is clearly evident in the actions of Ramzi Yousef and his uncle Khalid Sheik Muhammed, who was the mastermind of 9/11 attacks. In spite of several setbacks and failures, they tried till their purported missions became complete before they were captured. One such Al-Qaeda activist was Ali Muhammed, the double agent of FBI and Al-Qaeda who continued his double game with US law agencies till all the major missions he undertook were complete. Till then, he gave input to the CIA and FBI to make him safe, buying time and the opportunity to move around with the pretext of infiltrating the network but continued his support for Al-Qaeda.

Another example of an Al-Qaeda agent with sharp focus on his mission was Humam Khalil al-Balawi, a Jordanian doctor. Balawi, originally a supporter of Al-Qaeda and other Islamist militant groups, was recruited to Jordanian intelligence. They introduced him to the CIA. He passed information to both agencies for months, and CIA used his info for predator drone strikes. His initial information was accurate, but the targets were not of high value. He produced evidence of his knowledge in the terrain and the whereabouts of top Al-Qaeda leaders and produced photos with them as evidence. Having gained the CIA's trust, he was able to pass through the multi-tier CIA checkpoints into the CIA base at Khost, Afghanistan, known as Forward Operating Base Chapman. It was one of the two important CIA bases in Afghanistan directly run by the agency and was coordinating a drone programme. Usually not more than two officers would be present on informant debriefing. But then eight officers were present there, along with his Jordanian handler, Sharif Alibin Zeid. His info was considered very important, which was about the location of Ayman al-Zawahiri, the info they had been waiting for, for many years. When all were gathered, he exploded his suicide vest, killing five CIA officers, two CIA contractors, his Jordanian handler, and an Afghan. Six others were injured. This incident on 30 December 2009 was a major blow for the CIA. Before his debriefing, the White House had been informed of a possible major break. But unfortunately, the event turned out to be a major disaster for the USA with the loss of their top expert on Al-Qaeda.

The venue was chosen to include the base commander, Jennifer Lynne Matthews, who was considered a world-class expert on al-Qaeda and counterterrorism operations. She was an officer with twenty years' experience in CIA work at Alec Station, the CIA's Bin Laden unit, and was the chief of the counterterrorism branch in London. She was part of almost all rendition operations of Al-Qaeda leaders after 9/11. She was instrumental in the capture of several operatives and avoiding many terrorist plots, including aircraft hijackings. Within a few days, a video emerged with al-Balawi sitting next to militant leader Hakimullah Mahsud, the leader of Pakistani Taliban (Tehrik-e Taliban Pakistan [TTP]). In the video, al-Balawi said that he would be a martyr himself to avenge the killing of former leader Baitullah Mahsud in a US drone strike in 2009. Al-Qaeda also claimed responsibility for the same reason and for some other drone strikes. The area was a stronghold of another Taliban faction, the Haqqani network. Thus the attack was significant in that Al-Qaeda was organising coordinated attacks with TTP and the Haqqani network, a dangerous combination. But the suicide bomber, a young, well-educated man with a wife and two kids, worked hard, with constant vision and dedication lasting for months. It was his first visit to the facility, and there was no guarantee that he could kill a significant number of people. But still he went ahead with damn dedication to be a suicide bomber. Interestingly, his wife supported him and was proud of his martyrdom in her later interviews.

Perhaps the most important characteristic which distinguishes a person as a terrorist is they are free from fear. An average person will have fear of death, injury, torture, humiliation, social isolation, conviction, and of the laws of land. Most of the dreaded terrorists were already well prepared for their capture and interrogation and faced much of the torture including isolation bravely or tactically. When Ramzi Yousef was caught, he was comfortable chatting with his rendition agents and openly admitted most of the things he did. In the courtroom, he faced the judge bravely and accepted the charges without hesitation or repentance. When Khalid Sheikh Mohammed (KSM) was arrested in Pakistan initially, he refused to talk and insisted he should be questioned in the presence of his lawyer. The investigators have to use prolonged torture, isolation in dark rooms with complete isolation, and several attempts of waterboarding. It is believed that KSM underwent waterboarding more than 250 times and tolerated much more than others. It may have been a record. The same is true for many other Guantanamo Bay inmates. The value of torture to extract from the terrorists was not so often successful and reliable.

Another example for an exemplarily fearless man was Abu Musab al Zarqawi. People familiar with him recollect him facing very dangerous situations bravely close to committing suicide. A Jordanian intelligence officer, in his interview, recollected, 'Fear was not there in the dictionary of Zarqawi.' He had been injured five or six times in Afghanistan and Iraq and had narrowly missed many attacks on his life. Still he became more and more ruthless and finally succumbed to a massive bombing of his safe house. He was isolated in Al-Qaeda and received many warnings from them but continued his separate organization under his tight grip.

The story of Richard, a new white convert to Islam who became later known as Shoe Bomber, was also surprising. He tried to blow up American Airlines Flight 63 from Paris to Miami, wearing shoes packed with plastic explosives. He tried several times to detonate the fuse with matchsticks but was overpowered by fellow passengers and was later tried in America. During his trial, he claimed that he was an enemy of America, being part of Al-Qaeda and a soldier of God under the command of Osama Bin Laden. The judge, William Young, responded, 'You are not an enemy combatant, you are a terrorist. . . . You are not a soldier in any army, you are a terrorist. To call you a soldier gives you far too much stature. [Pointing to US flag.] You see that flag, Mr Reid? That is the flag of the United States of America. That flag will be here long after you are forgotten.' Reid was unrepentant about his actions and said, 'the flag will come down on the day of judgement.' Reid, a small-time petty criminal, spent many jail terms; when he was indoctrinated by the militant ideology, he became a stubborn man.

Some of the Al-Qaeda operatives were not so heroic or consistent. Fortunately many of the failed attempts were mainly due to ill-prepared and poorly motivated cadres. Some were just opportunists. Some were just petty criminals involved in terrorist activities for money and power. One example was Jamal al-Fadl. He was a corrupt man with some religious sentiment, but he was like an ordinary man of his age in his personal weakness and greed. He worked with Al-Qaeda for long years, embosomed a large amount of their money, and finally switched over his allegiance to America. At the same time, he was fortunate not to have been involved in heinous crimes by his own hands and could save himself from being a dreaded criminal. There are several individuals who changed their minds about being involved in terrorist plots; many such persons became witnesses in trials. There were far more foiled or aborted plots by Al-Qaeda than were executed. Many were avoided due to increased awareness, effective antiterrorism measures, and constant vigil of intelligence agencies throughout the world. It still remains the main strategy. At the same time, encouraging people to depart from manslaughter or supporting a terrorist plot is a need of the society and establishment. Such people who have denounced violence should be treated for their heroism and goodwill, avoiding prejudice or stigma; this may be a good strategy in terror combat!

Publicity is a crucial bonus and a necessity for many terrorists. Many terrorist leaders crave for attention by new missions. To be noticeable, a terror plot needs to be innovative and horrific. In spite of several setbacks, old terrorist leaders like Ayman al-Zawahiri and those in AQIM (Al-Qaeda in Islamic Maghreb) try hard to create news and attention though they are constantly losing recruits and prominence. Even among terrorists, most want to be leaders—if possible, the most notable. So they aggressively try to assert their position and control. Those with the most dreaded history, the offer of a huge reward for the head or being on the most-wanted list; all are medals of honour for a terrorist. Terrorism thrives on publicity. That is why they constantly attack civilian areas, malls, airports, aircrafts, metro rails, markets, and religious sites than army barracks—to attract media and ordinary peoples' attention. Modern media greatly assists the spread and existence of terrorists by projecting incidences, frequently publishing the threats and videos of dreaded terrorists. Thus terrorists get free advertisement to inspire their potential recruits and highlight their status and activity to the world. A horrific tragedy of someone may be regarded as apt punishment for others. Someone's villain may be hero of others. Extensive media projection of terrorist incidences offers enough fuel for terrorism, which the terrorists are desperately looking for. Unfortunately it is plenty and free. So also is polarization of society, hate campaigns, a sense of insecurity, and targeting communities.

CHAPTER 6

The Diary of a Terrorist

25 November 1996

In the name of God; most merciful and benevolent . . .

By the will of God, I am here in this prison cell in Swaqa. Today, by His grace, I returned to Allah. I had not been doing my *namaz* (daily prayer) for many months, I think never after the last *Ramzan*. Now I feel like the day when I first went to the school. I prayed to God all the day. Here in this faint light, I am writing this note. All five of my fellow jail mates here are sleeping. I don't know the time—maybe twelve o'clock midnight. Thanks to Allah I met a brother here, Arif, who is very kind and helpful. Yesterday he invited me to hear the lecture of Imam Maqdisi. I told Arif I didn't want to go, but he forced me. It was impossible to argue with a good friend like him. He was the only one who talked to me for many days when I came to this cell two months back. He introduced me to other cellmates. Now we all are good friends.

It was a meeting under a tree. Imam Maqdisi was standing over a small cement block, reciting the Quran. Arif and I joined the group of around fifteen prisoners sitting on the floor. I saw a prison guard watching the crowd from a distance. Imam Maqdisi, a man in his forties, had a special charm on his face. His voice was marvellous. He talked about youth. He talked about a Hadith which says, on the Day of Judgement, God will ask three questions to everyone: 'How devout were you with your namaz? What did you do with your money? And how did you spend your youth?' Imam asked, 'What answer will you give the Lord, my dear brothers?' After the speech, Arif introduced me to Amir Zarqawi. He was a young man of about thirty years with a small cap and a neatly trimmed beard. He was wearing the Afghan shalwar kameez. I don't know how he got it. He greeted me warmly with a tight embrace. He held my hands and said, 'Assalamu alaikkum va-rahmatullah,' and I reciprocated, 'Va alaikkumu salam va rahmatullahi va barakkatuhu [Let peace and blessings of God be with you].' He continued, 'Jazak Allahu ghayr [May God reward you]. It is inspiring that youth like you are reaching the path of Allah. It is his glory. May Allah take you to the right path! Welcome to our brotherhood. In sha Allah we meet you here next Thursday.' I saw a push in his eyes, an invitation and a command. I felt like I was being dragged into his mind.

That night, I thought again and again. Why was here? What was I doing? My father was a devout Muslim who never missed any namaz as far as I knew. My ummi (mother) was the centre of our household but later became ill following my father's death in an accident. She was also a good Muslim. Why was I here, caught by the police while snatching a bag from a woman along with my friends? They were not my friends. They were my enemies who spoiled me, who brought me here. When I was caught by a policeman, I stabbed him with a knife and wriggled out. I could not escape from other policemen running after me. Now I am here. All my friends escaped.

Before sleep, I asked Arif to call me also for the early-morning prayer. He was excited and said, 'Mashallah Mashallah [God willed it].' He hugged me and went to sleep. Today I feel so happy. Thank you, God; you put me in the right place. You gave me the right companions.

5 January 1997

Today I met my brother and sister. They came to meet me before the beginning of Ramzan. I told them by God's mercy I am now not missing any namaz and am in the company of good people. I requested them to take care of our ummi well. They bought a packet of big date fruits, which they brought from Irbid, my home city in Jordan. Now I feel very proud of my home town, a city that contributed hundreds of mujahideen to the Afghan war. In those days, I was not religious. I used to make fun of those Afghan Arabs wearing the Afghan shalwar kameez walking through the streets and talking about God and jihad in his path. More than half of my city's population was from Palestine; they had lost their homes and livelihood in one of the many Israeli aggressions. We were not so happy with those people, but now I feel sympathy for them. Many of them were rich people in Palestine, now living in small huts in the poor areas of Irbid. My friend Aslam used to tell me about the hardship his father and mother faced in Palestine, and finally, they sold their properties for a small sum and fled to Jordan. Today I talked to Arif for a long time about Amir and Imam. He said that their popularity in the jail is increasing and many of the jail staff are their supporters. But now all others are sleeping. Arif asked me to sleep not to disturb others and we would talk tomorrow.

25 January 1997

Today there was an iftar for all jail mates. Everybody was assembled in the kitchen hall before sunset. Imam Maqdisi was invited for a recitation from the Quran. After his recitation and brief explanation, Amir Zarqawi rose up and shouted, *'Allahu Akbar* [God is great)].' A large group sitting around him, maybe around thirty to forty rose up and shouted back, *'Allahu Akbar.'* In a hall with a few hundred people, their voices sounded like the voice of thousands. I wished I was part of the crowd. But I was new to this place and was sitting far behind that crowd. After that, everyone dispersed for food and prayer. I told Arif I wanted to be part of the group. He said, 'Let me see.'

2 January 1998

For a long time I could not write in the diary. I was always busy inside the cell with lessons from brother Arif. He taught me many chapters of the Quran. Now I meet Amir Zarqawi at least every week, and he treats me as one of his group members. With the grace of God, Brother Arif and I shifted to another block. To my great surprise, our cell is just opposite to Amir Zarqawi's. Occasionally we can see him. We see many jail guards when they pass through his cell greet him with 'salam' and respect. I see him many times reading the Quran. When he is free, he talks to his cellmates.

10 March 1998

Our wing is like a family. Amir Zarqawi is our leader. Everyone in the wing obeys him. No one dares to openly speak about him. He is kind to all of us. Now I think I am also part of their group. But in this wing, everyone is very serious. I used to watch TV in the other wing. But here no one touches TV; only Amir can start it. He put a black cloth over the TV to cover the screen not to display any female figure. If somebody wants, they can hear the voice of programmes. The only time the cover is removed is at eight o' clock night when Amir, with many of his close associates, comes to watch the news. He only pays attention to news about Afghanistan, Sudan, or Algeria. If someone makes much noise, his simple stare makes them instantly silent.

17 April 1998

After the dinner, I met Amir and promised my *bayat* that I would accept him as my imam, my leader, follow his orders unconditionally and fight for the cause of God. Everyone in the group embraced me and patted me, saying, 'Jazak Allahu ghayr [May Allah reward you].' Today I can't forget. *Insha Allah* (If God will), one day, I will be a martyr and reach heaven. Brother Arif talked to me for many hours. He spoke about Amir Zarqawi. He was not so religious like me and was from a humble background with little education. At the age of twenty-three, Zarqawi realized that he was leading an animal-like life and wanted to come out. It was Tablighi Jama'at (a Muslim organization doing preaching among Muslims and organizing prayer meetings or camps) people who took him back to Islam. He started to attend his prayers in his neighbouring Zarqa mosque. One day, he met a brother in his mosque inviting willing people to Afghanistan. He wanted to help the Afghan people to win the war against Russians. He was told about the millions of Palestinians who lost their land and lived in Jordan in inhumane situations. We should not allow that to happen to our Afghan brothers. The brother speaking to the gathering of a dozen believers asked who were willing to go for Afghan jihad. Only Zarqawi and a man in his late fifties raised their hand.

After a few days, in December 1989, Zarqawi and about twelve brothers went to Peshawar, Pakistan, to meet the mujahideen imam from Palestine, Sheik Abdulla Azzam. They were warmly welcomed by Sheik's son at the airport. He was taken care of by Sheik and other brothers from many Arab countries. Zarqawi was not his real name. His real name was Ahmad Fadeel al-Khalayleh. Later he took the name Abu Musab al-Zarqawi after the birth of his son Musab and in memory of his home town, Zarqa. Initially he was given a job in a mujahideen magazine as a reporter, but he was not so successful in writing. He wanted to become a fighter. His spirit was so high. He interacted with many mujahideen brothers who came from Jordan and Saudi Arabia. He was from a poor background. To his surprise, he saw many rich sheiks and young millionaires working hard in the name of God in poor conditions at Peshawar and Afghanistan. Soon he became friends with many of them.

Everyone was happy with his determination and valour. He fought battles along with many mujahideen. He was very brave and hated his enemies. He didn't hesitate to go in front of Russian soldiers and shoot them face-to-face. The conditions of mujahideen were not very good. He was just an ordinary fighter in Afghanistan among so many Arab commanders. One day, he happened to visit a wounded Jordanian man originally from Palestine, Salah al-Hami, who lost one of his legs in the battlefield. He was depressed and worried about his future. 'Who is going to marry a one-legged man?' Zarqawi offered his sister's hand; thus, he became his brother-in-law. The marriage was at Peshawar. It was attended by his mother and many of his friends.

Imam Zarqawi, before becoming a leader, had not been a learned man in Islam. He had a limited idea about the Quran. He was lonely in Afghanistan. He wanted to do something for the umma (the Islamic nation) but had no idea. During this time, Zarqawi met Imam Maqdisi in Afghanistan. He was also there to participate in Afghan jihad. Sheikh Abu Muhammed al-Maqdisi was born in the holy land of Palestine. His real name was Isam Mohammad Tahir al-Barqawi. Imam Maqdisi was a great scholar who studied in Saudi Arabia and was a true follower of ibn Taymiyyah and ibn Abdul Wahhab. For Zarqawi, he became like his own father, who had died long before, more than a great teacher. After the Afghan war and expulsion of Najibullah from Kabul, they came back to Jordan in 1993.

12 May 1998

I participated in the Quran lessons in our wing. Amir Zarqawi asked one of the brothers for *qira'at* recitation from the Quran and invited Imam Maqdisi for his lecture. Imam told us the need to be united under Amir Zarqawi to remove the man-made rules which were ruling our nation under King Hussein. Under his rule, the true Muslims like us were in jail. Every Muslim had the duty to establish the law of God in the world. Though we were a small community, by God willing, this small community of al-Tawhid would overthrow the oppressive rules against Allah from this land under the command of Amir. Everyone there shouted, '*Allahu Akbar* [God is great].' He reminded us that there was no Islam without assembly, no assembly without a leader, and no leader without obedient followers. 'Be loyal to your leader. No matter what hardship you face, don't be a traitor like many in the government. Traitors will be punished here and hereafter.' After his speech, Amir Zarqawi re-emphasized the need for jihad in the path of God. He said, 'Attainment of martyrdom is the ultimate bliss of a Muslim and sign of belief.' We finished the meeting with a prayer.

Back in our cell, I asked Brother Arif how Amir and Imam had landed in jail. Zarqawi had not had much political or religious knowledge when he went to Afghanistan. While being there with mujahideen he was changed altogether. Both of them reached Jordan with a vision. In his thoughts, Zarqawi wanted to overthrow the ruling king and establish an Islamic state. He was ready to do anything to make his dream of an Islamic state. He had no idea how. By this time, Maqdisi was touring all across Jordan preaching about Islam and reviving Islamism. He became famous in Jordan. Zarqawi found his friend from Afghanistan, Abu Muntassir, who was teaching geography in school and had good rapport with many Islamists of jihadi ideology. He taught Zarqawi many things about Islam and Muslim countries. Zarqawi invited Muntassir along with Maqdisi to start a new Islamic group. They called it al-Tawhid (the Monotheism).

They were frustrated initially as they found the country had changed a lot after they left for Afghanistan. Muslim Brotherhood was the only opposition party in Jordan distanced from the Islamic cause, and it wanted to become a recognized political party. A peace process between Israel and Palestine was in progress. Not many people were talking about jihad. Still, they could find some people who were unhappy with the Brotherhood's stand. But they were not very prepared. The first operation of the organization was to bomb a theatre showing vulgar movies. Zarqawi sent one of his followers with a bomb, but due to lack of *taqwa* (piety concentration), he was distracted by the movie shown there and the bomb exploded before he left, blowing off his leg. Zarqawi realised that *taqwa* for his followers was essential, and they should be kept away from all vulgar movies and TV.

But before they made more mistakes, they were arrested by the police after they found grenades in the house of Zarqawi. Maqdisi had brought those grenades from Afghanistan and had given them to Zarqawi for safe custody. But intelligence agencies were following Maqdisi due to his popularity. Their men infiltrated al-Tawhid that time. Both of them were arrested. Zarqawi told the judge that he had got the grenades from the street. But the judge did not believe him. Both were sentenced to fifteen years in jail for possessing weapons and being with an unlawful organization. But with the grace of God, his community was growing in jail and outside. Since he couldn't trust anyone, he shared his ideas only with those close to him. By the mercy of God, we were part of this group, to carry God's path. Now Zarqawi also became a scholar—he could recite more than six thousand *ayat* (verses) from the Quran. Now we call him amir, or prince, and Maqdisi our Imam. If Allah wills it, one day, we will make our Islamic state in this holy land of Levant. We will liberate Palestinians, Syrians, Iraqis, and Jordanians and lead them to the path of God. Amen!

10 May 1999

Allahu Akbar (Allah is great)! By the grace of God, today was a celebration for all of us. The new king in Jordan, King Abdullah II, had pardoned many prisoners. Amir Zarqawi was released. We all made a victory rally covering all the cells in our prison, shouting, 'Allahu Akbar!' If Allah helps, we all will assemble under his banner to make jihad in the path of God to make our Islamic state. I heard Imam will be released too. I will be released next year, and if God will, I will join with Amir wherever he will be. I heard that Imam Maqdisi writes for many magazines in the Internet about Islam and jihad. Thank God, with the support of some of our jail staff and our mothers and sisters visiting the jail, he could send his writings outside. Imam has a good Islamist friend in London named Sheik Abu Qatada al-Filistini, who is a person very knowledgeable in Salafism and jihad. He publishes these writings in several Islamic sites popular in Arab countries, Europe, and Africa.

25 February 2001

Today I reached Herat in Afghanistan. I joined with several of my brothers from Jordan and Iraq. By the grace of God, it is a large community. About five hundred mujahideen and their wives and some children are here. I spent the whole day talking to the brothers. I was promised by Brother Arif that we will meet Amir Zarqawi soon. Now he is busy with his work. Tomorrow, a large batch of mujahideen will be coming from Syria. Well-wishers from Saudi Arabia who were Amir Zarqawi's old friends in Afghanistan are helping generously. Some good Muslims from Europe and other countries are also helping Amir. Amir has some support from al-Qaeda through brother Saif al-Adel. I heard Sheik Osama had some dispute with Amir Zarqawi. I wish when Sheikh accepts the good work of Amir Zarqawi, it will be a great day for jihad. We had very good food prepared by our sisters who came with their mujahideen husbands. After a long time, I had such a rewarding dinner. All by the mercy of God!

14 April 2001

By the grace of God, today I met Amir Zarqawi. He is more charismatic now. He embraced me and greeted me heartily. When Brother Arif told him about me, that we had all been together in Swaqa Prison, Amir was very happy. He offered me black tea prepared by his wife. Brother Arif told him that I was well versed in the Internet. Amir asked me to be active with our Islamic sites and asked me if I could guide the Muslim brothers who were interested in donating or dedicating themselves to jihad. He reminded me to keep enough secrecy and avoid any lead about the location and Shura leaders. Our goal was Sham. 'By the grace of God, one day we will establish our Islamic state in Sham,' he said. He welcomed me to be in the select few in Jund al-Sham, soldiers of Levant. That was a great honour for me.

12 September 2001

Our Herat camp became a large community with more than two thousand members, including family members of brothers. There is great support from the Muslim Brotherhood leaders living in many countries in Europe. Large numbers of Brothers from Levant and even from Europe are ready to join us. But now the Americans have started bombing Afghanistan. Amir Zarqawi was against fighting with the Taliban, killing Muslim brothers from the Northern Alliance. They were not making any trouble for us. But now we have to fight with Americans if they come to Herat. Amir doesn't want his brothers to die here in Afghanistan. We have to make our Levant an Islamic country. Each one of us is valuable and just like his brothers. This is not our battlefield. Still, Amir assigned some of the brothers to fight against Americans.

10 December 2001

It was a bad day for all of us. American infidels bombed our camp. Some of our brothers were killed. Amir was also injured. He had a bad injury to his chest. He asked us to leave the camp. Many of the brothers and their families escaped to Iran. Some are trying to reach Pakistan. Amir asked me to get ready. We, about three hundred brothers, are packing all valuables into pickup vans. In the night, we may cross the border to Iran. He told us we will go one by one and cross the border at different places and will be in the border villages of Iran until further orders come.

2 April 2002

After wandering for months in Iran and Iraq, now we are settled down in the Kurdistan area of Iraq. Though we lost most of our arms and military materials, we could later collect many machine guns and lots of ammunition from Iranian agencies. They are helpful to us as we are not against them. We are against the Iraqi regime of Saddam Hussein and Americans. Amir Zarqawi doesn't believe Shia much. He was looking for Sunni brothers in Iraq for help. With the help of the Kurdish brothers of Ansar al-Islam, we are happy here in our camp. Luckily we are in a safe land protected by America and friendly Kurds, who are very kind to us. Saddam's forces cannot torture us here. But Amir is trying to get help from some Iraqi officials. They seem willing to help us as we are against Americans. They are planning to invade Iraq shortly.

5 February 2003

That was a great day for Jund al-Sham and Amir Zarqawi. Today, speaking in the United Nations, the American secretary of state, Colin Powell, certified that Amir Zarqawi was the senior Al-Qaeda leader in Iraq. He said Zarqawi was supported by Saddam Hussein. Though he was lying, it was a good comment for our ears, which made our Amir world-famous overnight. Everyone in the village we live in heard about the news and wondered. They could not believe that Amir Zarqawi was such an important man. There were several comments in the Internet and world media. For the first time we saw the satellite picture of our camp on TV and in the newspaper. Hundreds of people are now willing to donate or ready to join our fight from across the world. Amir is happy that Americans will be coming to Iraq. He wants revenge on them on this soil where they killed several children and innocent civilians through sanctions over several years, he told us. Though Saddam is a bad person, infidel Americans have no right to punish him. We all are excited to meet the Americans.

10 April 2003

Though the life in other parts of Iraq was horrible after the US invasion, we in Kurdistan are not affected. This has been a protected area by America for a long time. Now Amir Zarqawi is getting support from many Iraqi intelligence people and army men. Some of the senior army officers promised to join our group shortly if American forces continue to target them. Now Americans are looking for senior officers in Saddam's army and Iraqi intelligence Service (ISS). No one knows where Saddam is. Not a single nuclear or chemical bomb was found in Iraq by Americans as they lied to the world. We are also waiting for Saddam to go. Amir Zarqawi reminded us a ruined Iraq with American control was the right time to establish our Islamic state.

31 August, 2003

We got the first major chance to punish the Shia infidels. Yesterday we killed Ayatollah Mohammad Baqir al-Hakim, Iraqi Shia cleric, an agent of Iran and the leader of the Supreme Council for Islamic Revolution in Iraq. He was killed by a bomb blast which no one in Najaf ever thought about. Along with his fifteen bodyguards, more than hundred people were killed in the Shia city. This is the punishment we want to give those Shia leaders who are now ruling the country. No matter where they are—in a mosque, on the street, or in their homes, we will spill their blood. May Allah reward us! Senior brother Yassin Jarad volunteered to drive the car in front of their Shia shrine in Najaf to become a martyr. Before his death, he gave hand of his young daughter, who is fourteen, as the wife of Amir Zarqawi. May his soul reach heaven! Amen.

14 December 2003

Saddam has been captured. The people of Iraq have already started resistance against American and occupying countries. Americans have started killing innocent people. We will organize several attacks against the Americans. Amir Zarqawi ordered all his followers to target Americans, whoever they are and wherever they are. Still, he preferred to start the first major attack against the government of Jordan. Our brothers organized a car bombing in front of the Jordanian embassy of Iraq on August 7. We scared the Jordanians, but all those killed were Iraqis; five were Iraqi policemen protecting the wicked people.

Within a week, on 19 August 2003, another massive bomb grounded the UN headquarters in Baghdad. They were supporting the tyrant American president George Bush. The UN special representative and twenty others were killed. That was a shock to the world. We want to spill the blood of anyone who kills our people in Iraq. Several Muslims with jihadi tradition support our cause. Amir Zarqawi later announced in a press release, 'We destroyed the UN building, the protectors of Jews, the friends of the oppressors and aggressors. The UN has recognized the Americans as the masters of Iraq. Before that, they gave Palestine as a gift to the Jews so they can rape the land and humiliate our people. Do not forget Bosnia, Kashmir, Afghanistan, and Chechnya.'

Now thousands of people are willing to come to Iraq to wage war against the Americans. Since many borders of Iraq with Arab countries are controlled by Americans, it is difficult for many brothers to come in. Leaders from Al-Qaeda have more interest in us. Since we are already here, they are happy to help us. Every day, several hundreds of brothers are reaching Kurdistan to join our army. *Insha Allah* we will have a big army. Many of the brothers coming are bringing lots of money given by their family and well-wishers to support the jihad. Now many Iraqi army men have joined our army. Many have given us weapons. Some are willing to supply any weapon from the Iraqi army for money. We have many supporters throughout Iraq, even in

Baghdad and Fallujah. Amir has several safe houses and weapon stores. A large collection of weapons is hidden in the desert sand. Many friends of Amir from Saudi Arabia and Qatar promised any possible help we need.

24 November 2004

Now I am in Fallujah. This is a liberated city. Starting with a few young people here following the killing of innocent people of the city by Americans, the resistance became complete here. Hundreds of fighters are coming here from the Syrian border. In Jordan and Syria, our agents are recruiting young jihadis willing to work with us for God's cause. Amir likes Saudi recruits. They all are rich and bring lots of money, at least five thousand to six thousand dollars, and are always willing for fedayeen (suicide) attacks. I don't see anyone more willing than Saudis to become martyrs. They come here leaving their businesses, families, wives, and kids. The senior leadership of Al-Qaeda has recently accepted us as part of global jihad, and Zarqawi made his *bayat* (oath of allegiance) to Bin Laden in October. Zarqawi is now Amir of Al-Qaeda of the Land of Two Rivers. People say Amir Zarqawi is as great a jihadi as Osama bin Laden, as he has the same bounty of twenty-five million dollars on his head as Bin Laden. Now we have about three thousand fighters in the city. The city is surrounded by American fighters, maybe more than ten thousand. We are waiting for them.

Yesterday, our men killed several of them in the street. Their Humvees were blasting into the air only to hit their own army men. Thanks to support from army people, we know every street in this town. Ba'ath commanders, who are very good army men, better than those Americans, are now our friends. Under the leadership of Amir Zarqawi, they become ferocious fighters. Their brains work faster than lightening. Now we have lots of videos on the Internet. We put several pictures of the killing of Western tyrants. Amir wants the world to see how their blood spills when the heads are cut off. This is a lesson for all Western dogs who kill and rape our children and women. This is an inspiration to new fighters for the cause of Allah. But for me, some were just ordinary Americans helping Iraqis to get support and food. Though they were Westerners, they were not killers. They still had some humanity. Amir says, 'They are just agents of America just trying to know about us. They are infidels. Kill them wherever they are.' I don't know if we can kill all the Shia in this land. They are the majority. Every other day, there are attacks on Shia areas, in markets and mosques—our fedayeen blast them off. Amir wants the division to widen between Shia and Sunni. He says, 'We Sunni are not good fighters. More people should come out of their sleep and support the jihad—only then can we establish our Islamic state completely.' He asks us not to be distracted by the blood and cries of children and women. They all are infidels. If by mistake any good Muslims die, Allah will reward them with heaven.

5 April 2005

People have started to hate us. They distance from us in the mosque. People have started talking about us as a scourge on their land. They say we have killed lots of innocent Iraqis. Many Sunnis who were supporting us before are now fighting against us. Amir Zarqawi now tells us not to trust Iraqis too much. They can cheat us, joining with Americans. We Arabs should be free from the Western-made country limits and look for our Islamic state all over Levant as a model for the world. The path to that is difficult. Many have to spill blood. We need so many martyrs.

I wish we were like al-Nasser Salah al-Deen group. They are very religious; they only kill American soldiers, not ordinary Iraqis. I heard Amir Bin Laden and other leaders of Al-Qaeda are not happy with us. Not many foreign fighters are coming now. Most of the money is now coming from ransom. Some days, some of our brothers are sent to the road. They capture oil tanks and take them to our warehouses. From there, they will be sold in Syria or other parts of Iraq. We also get money from oil companies and their security agents. We offer them security from attack. Any rich Iraqi businessman in our neighbourhood will give money out of fear; in the past, that was mostly to support us. In some remote areas we have control over some oilfields. Though foreign donors are less, our pockets are rich. I was injured in a mine, and now, I can only walk very slowly. I am not going for any active jihad. I am maintaining our Internet connections and receive new recruits and supplies. I have to travel many Internet booths, as it is difficult to operate from our homes as they may be bombed by Americans.

10 November 2005

In my country, Jordan, people are generally sympathetic to jihad in Iraq. Many people are proud of us and Zarqawi. A Jordanian, Raed Mansour al-Banna, became a martyr on 28 February 2005. He killed 127 people and injured many hundreds of Iraqis lined up to join the police in the al-Hillah recruiting camp in Iraq. After his death, Banna's family in Jordan organized a heroic funeral in which many Jordanians participated. There was anger all over Iraq. Thousands of people gathered around the Jordanian embassy in Baghdad and demanded it to close.

But yesterday, everyone in Jordan cried. I was watching the horrific events in our home country of Jordan on TV. Three fedayeen blew up three large hotels in Amman, Jordan. The plan was to kill a large number of Americans and Israelis who usually stay at these hotels. It was retaliation for his old failed attack in 1999 at Radisson SAS and other hotels. At the Radisson Hotel, two suicide bombers, Ali Hussein Ali al-Shamari and his wife Sajida Mubarak, entered the ballroom at around 9 p.m. That was the grand wedding ceremony of Ashraf Akhras and his bride Nadia al-Alami with a large crowd of about nine hundred Jordanian and Palestinian guests. Sajida was the sister of a close associate of brother Zarqawi. She tried to detonate her suicide vest but failed. Her husband asked her to run outside. He then jumped to the middle of the dining table, detonating his bomb, killing thirty-six people immediately, including the fathers of both the bride and groom.

Many children, women, and men were injured, their beautiful clothes wet with blood. People were running frantically in all directions. I saw the videos on my TV. I saw my best friend and his wife stooped on the floor, holding their dead daughter in their injured arms. Plates and cloths were scattered everywhere. There was dust and blood all over. That was a scene I could not believe. I could not hold my tears. Oh my god! Is this jihad? If the suicide vest of Sajida had also exploded, it would have killed many more hundreds of innocent people there. Sixty people were killed and more than a hundred injured in the three hotel attacks.

15 November 2005

Jordanian people were burning in anger over the killings. Thousands of people in Amman came to the street shouting, 'Burn in hell, Abu Musab al-Zarqawi!' King Abdullah, after visiting the injured at hospitals, told the media, 'The pain you felt for the loss of your beloved ones, who were killed for no crime they committed, was shared by all Jordanians, regardless of their origins or religions.' That became now the feeling of all Jordanians. We have seen enough bloodshed and suffering. This time it was from the hands of the so-called protectors of Muslim. They are not waging jihad for Allah. These are massacres for Satan. Zarqawi's family, including his brother and the al-Khalayleh tribe, put a half-page advertisement in many Jordanian newspapers supporting the kingdom and blaming Zarqawi. It reads, 'We denounce in the clearest terms all the terrorist actions claimed by the so-called Ahmed Fadheel Nazzal al-Khalayleh, who calls himself Abu-Musab al-Zarqawi. We announce, and all the people are our witnesses, that we—the sons of the al-Khalayleh tribe—are innocent of him and all that emanates from him, whether action, assertion, or decision. We sever links with him until doomsday.' I want to follow these people. This is not jihad. This is not what Allah wishes. I want to come out of this devilish deed. Oh, Allah, help me!

16 December 2005

Many of us from Jordan who are now in Iraq under Zarqawi are not happy with events in Jordan. Some of us who called their families in Jordan are more worried that their families will ask them to come back. No one can talk openly. For the bombing of Jordan hotels Zarqawi chose only Iraqis. Jordanians may fail to bomb their own brothers and sisters living there, with only a little peace in the middle of several conflicts. For Zarqawi, blood, destruction, and anarchy are just basic needs to establish the Islamic state under his control. A real butcher of mankind! Many fools fight for him as he projected himself as his saviour. Anyone not following him is called kafir (non-believer)—no matter if he calls himself Muslim, is more knowledgeable, or does much more namaz than him. He has no hesitation about killing Jordanians or Iraqi Muslims in their mosques or markets or in their wedding gowns. Either they are his enemy or kafir, or if they are innocent, he is just assisting them to reach heaven! He has no hesitation about sending his father-in-law or close friend's sister to die wearing suicide vests. I want to come out of this animal gang. I want save my *iman* (belief), my *taqwa,* and I want to die as a Muslim, not as a killer of humanity. I know for Allah each innocent life on this earth is worth the value of all human beings on earth. Killing one is equal to humanity. Allah has been kind to me, not allowing me to be a killer though I was closely following these barbaric killers. I cannot believe these past few years. I curse my days when I was a devilish young man ending up in jail to reach such bad company as these inhuman animals. They don't understand Allah. They don't know Muhammed. They can never be Muslims. Allah cannot be with such murderers killing innocent children and women. Believers or non-believers that Allah has to decide. Who are we to decide someone's fear of God? They don't understand the sanctity of Allah's homes. May it is masjid or a church where his name is chanted thousands of times and believers engage in conversation with God, opening their hearts. I can't believe what kind of Islam I was looking for which kills people in namaz while they are in front of Allah. They slaughter Muslims and others during *Ramzan* and *Eid*. It can't be Islam. Zarqawi is not Muslim. He is not a soldier of Allah; he is the commander of Satan. Let him be burned in hell! Those who follow him here will follow him to hell.

14 February 2006

In Jordan, Imam Maqdisi criticized his old student as a deviant and opposed all his killing of innocent Muslims and Shia. I remember Zarqawi behaving more aggressive than Imam Maqdisi. He used to correct Zarqawi from calling other prison mates and Shia *kafir*. *Takfir* for him was more important than *shahada* (pledge on God). But strangely, now he has thousands of followers ready to do anything for him. Many other thousands are looking at him to relieve their frustration with the rulers of their countries and eager to establish an Islamic Khaliphate. If that won't happen, be a martyr and reach heaven. Here I am having seen all this bloodshed and having been with them in many attacks. I have called 'Allahu Akbar' at least a dozen times in war fronts along with my fellow warriors at the top of our voices. Some were attacks on so-called enemies, but they were fighting in this land for Iraqi people and their freedom. But most often, these attacks were on our own Muslim brothers, sisters, and children, who are the hope of the Muslim umma. I know where I am now. It is not a place God wants. For months now I have been looking for a way out. But I know it is not that easy. Being a member of the group of Zarqawi is like a lifelong commitment. No one can come out. Anyone leaving the group is a traitor, and they will face treatment worse than for enemies.

I see on many occasions young people running away that are caught by others. In the presence of everyone, their heads are chopped off by Zarqawi or his close associate. They cry like children for forgiveness and to be given at least one more chance to do better. But Zarqawi never gives pardon for a defector; for him, they are worse than a *murthat*, a defector from Islam. Cutting off the head of a Muslim who was fighting for him till the other day is just easy for him as killing a chicken. That is a lesson for everyone: whoever parts from him, this will be their fate. Zarqawi has a special death squad which is directly under his control. They don't usually go for fighting. They are only meant for special assassinations—for defectors, imams not loyal to him, and his own personal enemies. They are a select few; most of them are Chechens. Their reach is there all over Iraq and into the neighbouring countries. Zarqawi has many agents throughout Iraq, even in the army, police, and intelligence agencies. His location is not known to others except a few from his inner circle. He can be in any part of Iraq or even in neighbouring countries. Zarqawi has many homes, safe houses, and storage houses. He has many loyal people in the cities who don't usually fight but pass information or are just waiting for orders. So getting out of Zarqawi's network is not an easy task. I have decided to continue but lie low till I get a good chance.

Now I don't have much contact with my family or friends in Jordan. All I have is a few people around me. I don't want to tell anyone. Either my life or their lives will be at risk. It is suicidal to run away. I feel how lucky I am not to be with the inner circle of Zarqawi. My computer knowledge and accident saved me from hell!

8 June 2006

Finally that day came. Yesterday was the day I was waiting for. Zarqawi along with his newly found Islamic teacher and spiritual guide Sheik Abd-al-Rahman was killed in his house in an isolated area outside the city of Baqubah. The place was his stronghold, about 50 km from Baghdad. He met the end he deserved. His small child and one of his wives were also killed along with him. I was wishing his end would not be that easy. He died an hour after his home was bombed to rubble by American forces. All died immediately except Zarqawi, who was badly injured and was unable to move. I heard the US army men who reached there later beat him to death. It was news to celebrate for all Iraqi and Americans. It was my dream day. He will not trap youngsters like me any more to fight and kill for him. He cannot destroy this great religion any more. He cannot kill any more Iraqis, Americans, or anyone who love peace. *Alhamdu Lillah* (Glory to God)!

His empire was a gang of perverted youth looking for God's country even if that meant killing themselves and millions of others. His other friends were a bunch of hypocrites from the former Iraqi army and intelligence and smugglers who never believed his ideas but supported him because of hatred or for money or power. Zarqawi was not bothered about real infidels in his group. For him, all others—Muslims, Christians, Jews—were infidels if they didn't follow him. He didn't care how much they loved their God, how careful they were not to hurt others. He taught his youngsters killing was the greatest act and dying during killing was the ultimate way to reach heaven. Surely this thug created his own Islam. Al-Qaeda leaders like Bin Laden were far better than him. They did not want to kill innocent Muslims even if they always did. He did not have any good education or knowledge of Islam, politics, or about society like other Al-Qaeda leaders. He did not know what a society wanted from its rulers. There was no fun or light moments in their life. I can't say he was not bothered about life here as he lived with his three wives.

His group was always focused on jihad and hatred. His ego was too much for a Muslim; he believed he was the only one who was right and so were those who accepted his opinions. Those who did not follow him were projected as those not following God. Those who did not follow God, kill them. He never thought about his past; if any other jihadi like him would have found him before, he would have finished him. He forgot his past as a criminal, thief, rapist, pimp, and alcoholic. For him, there was nothing called mercy. Al-Qaeda under Osama was not a model for him. They were educated, cautious people from reputed families, unlike Zarqawi, who had nothing and nothing to be bothered about. He got his inspiration to kill anyone other than his group from al-Gama'a al-Islamiyya in Egypt; for them, all Egyptians were pagans and needed to be killed or changed. They killed Egyptians in suicide bombings and chopped off the heads of tourists. Their strategy of looting and raiding villages and cities came from the same group, al-Gama'a Islamiyya Musallaha in Algeria, also called GIA (Armed Islamic Group). They bombed civilians in cities and trains and looted people. They killed anyone other than their group, including their former leaders in the Islamic Salvation Front. That was a group of uneducated, marginalized people under senseless and unimportant leaders who could not find any place elsewhere. Here Zarqawi and his group followed the same strategy. A bunch of left-out people whom nobody respected, who had done nothing special for anyone in their life, were trying to make a country where only jihadis lived—no need for teachers, doctors, engineers. All they cared about was to train jihadis, treat them when they were injured, and make bombs and guns!

It is sure that without info from someone of his inner circle, Americans cannot find this safe house in this remote area among tall palm trees. The area is not easy to go to for Iraqi or American forces. I know his death is not going to be the end of Iraqi's suffering or the end of jihadis reaching Iraq like flies from across the world. So many attacks happen in Iraq every day. Zarqawi knew he would perish one day. Now many of his followers are ready to take over. Even among jihadis, most people want to be the amir, not just a suicide bomber killing himself in an attempt to kill a few people around.

30 June 2006

With no safe place to go, I have continued to work here—working part-time for them, watching the Internet and making occasional comments and replies on the Net. I pass the information to my carriers, who do the rest. If I go out of this area, I may be caught by American or Iraqi forces or even by men from our organization. Here on this street, most of the people know me, and I am just like one of them now. So the only place I can stay may be here in this small town. Al-Qaeda leaders were not so happy with Zarqawi, who had been killing Shia and Iraqi people just like chickens in slaughterhouses. But when Zarqawi was killed, they came with sympathy. Both Zawahiri and Osama Bin Laden praised him and blamed those who killed him.

On 23 June 2006, I saw on Al Jazeera TV a video of Ayman al-Zawahiri praising him as 'a soldier, a hero, an imam, and the prince of martyrs, and his death has defined the struggle between the crusaders and Islam in Iraq'. Later, I watched on the Internet an audio recording Osama released: 'Our Islamic nation was surprised to find its knight, the lion of jihad, the man of determination and will, Abu Musab al-Zarqawi, killed in a shameful American raid. We pray to Allah to bless him and accept him among the martyrs as he had hoped for.' He also said al-Zarqawi had 'clear instructions' to focus on US-led forces in Iraq and 'for those who stood to fight on the side of the crusaders against the Muslims, then he should kill them whoever they are, regardless of their sect or tribe.'

In a few days, I also saw another tape saying, 'Our brothers, the mujahedeen in the al-Qaeda organization, have chosen the dear brother Abu Hamza al-Muhajer as their leader to succeed the Amir Abu Musab al-Zarqawi. I advise him to focus his fighting on the Americans and everyone who supports them and allies himself with them in their war on the people of Islam and Iraq.' It seems veteran jihadis like Osama Bin Laden and Zawahiri need support from a martyr like Zarqawi. They now want to capture back their lost control in Iraq and want to claim all war in Iraq was part of their Al-Qaeda. They are just opportunistic like cheap politicians. They created monsters like Zarqawi. When they go madder than them or out of control, they deny them. When they die or people's memories fade about their horror, they become patrons of them; they project them as the greatest of martyrs. What an unholy mess this is! Allah saves our umma from these beasts!

9 July 2006

Glory to Allah! Today I am entering a new life. I am getting married. My bride is a beautiful Iraqi girl, the daughter of the owner of the shop where I have been working for the last two years. I have a couple of friends here now. I am Abid Hussein, am better and more obedient than before to Allah, and have turned twenty-nine now. People here are very helpful to me. For me, now this is my home, my country. I want to live peacefully for my family. I want to forget my past, the days when I was living on a devilish path, on someone's perverted thought. Thank God for a long time, I have not been on the payroll of AQI (Al-Qaeda in Iraq). My overseer in the organization with whom I had contact died last week in the hands of Shia militiamen. Now I have no contact with anyone in AQI. Thank God I am a free man now. My family cannot come today for my marriage as violence in Iraq is now part of everyday life. I phoned my brothers and sisters; they were very excited. They blessed me and promised to come to see me and my wife when the situations in Iraq become calm. They asked me not to come to Jordan soon as police and intelligence people are looking for all those that have been to Iraq and Afghanistan.

My neighbourhood here is calm, but other parts of Iraq are burning in hellfire. Today in Baghdad, Shia militiamen killed forty Sunnis. They created check posts in the jihad neighbourhood of Baghdad, pulled out people from their cars, and killed whomever they found as Sunni. It was probably in retaliation for a suicide bombing in a Shia shrine yesterday which killed two people. I saw on TV, in another area in Baghdad, two suicide car bombs killed twenty-five people in a Shia mosque in the Kasra district of Baghdad. The seeds sown by Zarqawi are working. Iraq is going into a Shia–Sunni battlefield; every day there are several killings. Even the firebrand Shia cleric Moqtada Sadr, whose men are behind most of the Shia violence, appealed for peace and asked, 'Put our hands together for the sake of Iraq's independence and stability.' Now not only followers of Zarqawi but also many Sunni tribes and former Ba'ath leaders are all behind the daily bloodshed in Iraq. Violence unites all bloodthirsty people.

Hatred can breed hatred only. I know it is easy to sow seeds of hatred but very difficult to bring peace. For peace, only a few people are coming forward, coming out of their sects or political belief. I am looking for them, those who are honestly working for the people, for this rich country, their own families, the future of their kids, and most importantly, for Allah on his path, *fi sabilillah*—the true path of God! Let me lead my private life till then. I know your prayers are with me . . .

(Note: Abid Hussein is a fictional character. The story is based on many testimonies and sociopolitical situations in the Middle East. All the major political events in this story are historical. Most of the Arabic words are in italics.)

CHAPTER 7

The New Generation Al-Qaeda-ISIS and Jabhat al-Nusra

The situation isn't like the West portrays it, that there is an "organization" with a specific name (such as "al-Qai`dah") and so on. That particular name is very old. It was born without any intention from us. Brother Abu Ubaidah al-Banshiri created a military base to train the young men to fight against the vicious, arrogant, brutal, terrorizing soviet empire . . . So this place was called "The Base" ("Al-Qai`dah"), as in a training base, so this name grew and became. We aren't separated from this nation (Ummah). We are the children of a nation, and we are an inseparable part of it, and from those public demonstrations which spread from the far east, from the Philippines, to Indonesia, to Malaysia, to India, to Pakistan, reaching Mauritania . . . and so we discuss the conscience of this nation (Ummah).

Osama Bin Laden

Middle East—Political Map

That was the real description of Al-Qaeda. The word *'Al-Qaeda*
is seldom used by its members. The organization is just a loose
amalgam of people connected with a common ideology. But for one to
understand its roots and many of its offshoots, precise classification
is just a learning tool. Several organizations with the black banners
of Al-Qaeda and from inspiration from its founders are there all
across the world. Some are closely connected with endorsement and
overseeing; some are just local versions. Sometimes they are more
refined, many times more viral than their parent organization. In any
case, now we are going through a generation where organizations
with ideological roots with Al-Qaeda now control a vaster area of
land than ever before. Contrary to general expectation that banning
an organization will prevent people from being supportive of its cause
or being part of it, history has proven otherwise.

The brand endorsement of Al-Qaeda makes a militant organization more authentic, instantly gaining it worldwide attention. There is contempt from many quarters; so also is there support from a host of sympathizers, financiers, and willing young men looking for venues for jihad. Also the portrayal of horror or brutality has a mixed response to it and belief in media stories. Most people who are indoctrinated in violent jihad do not believe any public opinion or media portrayal. They believe it is just propaganda of Islam's enemies. Support for violent extremism often comes from faraway places, where people are not aware of disruption of the normal lives of ordinary people in those lands. For them, support is just help in the path of God. For the people in the hotbed of terrorism, they can be either with terrorists or against them. But for those people watching abroad or receiving campaigns to support, there are lots of grey zones in their idea. This makes one man's 'enemy of mankind' other one's 'vanguard of God's own army'. Looking at the rapid spread of Al-Qaeda's root ideology in the Middle East and Africa and their supporters worldwide takes us to this reality.

Al-Qaeda evolved though the Azzam era of religious renaissance, Bin Laden's era of jihadi activism, and the practical jihad era of Ayman al-Zawahiri, stretching to this new-generation era of Al-Qaeda states. The old ideology and new brands are seen in some areas together, and a group of elders of old Al-Qaeda who escaped 'martyrdom', like Ayman al-Zawahiri, are now working as mostly referees sitting at their hideouts in restive areas of Af-Pak and rebel strongholds of Yemen. The Al-Qaeda central command is still active with mediation and endorsement of ideological warriors in different parts of world. Their 'certification' is valuable among jihadi circles. One of the most violent and aggressive offshoots of Al-Qaeda ideology representing the extreme end of the new-generation Al-Qaeda is the Islamic State of Iraq and Syria (ISIS).

ISIS evolved over the years from the crude, sadistic self-proclaimed amir of Levant, Abu Musab al-Zarqawi from his Jama'at al-Tawhid wal-Jihad. In October 2004, Zarqawi proclaimed his allegiance to Osama bin Laden. That was after several months of negotiation to make his outfit independent from tight control by central leaders and labelled his organization as Tanẓīm Qāidat al-Jihad fi Bilad al-Rāfidayn (The Organization of Jihad's Base in the Country of the Two Rivers) known for short as "Al-Qaeda in Iraq (AQI). It was later expanded to include some small Iraqi Sunni tribes who shared his ideas to form the Mujahideen Shura Council in January 2006. When Zarqawi was killed after a long chase in his hideout in June 2006, by American and Iraqi forces with inputs from Jordanian intelligence agencies, two other radicals emerged as leaders of the terror outfit. A mastermind of terror and favourite of central Al-Qaeda, Abu Ayyub al-Masri, known as Abu Hamza al-Muhajir, was the obvious choice. But he was an Egyptian. Soon dissidence spread, as most in the organization were looking for an Iraqi. Thus, an Iraqi, Abu Abdullah al-Rashid al-Baghdadi, also called Abu Omar al-Baghdadi, became the figurehead, with actual power resting with al-Muhajir. They also pursued the aggressive campaign of Zarqawi with suicide bombings, Shia massacres, kidnapping, ransom collection, beheadings, and torture.

In 13 October 2006, they declared Dawlat al-Iraq al-Islamiyah, or Islamic State of Iraq (ISI), and declared a state throughout Iraq with a cabinet and Omer al-Baghdadi as amir. ISI had backup with many militiamen and Sunni tribes. Many former Ba'ath leaders and army men gave them strategic advice and military training. A former Iraqi army colonel named Haji Bakr was the chief consultant of Omer al-Baghdadi, coordinating contacts with former Ba'ath commanders. They provided operational knowledge, planning strategies and communication methods. Both Omar al-Baghdadi and al-Muhajir were killed in April 2010 by a missile attack followed by a ground offensive by the US and Iraqi army. Following their death, a relatively unknown, not a member of leadership council of ISI, Abu Bakr al-Baghdadi was chosen by Haji Bakr as the successor. Shortly, he became the unquestionable leader of the outfit with real power in the hands of Haji Bakr. Haji Bakr orchestrated a cleaning of the outfit by assassinating all dissidents against Baghdadi within the group and consolidating their power.

Abu Bakr al-Baghdadi reconstituted the leadership council with exclusively Iraqi nationals as he did not trust anyone other than Iraqi. Haji Bakr was initially a Western-styled man without a beard, which was unimaginable for others in the jihadi outfit. He later changed his appearance with a beard and mannerisms suitable for ISI. The ISI leader was almost unknown; his whereabouts were known only to a select core. He never used to meet his subordinates; he just passed his orders through a council. Its members were strictly prohibited to enquire about its leaders as enquiry meant doubt; doubt meant a break in loyalty, which invited death.

Money was not a big problem for the group. Just like his predecessors, Abu Bakr al-Baghdadi continued confiscating valuables of Shia, Christians, non-Muslims, and any regime supporters; it did not matter whether he was Sunni or not. They controlled oil sources, fuel plants, and government factories or any financial source to extract money in the areas they controlled. If they couldn't fully manage a large factory, they would threaten to kill the owner or blow it up in exchange for monthly protection money. They regularly put check posts in their area of influence to collect money from trucks and confiscate oil tankers. Then there were foreign groups donating money in support for the anti-American campaign or for anti-Shia activities. Many new recruits also used to bring money they collected from their families. Agents were there who collected donations from private donors in other countries. Selling of oil, fuel, and other goods through several agents also brought lots of money. When they occupied lands, banks were looted to fill their coffers. With all this money, they could pay recruits if needed, bribe officials, and buy enough arms from the government guards or from arm dealers. The money power also attracted local recruits to the payroll and support from greedy tribal leaders.

The impact of ISI on Iraq and its population has been devastating from the beginning of their massacres in 2003 and is still continuing. According to a study published in a Lancet medical journal in September 2011 aided by an Iraqi body count from 2003 to 2010. There were 1,003 documented suicide bombing events. It caused

12,284 deaths and injuries of 30,644 people. Among this, 14 per cent were children. Children are more vulnerable than adults to death and serious injuries. Undoubtedly, most of those acts were carried out by ISI and their early versions. Among all these, the death toll of coalition forces was 200, of which 175 were US soldiers from 76 events, and the rest from Italy, Britain, Bulgaria, and Thailand in three other incidents. Unlike a bomb blast or an ambush; in a suicide attack the target would be precise. That translates as out of 1,003 attacks, only 79 were targeted on foreign soldiers. On analysis 61 Iraqis died for every single coalition force trooper who died from suicide bombing. A total of 108,624 Iraqi civilians died during this period due to violence, and 117,165 people were seriously injured. Most of the injured had multiple injuries, fractures, multi-organ injuries, or injuries to eyes or ears, causing lifelong disabilities. A total of 4,804 coalition force members died during that time from war and insurgency.

For ISI, not only the foreign forces were their enemies. The Iraqi policemen and army men maintaining the law and integrity of their country, any Shia, any non-Muslim, or even any Sunni Muslim who didn't believe in them or did not follow their version of Islam or government was their enemy or an infidel. They chopped off the heads of Sunni sheikhs who refused to pledge their alliance, cut off the fingers of men found smoking (which they viewed as strongly un-Islamic), collected huge extortion money, and looted banks and gold shops. In spite of all these brutalities, how could they survive all these years? That was thanks to their strategy and focus. Also the power of the sectarian divide they created in Iraq and in the Middle East. Attacks and counter-attacks by both sects are now tearing apart the collective human conscience of Iraqi people.

Following the civil war in Syria, ISI leadership was forced by their cadres to expand their activities to Syria. ISI quickly expanded its inroads into Syria, taking a significant presence in areas like Aleppo, Idlib, and Ar-Raqqa. After the expansion into Syria, the group adopted a new name on 9 April 2013, Islamic State of Iraq and the Levant, also known as Islamic State of Iraq and al-Sham, abbreviated as ISIS or ISIL. The Arabic word *Sham* refers to Syria, but in the context of global jihad, it means that Levant or Greater Syria include Iraq, Syria, and Palestine. Though it was declared an Islamic state in Iraq long ago, it did not have much territorial control in any part of Iraq consistently. But their expansion into Syria transformed it from a terrorist group to a militia with territorial control. It also rejuvenated the recruitment with thousands of new recruits coming to join. Unlike the terrorist attacks in Iraq with mostly a hit-and-run strategy, in Syria, they fought like a military force against a professional Syrian army. That gained them a lot of battleground experience and experienced soldiers in spite of casualties. In Syria, they adopted a strategy to control territories. In a war-torn Syria with no law and order or support to people suffering from war and lawlessness, the arrival of ISIL fighters was a relief initially. They bought medicines and food materials for the population. Their presence forced petty criminals who were looting and robbing the general public to run away. They tried to provide electricity, water, and transportation services. They provided security to school and hospitals. All these gained popular support. Many local people enlisted in the group. But that was just initial advertisement and a public relations campaign.

Once they established their control in the area, they chased away other more liberal fighters from the Free Syrian Army and other groups. They compelled them to join them or face their ire. For ISIS, the punishment for an enemy is death. They started killing other rebels. Summary executions, hanging, and even crucifixion became regular punishments for enemies. For civilians, they started their brutal implementation of their own version of sharia. Torture by flogging, summary judgements, imprisonments, and summary executions became common. Schools and hospitals in the cities they controlled became their jails and headquarters. Any westerner or journalist in their area of control was killed, imprisoned, or exchanged for heavy ransom. Smoking was banned, and smokers were given brutal punishment, including chopping of fingers. Women were not allowed to go out alone, and a strict dress code for men and women was enforced. Violators were punished harshly. People started to run away from their areas. More than the Syrian regime, they targeted other rebels, who were forced to fight back. ISIL became isolated. This saved them from the Syrian army to an extent as their targets were mostly rebels, thus helping the Syrian forces indirectly. During this time, the Syrian air force purposefully avoided their conspicuous headquarters from bombing while even many smaller bases of other rebels were targeted.

They had to abandon many of the territories they initially controlled. Towards April 2014, they were restricted to areas of Ar-Raqqah and those close to Iraq. But this was the area of most of the Syrian oilfields. They gained control over them. They also got control over power plants, water sources, and dams. They also got involved in the trade of raw materials and archaeological artefacts. All these gave them enough money and tactical advantage. In fact, they sold oil, power, and water to even the Syrian government for money. The Syrian experience was a boost despite many setbacks. It helped them to gain experience, more fighters, more money, and more arms. When their prospects in Syria became dim, they turned back to Iraq.

Iraq, by June 2014, was more weakened by the power struggle between the Shia-led coalition, which won the maximum seats in the recently held national election, and various Sunni and Kurdish factions. They were fighting against the government under Nouri al-Maliki. American forces left Iraq. President Barack Obama was no longer interested in any military activity in Iraq. The Iraq army became a loose, demoralized force running on loyalties rather than professionalism and was embedded in corruption. Many Sunnis felt alienated by the Shia-led government and wanted to get rid of it at any cost. Against this backdrop, ISIL launched a massive attack on Iraqi territories, easily conquering a vast area of northern Iraq close to the Syrian border. They occupied a host of Iraqi cities, including the second largest city of Iraq, Mosul. It was not a fight even. A small army of eight hundred ISIL soldiers quickly gained control of a large city with a two-million population guarded by more than ten thousand army men and air force personnel and thousands of policemen. Nothing was as unbelievable as the military takeover of Mosul by ISIL in the conflict. How did they orchestrate this unusual victory?

Following their conquests in Iraq, they renamed the organization as Islamic State or al-Dawlah al-Islamiyah and declared Abu Bakr al-Baghdadi as Khalifa of global Muslims and changed himself to Amirul Mu'mineen Khalifa Ibrahim.

People watching the new developments in Iraq can dub it as silly madness. But reality is bit more than this. According to estimates, by June 2014, Islamic State or its former label, ISIL, had six thousand fighters in Iraq and three thousand to five thousand in Syria. About three thousand of them may be foreigners, a substantial number of about one thousand from Chechnya and perhaps five hundred or so more from France, Britain, and other European countries. The forces behave like a well-trained national force with a top-to-bottom commanding structure, having a communication system connecting all levels. Their soldiers are well equipped with almost all types of modern military equipment. They wear American combat dress and work with night-vision goggles. Trained fighters operate tanks, missiles, anti-aircraft guns, and modern military vehicles. Many of them they grabbed when they took control over various armouries in Syria, Iraq, and former American bases in Iraq. When they captured Mosul, they also took over many military helicopters, commercial carrier aircrafts, and even ballistic missiles and nuclear materials. How they are going to make use of them is still a question.

They also looted a substantial amount of money and bullions they stashed from the central bank in Mosul, estimated to be worth US $429 million. Islamic State is not just a small terrorist group working with few thousand dollars and a few secret members but a well-oiled organization with about US $2 billion assets, most of it acquired recently from Mosul. It is enough to pay the usual salary of $600 a month for about sixty thousand new recruits for more than a year, making it the richest terrorist organization or militia in the world at present. The enormous money power it gained is one of the major factors it can bribe army commanders to desert their bases, leaving leaderless army men either to run away or surrender. They also manage the tribal militia and leaders with money, threats, or luring. It is believed that the tribes actually control the territories with a token of

Islamic State soldiers directing them, showing their presence only on the street and manning check posts. They have also freed thousands of prisoners from Mosul jails. Many of them were their associates, who promptly joined the fight on battlefields along with them.

The rise and spread of Islamic State in Iraq and Syria can be equated with the rise of Taliban in the post-Soviet-war Afghanistan. Both superficially appeared to be a bunch of amateur jihadists but, in fact, were professional armed forces backed by senior military experts. For Taliban, they were guided by the Pakistan army and their intelligence agency (ISI). But for Islamic State, the old Iraqi army officers and Ba'ath leaders take the military command. Some Ba'ath army and intelligence agencies from Syrian forces also joined the group. An unending supply of Arab youths and spirited people from world over make the mass of this masked armed militia. Many Sunnis in Iraq were also attracted to the cadres to punish the Shia, Yezidis, and Kurds in the Iraqi atmosphere of sectarian hatred.

Islamic State initially enjoyed the apathy of the population they conquered and their silent support, having forgotten the past and the history of such criminal gangs elsewhere. Although millions of people have fled from their territories, others continue their lives till they feel it is intolerable. Till then, people will be amused with the loosening of traffic control, the free flow of traffic without check posts, and continuous electricity and fuel supply, which they have implemented in the conquered cities of Iraq initially. Islamic State, or ISIL, in their areas of influence, acted more or less like a state with their own security, courts, jails, and occasional public relations exercises. Most of their cadres were masked men; no one knew who they were. So there were also no question of identifying them and knowing their leaders, reporting them to higher authorities if anyone of them commits any atrocity which is not expected from even a militant jihadist. Over a period of time they started exposing their identities.

ISIL, or Islamic State, recruits, no matter how learned, undergo a mandatory training course on Islam and the Islamic state of their own version and principles. Then they undergo arms training. Mostly they are deployed to a new area. All the cadres working in an area are usually new to the place, so they implement ruthlessly what they were taught. Defection or going back is a serious crime with brutal punishment. So once a cadre, it means till his end he has to be in the organization. No question of authority and no doubt on seniors is permitted. So most of the younger fighters have no idea under whom they are working. ISIL and Islamic State maintain a major public relations department much more organized than that of many multinational companies.

Several units are involved in various public relations campaigns flooding the Internet with propaganda materials. They publish many videos of gruesome beheadings and killings on the Net to scare enemies and give a glimpse of their activities to potential recruits. From 2012, they have published their annual reports containing details of figures of operations, assassination, bombings (mortars, grenade launchers, and rockets), suicide missions, knife attacks, apostates who have repented and joined the ISIL cause, cities taken over, and checkpoints set up, etc., just like corporate houses publishing annual returns. This is to attract their donors and potential recruits and boast of their capabilities. As per the latest report, titled 'Naba' (the news), ISIL has carried out 9,540 attacks in 2013, including 1,047 assassinations and 4,465 roadside time bombings and has freed hundreds of prisoners, substantially higher than the figures for the previous year.

Shortly after the creation of the Islamic State of Iraq in 2006, the group established the al-Furqan Institute for Media Production, involved in making DVDs, posters, pamphlets on ISI ideology, and web-related propaganda products. ISIS in 2013 started its main media outlet, al-I'tisaam Media Foundation, distributed through the Global Islamic Media Front (GIMF). In 2014, ISIS established the al-Hayat Media Center, targeting a Western audience, producing materials in English, German, Russian, and French languages. They are also active in social media like Twitter with several hashtag campaigns.

Till recently, the identity of al-Baghdadi, amir of Islamic State, was a closely held secret with no official videos or photographs. He used to wear a mask even when he addressed his commanders, which earned him the nickname 'the Invisible Sheikh'. After the Mosul invasion, a video emerged showing al-Baghdadi giving a sermon in the historic mosque of Mosul. Abu Bakr al-Baghdadi is projected as a descendant of Prophet Muhammed. But those familiar with him identify him as Ibrahim al-Badri, a lecturer of Islamic studies who worked as a cleric in Baghdad and the Fallujah Mosque. He belongs to the Bou Abbas clan of Samara, not a member of the Quraishi tribe (tribe of Prophet Muhammad), as claimed by his followers. Since no one in his organization dares to question his status as long as he is alive, he will be the sole front leader of the Islamic State. The evolution of political scenes in the Middle East is beyond prediction. They control a large part of Syria and Iraq, which is one-third each of both countries by August 2015.

Islamic State fighters continued to expand to Kurdish areas of Iraq and started ethnic cleansing of Kurds and Yezidis. Kurdish areas of Iraq were under patronage by the US since the Kuwait war. An impending humanitarian catastrophe prompted a US military response. US president Barack Obama was adamant not to get involved in another war in Iraq. But widespread criticism in the USA against his policy of non-interference in Iraq, rapidly advancing Islamic State fighters, expanding across borders, and capturing strategic assets and their brutal pogroms in the captured areas provoked the USA to start air strikes in Islamic State targets. When the air strikes started in August 2014, Islamic State fighters changed their target from Iraqi areas to Syria. They had already established a contiguous Syria–Iraq landscape with no existing border between Syria and Iraq along the Eastern Syria. During the ongoing US air strikes in Iraqi targets, Islamic State captured the last airfield in Raqqa province in Syria from the Syrian army. Islamic State was already considering Raqqa as their capital. These events necessitated that any major military campaign to eliminate or restrict Islamic State needed a combined action in their Iraqi and Syrian territories. Attack of Islamic State targets in Syria might indirectly help the Assad regime, making that option a difficult choice.

A broad coalition against these forces was emerging which might ultimately limit their relentless march crossing over national boundaries. Their attacks on Saudi, Jordan, and Turkish territories exposed the vulnerability of neighbours of Iraq and Syria and to take serious steps against them for the survival of these countries, no matter whether they helped the group in the past or not. The bombing of a Russian passenger aircraft in Sinai (Egypt) and the Paris attack on November 2015 galvanized a broad front against Islamic State with massive individual attacks by France, Russia, and US forces on selected targets of Islamic State.

A reasonably refined version of Al-Qaeda emerged from ISIL in Syria during the Syrian civil war, known as Jabhat-al Nusra, or Al-Nusra Front. When the Syrian people start their revolt against Bashar al-Assad regime in 2011, many in the ISI, especially those from Syria started hoping for acting in Syria. Abu Bakr-al-Baghdadi was disinterested to interfere in the Syrian fight. He initially thought it was going the way of democratic resistance and of no interest to his ideology. But later, when armed resistance started, many in the ISI were keen to participate in the civil war, reaching the verge of rebellion in the ISI against their leadership. At this point, al-Baghdadi and Haji Bakr decided to form a non-Iraqi battalion to go to Syria under a Syrian commander and forbade Iraqis moving to Syria to safeguard against defection and collapse of the outfit. That was the beginning of Al-Nusra Front, formed in December 2011 under Abu Mohammed al-Golani, who was a close aide of al-Baghdadi. The whereabouts of Golani are not much known, but the name Golani, surely a nom de guerre, means he is from the Golan heights of Syria. But once in Syria, Al-Nusra Front soon became famous, attracting jihadists from Arabia, North Africa, Yemen and from Europe. Baghdadi and Haji Bakr feared this sudden raise since the new recruits may not pledge their allegiance to ISI and Baghdadi. Soon they sent a message to Golani to announce that al-Nusra Front was under the ISI and Baghdadi's leadership. Golani sent a reply that he would think about it. After a repeat warning from al-Baghdadi, he replied that he had consulted with his Majlis-ash-Shura (Consultative Council)—a small group of top leaders—that it won't be in the interest of the revolution. This infuriated Baghdadi.

The envy worsened with later developments in Syria like territorial gains by Al-Nusra Front, the declaration of Al-Nusra Front as a terrorist organization by the USA on December 2012, and Golani becoming the most wanted man in Syria. Golani was given a test of loyalty, and he was asked to attack Free Syrian Army leaders. But he declined. By now, Baghdadi and Bakr decided to interfere. Baghdadi declared a new organization called ISIL (Islamic State of Iraq and Levant), or ISIS, to extend their activity to Syria and asked for the dissolution of Al-Nusra front and to merge it with ISIL on 8 April 2013. Golani refused the offer and instead pledged direct alliance to Al-Qaeda Amir, Ayman al-Zawahiri after two days. By the declaration of ISIL, some of the cadres of Al-Nusra Front joined ISIL. The rest remained with Al-Nusra Front. Baghdadi made plans to murder Golani and his commanders. Sensing trouble, Golani asked for mediation by Zawahiri. Zawahiri authorized senior Al-Qaeda leader Nasir al-Wuhyshi to mediate. But it failed as Baghdadi refused to entertain them. Baghdadi claimed that he was a head of state and could not accept any mediation from groups, under guidance from Haji Bakr. Zawahiri declared Al-Nusra Front as the only authorized unit of Al-Qaeda in Syria and ISIL formation as invalid. He asked ISIL cadres to return to Iraq, continuing with their ISI. That created an ideological split of ISIL with central Al-Qaeda leadership. The fight between Al-Nusra Front and ISIL intensified, leading to thousands of deaths of cadres (about three thousand fighters by March 2014) and many civilian casualties in their contested areas. Al-Nusra Front aligned with FSA and continued their offensive both against the Syrian Army and ISIL. ISIL fought against rebels and gained their independent territories. Al-Nusra Front found strong support from Qatar, and ISIL maintained their support from Saudi Arabia, Bahrain, and Kuwait jihadi supporters. Apparently, government agencies of Saudi Arabia actively supported ISIL, and Qatar supported Nusra Front.

Al-Nusra Front started their anti-government activities in Syria on 6 January 2012 with a suicide bombing in central Damascus on a bus carrying riot police to protest areas. It killed 26 personnel and injured 63 others. A video of Al-Nusra claimed the responsibility of the 'martyrdom-seeking operation' in retaliation for the regime force's atrocities in Homs. Before this, on 23 December 2011, two coordinated suicide attacks in the Syrian capital, Damascus, killed 44 people and injured 166. It was the first ever suicide attack in the Syrian war. It was possibly carried out by Al-Nusra Front. The first car bomb attack was in front of the Syrian military intelligence building. A second car jammed the building gate and exploded when guards came out to look at the first attack. Most of the victims were civilians. Al-Nusra Front was not known in Syria at that time. Apparently, due to heavy civilian casualties, the front did not come with any claim. It was believed to be have been carried out by two female suicide attackers from Iraq. The FSA blamed Syrian government, and the government blamed the rebel FSA. FSA never justified or proved to have carried out any suicide attacks. Till June 2013, the al-Nusra Front had claimed responsibility for 57 of the 70 suicide attacks in Syria during the conflict. The rest were unclaimed by them or some were the handiwork of other rival Al-Qaeda group, ISIL.

Al-Nusra Front was a highly motivated force. They worked like a professional army. This gained them respect among the rebels. Many of them were among the most trained soldiers in Iraq under Zarqawi. They had more sophisticated weapons than FSA soldiers, including anti-aircraft shoulder-fired missiles, which were possibly supplied by Qatar. They got a liberal supply of arms, materials, and money from foreign countries. ISI contributed about half of their budget in the initial period prior to the rivalry with the group. Apart from the militant activities with suicide bombing and IED attacks, they also took part in many military campaigns. Many times, along with FSA soldiers, they fought against the Assad regime as their common enemy. All these gained them support from other rebel groups. Many of them protested when the USA labelled Al-Nusra Front as a terrorist organization in December 2012. There were also mass rallies against the move with thousands rallying in Syrian streets on 14 December 2012, shouting, 'There is no terrorism in Syria except that of Assad.'

Al-Nusra Front regarded the Assad regime as the current enemy of Syria and must be removed. They wanted to establish an Islamic caliphate under sharia rule when they came to power. In those areas where Al-Nusra Front, had independent control, they enforced sharia law but not as forcefully as ISIL. This made them separate from secular FSA, causing ideological conflict. The relatively mild stand of Al-Nusra on controlling territory as their own and slowness in implementation of sharia in their strongholds are part of their strategy. As pointed out by Dr Sami al-Oraidi, a top sharia official in the group in early 2014 in an interview, his group was influenced by the teachings of Abu Musab al-Suri, a Syrian jihadist and prolific writer of jihadi ideology in social media. They followed the strategies from Abu Musab's guidelines to win hearts and minds amongst local Muslim communities. It included providing services to people, avoiding being seen as extremists, and maintaining strong relationships with communities and other fighting groups. They focused on fighting the regime. But their ultimate goal was establishment of the caliphate. The group maintained that they had no intention of attacking foreign countries.

Al-Nusra Front maintains a massive propaganda campaign in the media and Internet. Their media outlet, al-Manarah al-Bayda (the White Minaret) releases their videos through the web forum Shamoukh al-Islam. Al-Nusra and ISIL compete in the border areas to absorb foreign jihadists coming to wage war in Syria. Both have an extensive network to canvass foreigners reaching Syrian borders. All new recruits undertake a ten-day religious training course to orient themselves about the organization, followed by fifteen to twenty days of a military training programme. There are hundreds of recruits from European countries, mostly from Chechnya. A number of people from the USA also worked with Al-Nusra. On one such event, an American recruit, Abu Huraira al-Amriki, carried out a suicide truck bombing at Idlib on 25 May 2014.

Al-Nusra can be regarded as an evolved new-generation Al-Qaeda outfit with direct patronage from central Al-Qaeda. Though it has a pan-national Islamic agenda, now its activity is restricted to Syria, focusing on the near enemy alone. Ideologically they are against USA and Israel and consider them as enemies, and they do not want any Western intervention in Syria. By January 2014, Nusra Front controlled about a dozen Syrian towns, carrying out government services and maintaining sharia courts. It maintains electricity services, security, and food distribution in areas they control. These areas include parts of Idlib, Aleppo, Daraa, Homs, Hama, and Damascus outskirts. It controls many border posts of Syria with Lebanon. Many citizens are unhappy about their militant Islamic ideology; some others support them in those areas. It has access to Turkish border posts and parts of the Iraq border. Though it maintained mostly a tolerant stand, in December 2013, Al-Nusra fighters kidnapped thirteen nuns from the Christian town of Maloula and took them out of the country to Lebanon. After direct intervention of Qatari Amir with the group and negotiation of Syrian and Lebanese authorities, all the hostages were released unharmed in March 2014. Upon release, the nuns expressed their gratitude to Qatar Amir. It is believed that the release was in exchange for the release of more than hundred associates of Al-Nusra front from prison. Qatar was believed to have paid one million dollars for each nun, a claim all parties denied openly. This event exposed the intolerant attitude of Al-Nusra Front and involvement of Qatar in the terror outfit. They fought with Hizbullah fighters in Syria who were supporting Assad regime. The outfit organized suicide attacks in Lebanon on Hizbullah targets and reasoned them as legitimate attacks.

Though the Syrian fighters in Al-Nusra claim no other territorial interest, there is a growing number of foreigners trained in warfare, and their return to their respective countries may pose a significant security threat. Also as long as Assad remains in power, the regime will remain their major enemy. Once their regime goes, the other rebels may have to fight with them for power. Once they have access to power, their territorial interests may change, posing a significant challenge to the neighbouring countries. There are reports that the group acquired chemical weapons when they conquered a Syrian government armoury in Aleppo. Some of their members were arrested in Turkey trying to acquire raw materials for chemical weapons. The human rights watch in June 2014 blamed them for recruiting child soldiers. Al-Nusra, with an army of about seven thousand soldiers by early 2014, is believed to have infiltrated the Syrian army, intelligence agencies, and police, probably much more than any other rebel group, making them a formidable opposition group, at least for the near future. A radical terror outfit gaining roots and stability in a volatile land like Syria may pose a significant threat to peace in other parts of the world. Their polished attitude of tolerance is more a problem than a virtue since that makes their survival more durable and invites a callous attitude towards their activity and spread, making them seem less dangerous or even acceptable to some people. That makes the threat posed by such group more dangerous, probably more than more notorious terror outfits like ISIL which make more news with their constant brutality drawing more attention and retaliation.

In a constantly changing political situation in Syria and Iraq, the grounds of Al-Nusra and other militant ideologies is constantly changing every day. Past history shows the basic tendency of militant groups to germinate from even a single left-out seed to a large violent organization controlling big swathes of land, necessitating prolonged, massive counter-insurgency operations, materials, and human cost.

In January 2014, Haji Bakr, the shadow commander of ISIL and close aide-cum-mentor of al-Baghdadi, was killed in Tal Rifat, on the outskirts of Aleppo. He was killed after fierce fighting when his home had been surrounded by Syrian Martyrs' Brigade, an associate of Free Syrian Army. After his death, his identity was confirmed by his associates; his wife and son were captured. His wife, who was sporting an automatic machine gun, was also injured. His son was a clean-shaven thirty-year-old businessman in a suit, dedicated as an envoy of ISIL, who travelled internationally. In the house they found many documents, including a reference to ISIL confiscation of fifteen truckloads of a French shipment of anti-aircraft missiles to Syrian rebels and several passports. Curiously, several articles to disguise the figure like coloured contact lenses and a half-finished bottle of Johnnie Walker whiskey were found along with his body. That was the hypocrisy of the Islamic State: the ultra-orthodox jihadi outfit that amputated people's hands for smoking or drinking and whipped people for dressing below their ankle!

Haji Bakr was a member of the secular Ba'ath party. His real name was Samir Abd Mouhammd al-Khlifawi, and he worked as a colonel of Saddam Hussein's army. After the US–UK invasion of Iraq, he was captured and sent to Camp Bucca prison, where he probably spent four years. While in jail, he met al-Baghdadi and five others who later became the top leaders in the ISIL. In the corridors of that high-security prison, a unique revenge squad was formed, one advocating orthodox jihadi Islam and the other a group of trained non-religious soldiers determined to revenge foreign powers and anti-Saddam forces in Iraq, including the Shia majority. That was a lethal combination—the power of jihadi spirit and the expertise of the Ba'ath special forces of Saddam's army!

Haji Bakr could not see the fruits of his work when his brainchild terror outfit declared an Islamic caliphate and conquered more than one-third of Syria and Iraq. But still their terror journey continues. His other military colleagues like Abu Ayman al-Iraqi are there to take the lead. It is also believed that several Syrian army and intelligence officers now work with Islamic State. In spite of being controlled by faceless men and shadow leaders to whom they force people to take the oath of loyalty, the recruits to the outfit are not drying up. It is believed that Islamic State rapidly swelled to a strength of fifty thousand fighters by August 2014 after declaring the caliphate. No matter if others call them terrorists; no matter if they are asked to kill anyone who will not accept their version of Islam and their rule. Masked men in black fatigue wielding black flags are making another wave of polarization. Moderates are becoming marginalized. Al-Nusra and FSA camps are rapidly becoming deserted to join the power and brutality of the so-called Islamic State. It is crossing borders. Iraq and Syria have borders with Turkey, Jordan, Lebanon, Saudi Arabia, and Iran. All are under threat, as the Islamic State can spread in any direction. It does not matter whether one supported them before. No matter if their country is Sunni or Shia. Terrorists don't respect borders; they have no permanent loyalty. A broad coalition is grooming against them, including world powers and all regional countries, which is going to make the story different.

CHAPTER 8

The New-Generation Al-Qaeda Ansar Al-Sharia

The Ansar Al-Sharia came out to make Dawah to the Muslims to implement the Sharia and defend it, and fought for that, and they are still on their path to liberate Palestine and all the lands of Muslims.

Sheikh Abu al-Mundhir al-Shinqiti, a senior Jihadi ideologue

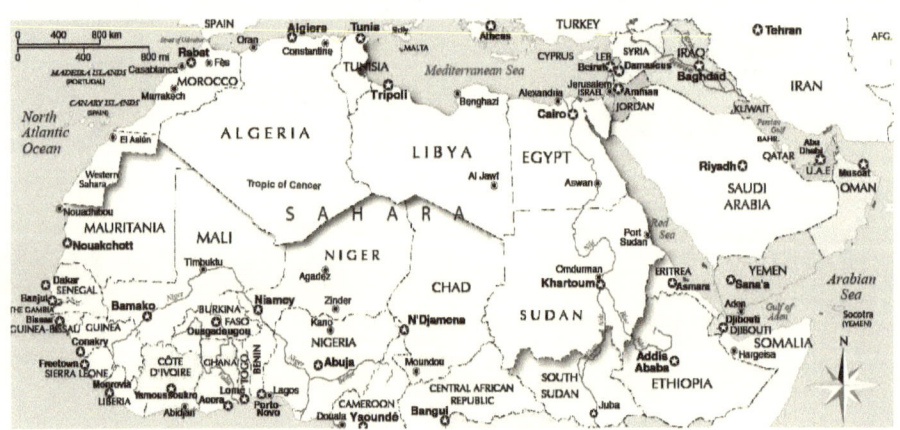

Map of North Africa

Al-Qaeda in Arabian Peninsula (AQAP) rebranded itself as Ansar al-Sharia in April 2011 following the Arab Spring and death of Osama Bin Laden. The name change was probably inspired by the advice of Bin Laden near to his death. He suggested a name change to closely reflect the affiliation to Islam, though the name did not figure in any of his possible suggestions. Ansar al-Sharia, literally translated as 'supporters of Islamic law' wanted to re-emphasize proselytation (*dawah*) to Muslims for more recruits, then carry on with their work on *hisba* and jihad with the aim to establish their own version of sharia in the Islamic world and possibly everywhere else. Though the name appeared in Yemen to call the Al-Qaeda there, soon organizations with the same name sprouted up in Egypt, Morocco, Tunisia, and Libya. Though all these organizations acted almost independently, most of their founders and senior leaders were known jihadis who fought in Afghanistan or elsewhere with a strong Al-Qaeda connection. There was no evidence to suggest that they were unified by a central command of Al-Qaeda in Pakistan. Their nature can be revealed by the fatwa of Sheikh Abu al-Mundhir al-Shinqiti, a Moroccan jihadist ideologue. He was actively engaged in jihadi propaganda, mainly through the Internet, and was the author of many dozens of fatwa advocating militancy. He released a fatwa in June 2011 asking Muslims to establish their own version of Ansar al-Sharia in their respective countries and then uniting them to a conglomerate. Even before his public advice, most of the Ansar al-Sharia groups were already established. Ansar al-Sharia in Yemen was somewhat different than other groups. It was already a well-established organization in Yemen, and it was just a name change to attract more people and divert the attention of the world from Al-Qaeda. It had already established an administrative presence in South Yemen, mainly in Abyan and Shabwan provinces, by April 2011 when the new entity was declared by Shaykh Abu Zubayr. He was AQAP's chief religious figure and claimed, 'The name Ansar al-Sharia is what we use to introduce ourselves in areas where we work to tell people about our work and goals.'

AQAP was, in fact, one of the very first active divisions of Al-Qaeda since its formation. Al-Qaeda's terrorist and military activities of the Islamic world evolved in Saudi Arabia and Yemen in the early Sudan years of Bin Laden. During these years, separate groups controlled activities in Saudi Arabia and Yemen. In January 2009, both branches officially merged together to form the AQAP. In December 2009, the USA designated Al-Qaeda in Yemen as a terrorist organization. In Saudi Arabia, Al-Qaeda organized several terrorist plots, bombings, and assassinations, including the 1996 al-Khobar Tower bombings.

Most of their activists were captured and executed there by substantially reducing their activities in Saudi Arabia. Many of them escaped into lawless Yemen, where another Al-Qaeda group was actively working with support from the ruling class.

In the 1990s, Yemen was going through separatism with fight between South Yemen and North Yemen. Al-Qaeda supported the North Yemen initiative by its long-time president, Ali Abdullah Saleh. When the rule of Saleh started losing ground, Al-Qaeda gained support, and many parts of Yemen became their strongholds. After the resignation of Saleh, Al-Qaeda mounted pitched battles against Yemeni forces, and they became a threat to the government, even at the capital, Sana'a. US forces started assisting Yemeni forces against Al-Qaeda with drone strikes. Several AQAP leaders were killed by US drone attacks. The list included Kamal Derwish, Anwar al-Awlaki (a top leader and recruiter), and Samir Khan (the editor of the English-language magazine of Al-Qaeda, *Inspire*). All three were US citizens. Several citizens from Western countries, including USA and Britain, went to Yemen to be trained and to participate in Al-Qaeda activities.

Following the 2011 Yemen revolution against the rule of Saleh during the Arab Spring, Al-Qaeda gained territories as the grip of government loosened. On 31 March 2011, AQAP declared an Islamic emirate in the southern Abyan Governorate with Zinjibar as capital. Immediately following this Ansar al-Sharia emerged in AQAP strongholds and officially declared their rebranding in April 2011. By 2012, they lost most of the territories and cities to Yemeni forces. When they withdrew from the territories, they planted thousands of mines in the territories, which later killed at least seventy-three civilians. After their withdrawal, about three thousand mines were removed from Zinjibar and Jaar. Apart from the name change, the new Al-Qaeda brand, Ansar al-Sharia Yemen (ASY), had a major facelift by being involved in services, filling the vacuum left by the government's inability or unwillingness. In a video series released by ASY through Madad News Agency, titled 'Eyes on the Events'; the organization boasted about their role in providing water, electricity, security, education, and justice. Though their law and order was based on their rigid version of sharia with little enthusiasm among people, their governance initiatives were largely popular in those lawless and neglected areas by government.

AQAP and Ansar Al-Sharia Yemen (ASY) continued as the only significant continuation of Al-Qaeda. They continued to mount regional and global terrorist activities after the central leadership of Al-Qaeda based in Pakistan became weak. In May 2012, a suicide attack on a military parade rehearsal for upcoming Yemen's Unity Day killed 120 people and injured 200 others. It was the deadliest terrorist attack in Yemen's history till then. On 5 December 2013, a series of bomb and gun battles in Sana'a targeting Yemen's Defense Ministry killed at least 56 people. Yemeni television showed footage of the attack, including on a hospital within the ministry compound, and the killing of medical personnel and patients. The AQAP chief apologized for the hospital attack and claimed they had not sanctioned the attack on hospital but that the attackers went ahead with it.

AQAP dominated the attacks against Western targets after 2001, as the central leadership was mostly on the run. In October 2000, AQAP carried out the USS *Cole* bombing in the southern port of Aden, killing seventeen US sailors, injuring thirty-nine others, and substantially damaging the vessel. It was one of the few successful major attacks on US naval vessels ever. In 2002, Al-Qaeda carried out an attack on a French supertanker, causing damage in the Gulf of Eden. In 2004, they orchestrated a Khobar massacre in Saudi Arabia, killing twenty-two and injuring twenty-five others. Most of the victims were construction workers from other countries, including eight persons from India. It was committed in the name of the Jerusalem Squadron. AQAP was associated with the Little Rock recruiting office shooting in Arkansas, USA, in June 2009. They attempted a Christmas Day bombing of Northwest Airlines Flight 253. They were also behind the crash of UPS Boeing 747-400 cargo plane in Dubai on 3 September 2010. Intelligence input foiled a plot on 29 October 2010, when two packages containing bombs were found on cargo planes with the help of UAE and British agencies. The packages originated from Yemen.

Later, AQAP claimed responsibility and threatened more such attacks on passenger flights targeting American interests and their allies.

AQAP and its new avatar, ASY, were headed by Nasir al-Wuhayshi, a close aide of Bin Laden and his secretary. He had coordinated most of the Al-Qaeda activities during the Afghan era on behalf of Bin Laden. He was the liaison of Al-Qaeda in Iraq and Pakistani Taliban leaders. Many letters of Bin Laden were addressed to him or by him. Following the US invasion of Afghanistan in 2001, he left Afghanistan and was arrested in Iran. Spending two years in Iranian prison, he was extradited to his native country, Yemen, where he was imprisoned without trial. In February 2006, he along with twenty-eight other prisoners escaped from a high-security prison in Sana, Yemen, through a three-hundred–metre-long tunnel dug in their prison compound. He became the most wanted man in Saudi Arabia and Yemen.

His letter to Bin Laden reveals his close association and obedience to Bin Laden's ideas. Some of the last letters of Bin Laden advocating the need for change in Al-Qaeda strategies and the issue of name change were probably addressed to him. He went ahead as advised by Bin Laden with a new facelift for AQAP and the emergence of ASY and other Ansar al-Sharia offshoots elsewhere in North Africa. Wuhayshi was the second in command of central Al-Qaeda after Ayman al-Zawahiri, who was designated as general manger of central Al-Qaeda and 'amir' of mujahideen in Yemen. He was on the list of terrorists facing sanctions by the UN for kidnapping and killing of tourists, aide workers, and counterterrorism officials. He was also involved in planning and organizing attacks on the US embassy and oil facilities in Yemen. Wuhayshi was ultimately killed in a US drone attack in June 2015 at Hadharamauth in Yemen. Continued war with the Yemen army and air force and constant hunting by US drones are changing the influence of Ansar al-Sharia in the impoverished, almost failing nation of Yemen.

Tunisia was mostly a secular country during the reign of Zine El Abidine Ben Ali. Many extremists were jailed, and many others went to exile to neighbouring countries. But following the 2011 Tunisian Revolution, Islamist party Ennahda came to power, which was soft on Islamists. They released most of the hard-line Islamist extremists from prisons. They tried to build a state based on Islamic sharia and persuaded the extremists to join the mainstream. One such known jihadi released was Seifallah Ben Hassine, also known as Abu Ayadh al-Tunisi. In the jail, he met many of his future associates, like Hassan Ben Brik, and started working on their future plan. Abu Ayadh was an active jihad figure who spent a long life in exile in the United Kingdom. There he met his jihadi ideologue, Abu Qatada al-Filastini, who became a mentor for Abu Ayad. Abu Qatada was an active jihadi ideologue in Europe associated with inspiring, recruiting, and organizing several terrorist plots in European countries, which were done by Al-Qaeda.

Abu Ayadh also lived in Afghanistan, and there he formed the Tunisian Combatant Group (TCG) along with Tarek Maaroufi in 2000. It took the subcontract from Osama Bin Laden to assassinate the Northern Alliance leader Ahmad Shah Massoud. He was executed in a suicide attack just a few days before 9/11 attacks by two Tunisians disguised as journalists. Abu Ayad was arrested by Turkish authorities in 2003 and was extradited to Tunisia. He was sentenced to forty-three years in prison for militant activities. Immediately following his release after the Tunisian Revolution, he formed Ansar al-Sharia in Tunisia (AST) in April 2011, along with his other jihadi jail mates. It was almost the same time as the entity was announced in Yemen. In April 2011, they organized the first national conference of AST with a few hundred participants. During the next year's conference in May 2012 at Kairouan, the participants reached about four thousand to ten thousand activists, which was their largest public demonstration of strength. They continued to grow, but the government banned their third annular conference on May 2013. By this time, they had apparently reached an activist strength of ten thousand with about one hundred thousand sympathizers and controlled about four hundred mosques in Tunisia.

Unlike previous Al-Qaeda groups, this group followed a more cautious approach, probably following the advice of the Jordanian cleric Sheik Muhammed al-Maqdisi for 'pure jihad'. He advocated focusing on *qital al-takmin* (fighting to consolidate one's power) rather than *qital al-nikayya* (fighting to hurt or damage the enemy). The later would give only short-term tactical victories, whereas the former would provide a long-term base, making a framework for consolidating an Islamic state. Al-Qaeda's morale in Islamic world was deeply shattered following the heavy atrocities committed by Al-Qaeda in Iraq under Zarqawi, his followers, and Taliban in Afghanistan. Al-Qaeda's appeal was further shattered after the Arab Spring, which proved a welfare state in the Islamic world could be created by mass agitation using democratic means, which was a major blow to violent jihadi ideology. At this critical juncture, Al-Qaeda and affiliated groups changed their strategy.

They went for drastic name changes, concentrated on needs of the population, tried to provide services, and provided administrative support in their areas of influence, ideas with which they had not been familiar before. These changes happened with Al-Shabab in Somalia, AQAP in Yemen, Tunisia, and other parts of Africa. This strategy enabled them to exist in areas with law and order and find a support base without drawing undue attention from the government or alienation by the people. With the deep aspiration of violent means in mind, they went with a triple strategy of *dawa, hisba*, and jihad.

Immediately after the formation of AST, it went for new recruits, doing *dawa* or preaching about Islam, sharia, and the need for an Islamic society. Holding *dawa* events at markets, universities, mosques and public places made their presence felt. They organized public protests on issues of public interest and organized debates, discussions, and membership drives. Since the organization was not banned and was not involved in any illegal activities initially, they got some audience among young students and religiously inclined people. Along with this, they started organizing social services by distributing food, clothes, and medicines for the needy people. Weekly caravans of AST with large-supply materials were common in many areas of Tunisia, which gained public attention and interest.

But the overall number of Salafi ideologues in Tunisia was less than ten thousand and Salafi jihadis less than four thousand at any time. When the Syrian uprising began, many campus groups started campaigns to support the Syrian rebels. Many AST activists, about four hundred to eight hundred by estimate, went to Syria to participating in the war. The government recognized jihadis getting trained in Syria and coming back as future threats with extremism. They went for a crackdown on potential jihadi migrants, preventing about eight thousand youngsters from travelling to Syria and conflict zones. Though AST used to collect money from local population, a substantial amount might have come from abroad. AST openly acknowledged the medical assistance from Kuwait-based charity RIHS (Revival of Islamic Heritage Society), which the US treasury department alleged to have supplied money and material support for Al-Qaeda and their affiliated organizations in the past. Most of their literature materials for *dawa* events originated from Salafi publishers from Saudi Arabia.

Hisba is a general Arabic term for 'forbidding wrong', a concept from the Quran itself. But for groups like AST, *hisba* necessitates violence and is directed against Muslims, in contrast to jihad, which is against non-believers. Particularly for AST, *hisba* is Salafist vigilantism in a Tunisian context. Much of the Salafi vigilantism in Tunisia can be attributed to AST, but some may be perpetrated by others. But apart from a few public figures of AST involved in service activities, many of their activists were involved in clandestine activities and rarely came into the public face. So their involvement need not be open. Tunisia was one of the most liberal societies in the Arab world. After the revolution, more and more women were compelled to wear hijab, fearing social pressure and harassment. Violence against women, prostitutes, and anyone wearing modern dress became frequent. In October 2011, a theatre screening of a film, *Necropolis*, was attacked by a mob followed by a violent attack on the theatre owner in spite of his public apology. The conservative Muslims found a scene in the movie depicting God as blasphemous and went for a violent attack. Later, a court imposed a fine for screening the movie for 'disturbing public order and attacking moral values' rather than curbing the violent reaction. Salafists insulted many imams on several occasions, accusing them of collaborating with the old regime. This eventually led to a Salafist takeover of more than four hundred mosques. About thirty-five Sufi shrines were attacked in 2013. There were incidents of attacks on Christians and churches. In September 2011, Salafists in the city of El Kef occupied a Christian basilica to turn it to a mosque. Several attacks on universities, colleges, and schools by conservative Salafists trying to impose strict niqab covering the face created tension with secular students and teachers. There were several violent attacks on hotels and bars throughout Tunisia. Several secular activists and trade union leaders were attacked, threatened, or even killed. Police were largely inactive against the culprits, as they were threatened personally or due to the threat of widespread violence. Such vigilantism resulted in death of two prominent Tunisian politicians, Chokri Belaid (in February 2013) and Mohamed Brahmi (in July 2013), which caused a widespread outburst against extremists, including AST.

Though AST claims that at present they do not support jihad in Tunisia, they are not averse to jihad abroad. They actively participated in Syrian war, though their leaders resisted a mass exodus of their activists from Tunisia to concentrate on activities there. Most of those fighters reached ISIL, and some were recruited to Al-Nusra Front and other opposition groups. AQIM (Al-Qaeda in Islamic Maghreb) was directly affiliated with ISIL from the Zarqawi era and not with the central Al-Qaeda. When Islamic extremists took over parts of Mali, fighters from AST participated in it as done by AQIM cadres. Their commitments to jihad in the future were reinforced by the fact that many activists were arms-trained and they stocked arms and ammunition. ATS, through social media, organized a protest in front of the US embassy in Tunis against the film *Innocence of Muslims*. Many Islamists joined the protest, thinking it was peaceful. But AST went ahead with a violent attack on the embassy, setting it on fire, prompting the departure of all non-essential US embassy staff from Tunisia. They also set fire on a nearby American school. These incidences resulted in four deaths and the injuries of forty-five people.

The strength of Al-Qaeda was tested in the agitation against this film worldwide, with many protests turning violent, causing several casualties. About sixty-five countries were affected; many of them were organized by known Islamic groups in those countries with no recognized Al-Qaeda connection, as in India, Sri Lanka, Japan, Singapore, Hong Kong, etc. In India, Tamilnadu Muslim Munnetta Kazhagam organized a massive rally of hundreds of workers in front of the US embassy at Chennai. The protesters turned violent, causing widespread destruction of the building and disruption of embassy work. This widespread agitation against a simply negligible and unimportant amateur film with little professional value or substance and watched by a select few was strange and unprecedented. Almost all those agitated had never watched that movie, and many of them had probably not even seen any YouTube video in their life. Many governments did not recognize the selected timing after September 11, selective targeting of US interests, organized nature throughout the world, and possible Al-Qaeda connections. Rather than dubbing it just as a spontaneous response of Muslims against an insult to their prophet, a thorough scrutiny into the source and organizers of those agitations might have saved them from similar future violent agitations on namesake issues and a hidden Al-Qaeda nexus in those countries.

Illegal arms smuggling into Tunisia often resulted in a violent confrontation with security forces at borders, mainly on Algerian borders. In early 2013, Al-Qaeda of Islamic Maghreb (AQIM), based mostly in Algeria, declared their association with AST. On 27 March 2013, Abu Ayadh threatened to overthrow the Tunisian government if it interfered with the activities of AST. Another Tunisian organization connected to AQIM and AST called Okba Ibn Nafaa Brigade attacked army posts with RPG and assault rifles near Algerian border in May 2013, killing fourteen Tunisian soldiers. A group of thirty terrorists, who were partly from Algeria and the rest from Tunisia, was behind the attack. The militants made the mountainous area close to Algeria into training camps and military headquarters with a large ammunition warehouse. There was a report of a merger of AST and the Brigade in early 2014, orchestrated by AQIM. In May 2013, Prime Minister Ali Larayedh officially declared AST an illegal organization and linked it to terrorism.

Abu Ayadh declared that acting against AST will prompt the youth to defend Islam as what had happened in Afghanistan, Chechnya, Iraq, Somalia, and Syria. Ayman al-Zawahiri released a video during this time and blasted the Tunisian government for purported anti-Islamic activities, thus endorsing and supporting the AST. Many jihadi supporters of AST asked them to restrain in that situation of Tunisia until it gained wider support. Various degrees of cooperation exist between AQIM and other Ansar al-Sharia organizations, especially in Libya. The threat posed by these radical elements, though small, can cause security and administrative issues in a nascent democracy like Tunisia, though the possibility of threatening the very existence of the state may be very remote. Developments in Libya can influence the security and politics of Tunisia due to active Ansar al-Sharia groups in both of these countries, their porous borders, and socio-cultural interaction of both countries. Tunisian society started responding to such radicals, and their influence in the public sphere is decreasing, but these can make them more viral as what happened with the Islamic State of Iraq.

Libya was gradually transforming from a ruthless dictatorship to a primitive democracy. It was struggling to cope up with fatally broken police, army, and security apparatus, torn down by dozens of militia and armed extremists controlling the streets and villages. In this fertile ground for Islamic extremism, a number of groups use the name Ansar al-Sharia. Two of the more prominent groups are Katibat Ansar al-Sharia in Benghazi (ASB) and the more elusive Ansar al-Sharia in Derna (ASD), led by former Guantanamo Bay inmate Abu Sufian bin Qumu. Both groups were independent and were established after the death of former Libyan leader Muammar al-Qaddafi. The formation of ASB was first announced in February 2012, led by Muhammad al-Zahawi, who was imprisoned in the infamous Abu Salim prison of Gaddafi.

ASB hosted the first annual conference in June 2012, with about one thousand attendees. A number of people were from other smaller militias; all joined for the meeting calling to implement sharia. Like Ansar al-Sharia in Tunisia, ASB has been providing local services like maintaining roads, providing aid during Ramadan, and providing security at key installations like hospitals in Benghazi. Though they were not averse to promoting their aggressive religious ideology, destroying shrines and tombs, they were also involved in some service activities in situations where the government was practically a nonentity. The first major military demonstration by the group was organized on 7 June 2012, when they organized a rally of as many as two hundred pickup trucks mounted with artillery and other weapons along Benghazi's Tahrir Square, demanding imposition of sharia law. The *New York Times* commented, 'Western diplomats who watched said they were stunned by the scale and weaponry on the display.'

On the evening of 11 September 2012, a group of about one hundred men attacked the American diplomatic compound in Benghazi, killing US ambassador J. Christopher Stevens and US Foreign Service information management officer Sean Smith. A few hours later, a second assault on another location a mile away killed two CIA contractors and injured ten others. Persons who witnessed the event saw that vehicles involved in the embassy carried the Ansar al-Sharia logo, and their activists claimed their affiliation with the ASB to local people. ASB commander Ahmed Abu Khattala was found to be leading the attack. US delta forces arrested him on 15 June 2014 on a raid in Libya, and he was taken to the USA for trial. ASB claimed they were not solely responsible for the events but that it was a spontaneous reaction against the film *Innocence of Muslims*. These attacks provoked massive public rallies against extremists, and they attacked their compounds and militia headquarters on 21 September 2012, confiscating arms. Eventually, the militants were expelled from the city the next day. By March 2013, the group returned back to

Benghazi. They started patrolling hospitals, manning check posts, and providing humanitarian services to residents.

Another group established Ansar al-Sharia in Derna after the 2011 revolution under Abu Sufian bin Qumu, a former Guantanamo Bay detainee. The group disbanded their activities following the September 12 Benghazi US embassy attacks. It re-emerged as a branch of Ansar al-Sharia Benghazi in late 2013 with the slogan 'A step toward building the Islamic state'. The ASB also has a presence in other Libyan cities like Ajdabiya and Sirte.

With the re-entry of Ansar al-Sharia in Benghazi, the already fragile security situation became worse. The government was trying to disarm the militia formed during the revolution, but Ansar al-Sharia refused. On November 2013, a major clash broke out between Ansar fighters and the army, killing at least nine and injuring forty-seven people. Army declared a 'state of alert' in Benghazi and called all troops to report for duty. On 11 January 2014, deputy industry minister of transition government Hassan al-Droui was shot dead by unknown assailants in Sirte, his home town. This was the first assassination of a minister in the newly formed government. The Libyan Parliament had been attacked many times in the past by militants. On 10 October, 2013, Prime Minister Ali Zeidan was kidnapped by gunmen from a Tripoli hotel and released many hours later. The security situation in Libya worsened further in early 2014, with criminal gangs roaming freely in major cities like Tripoli and Benghazi with no effective national police or security forces on ground.

On 17 May 2014, a former army major general, Khalifa Haftar, emerged with support from many army factions and tribal leaders. Fighting broke out in Benghazi, resulting in the death of twenty-four people and injury of ninety others. Haftar vowed to quash all rebels of Ansar al-Sharia from Benghazi and Libya. The initiative got a mixed response, as a large number of people were fed up with the worsening security situation at the hands of criminals and extremists and were convinced the government inaction supported the move. But the government maintained that he and his group had no authority to impose any military action.

Ansar al-Sharia is also active in Egypt, Morocco (as Ansar al-Sharia of Islamic Maghreb), Mali, and Mauritania. They are, at present, mostly engaged in *dawa* work and recruiting supporters. Local versions of Al-Qaeda have been a trend of the last two decades. In Mali, over a period of months, an Al-Qaeda–linked organization called Ansar al-Dine (Helpers of Islamic religion) captured a large part of Northern Mali and declared it an emirate. They started implementing their version of sharia with brutal punishments like flogging and amputation in 2012. Later, a French intervention expelled the rebels, and they were mostly chased and many were killed in remote desert areas of Sahara. In Nigeria, a group with Al-Qaeda inspiration called Boko Haram (Western education forbidden) carried out widespread attacks on security forces and frequent raids in villages and towns. They also engaged in destruction of schools and abduction of schoolgirls and took them captive, causing a worldwide outrage. Al-Shabab militants in Somalia already affiliated with Al-Qaeda control a vast area of Somalia, including the most fertile areas of Somalia. Almost all countries in North Africa have rebels under different names, many with Al-Qaeda links.

With a wide number of organizations riddled with frequent name changes, strategic dismantling, regrouping, and increased geographical control in difficult terrains or lawless areas of the world, Al-Qaeda is becoming more complex. They have transformed from urban Islamists to rebel militia controlling lands. The fight against new-generation al-Qaeda is an increasingly difficult and dangerous affair. In spite of constant chases, hunts, sanctions, and political mobilizations, newer and newer territories are falling under the grip of Al-Qaeda. When one group becomes weak, another emerges in some other part, making the fight like chasing a mirage. Many countries that are in the forefront of fighting terrorism are already tired because of growing frustration and the spread of violence from territory to territory. All this needs deeper and more consistent understanding of the catastrophe of the ideology of hatred becoming an uncontrollable chain reaction! All this indicates pitfalls in assessing conflicts and arresting their spread.

CHAPTER 9

Anatomy of Terrorist Breeding Grounds

We believe it would be a fatal mistake to commit ground troops . . . If our troops went in, the situation in your country would not improve. On the contrary, it would get worse. Our troops would have to struggle not only with external aggressor, but with a significant part of your own people. And the people would never forgive such things.

Alexei Kosygin, the chairman of the USSR Council of Ministers in response to Afghan President Nur Muhammad Taraki's request for Soviet presence in Afghanistan to support his administration in 1979

Map of Western Pakistan and Afghanistan

It is common knowledge that two major events shaped the rise of Islamic fundamentalism and jihadi terrorism in the world. One was the rise of Israel with marginalization of Palestinians and their plight from their territories. The other was Soviet invasion of Afghanistan and the ensuing Afghan war. All major Al-Qaeda leaders were veterans of Afghan jihad. Either they directly participated or were trained during or shortly after the Afghan mujahedeen's fight with Soviet forces from 1979 to 1989. Were the Soviets such ruthless invaders in a Muslim country, shattering the dreams and destinies of their countrymen? Did the response to Soviet invasion in Afghanistan need such a massive response from a host of about fifty countries in the world? It resulted in the deaths of about 1.5 million Afghan civilians, close to 100,000 mujahideen deaths, and about 15,000 deaths of Soviet forces and civilians. Millions incurred injuries, including loss of limbs, vision, and hearing. About 5 million Afghans were forced to leave their country; many of them could never return to their homes. An entire country, reasonably prosperous, was ravaged, with no livelihood, deserted farmlands, ruined factories, roads, and homes. A large number of people were left struggling for survival, ready to engage in anything from looting, robbing, smuggling, to killing. Shattered families and orphans were plenty and also people with serious psychological trauma and mental illness. No place was really safe. Criminals roamed in the streets. Land everywhere was so treacherous, with millions of mines making farming, walking, and digging on any unexplored area dangerous. That was the Afghanistan when Soviets left. There was no viable government on the horizon. The fight was still going on between different mujahedeen factions those who were mostly united against Soviets till then were fighting for their pie when their Russian enemies left.

For the rest of the world, things were not anything great too. Common people trained in arms and ammunitions fought in Afghanistan and returned to their native countries finding an entire world had changed around them. Some started terrorist groups, some became gangsters or criminals, and many went back, looking for their jihadi friends fighting in other conflict zones of the world. The Afghan mujahideen volunteers were not just from a few isolated countries. They were mobilized from far and wide—from America to Indonesia or the Philippines, from Russia to Mauritius. In countries in the crossroads to Afghanistan, as in Pakistan, the entire sociocultural-political atmosphere changed, changed forever. Campuses witnessed extremism and violent student clashes, with veteran boys of the Afghan war fighting with their fellow students with AK-47 machine guns and time bombs. Many cities close to Afghanistan were flooded with drugs and weapons in mushrooming illegal bazaars, ready to sell to any buyer from any part of the world. Was all this preventable? Did these history lessons of Cold War politics change the world in terms of undue indulgence in internal problems of other sovereign countries?

In 1973, Mohammed Daoud Khan, a former prime minister of Afghanistan, staged a bloodless coup d'état against the long-reigning king of Afghanistan, Zahir Shah, while he was undergoing treatment in Italy. Daoud Khan, a first cousin of King Zahir Shah who was married to the sister of Shah, was forced to resign by him a decade earlier from his prime minister post. He had held the post from 1954 to 1963. In 1933, Zahir Shah became the king of Afghanistan when he was nineteen years old, after his father's assassination. He ruled the country for four decades. The Republic of Afghanistan was established by Daoud Khan with help from the Afghan army, and he became its first president. He alleged corruption and poor economic conditions against the king's government. He was supported by a growing but still small communist party, People's Democratic Party of Afghanistan (PDPA), which had close ties to the Soviet Union. After the coup, the loya jirga, a traditional Afghan tribal elders' body, approved Daoud's new constitution. Thus, he established a presidential one-party system of government in January 1977 with only his newly established National Revolutionary Party as only official party. The new constitution alienated Daoud from many of his political allies, including PDPA. Daoud Khan introduced many reforms in Afghanistan which were largely popular. He was secular and known for his stand on equality and education of women. He became close to the United States and other Western countries and was not very inclined to the

Soviet Union, the traditional main backer of Afghanistan. He improved relations with emerging oil powers like Saudi Arabia, Kuwait, Iraq, and Iran in addition to India and Egypt. Under an arrangement with Egypt, the Afghan army and military started getting training from Egypt. Egypt was a very close ally of USSR, which had supported them heavily before like Afghanistan. They were then becoming more pro with US and Israel. All this worried the Soviet Union, which by this time had several interests in Afghanistan, and they feared the United States would eventually control Afghanistan. The relations worsened after the visit of Daoud to Moscow in 1977 where he bluntly stated to the Russian leader Leonid Brezhnev that Afghanistan would remain free from Russian control and never allow Russia to dictate terms.

During his early prime ministership under King Zahir Shah, Daoud revived Pashtun nationalism and tried to integrate Pashtun areas in Pakistan with Afghanistan. With the formation of independent Pakistan separated by an arbitrarily drawn Durand line with Afghanistan, the conflict turned to extremism. Daoud, who was also minister of defense under King Zahir Shah, supported the armed militia along the Durand line. Finally, this resulted in Pakistan closing the borders with Afghanistan, causing economic crisis and dependency on USSR. Shortly, USSR became the major trading partner. They sent a large contingent of arms, including fighter planes and tanks at a heavy discount. In 1962, Daoud sent his army to participate in an armed struggle in the Bejaur region of Pakistan to rake up the Pashtunistan issue, which escalated tension with Pakistan. This was settled only with his forced resignation by the king in 1963. When Daoud became the sole ruler of Afghanistan as the president, he again raised the Pashtunistan issue and started a proxy war with Pakistan in 1976. This created worsening relations with Pakistan, including trade and transit agreements with the landlocked Afghanistan. Pakistan retaliated by supporting the Islamic fundamentalist movement in Afghanistan, which soon became a problem in Afghanistan. Daoud could suppress the militant struggle to overthrow his government. This was under the Jamiat Islami party. Many of their leaders went to refuge in Pakistan;

where they got support from Prime Minister Zulfiqar Ali Bhutto, who encouraged them to fight against Daoud.

On 17 April 1978, Mir Akbar Khyber, a prominent Afghan intellectual and a leader of PDPA, was assassinated outside his home. Nur Mohammad Taraki of the PDPA blamed the government as behind the killing, a belief much of the Kabul intelligentsia shared. The Daoud regime put the blame for Kyber's death on Hekmatyar's Hezbi Islami. Conflicting claims were there on the perpetrators, including rival PDPA faction leader Hafizullah Amin. His death provoked massive agitation. On April 19, about fifteen thousand PDPA sympathizers gathered in Kabul for his funeral. They paraded through the streets shouting slogans against the CIA and the SAVAK, Iran's secret police. Alarmed by this reviving communist strength, Daoud ordered an immediate crackdown on the PDPA leadership. Most of the top leaders were arrested by April 26. Hafizullah Amin was not imprisoned immediately but was put on house arrest. That gave him time to order his followers in the army to launch a military coup that became known as the Saur (referring to Taurus, star of the second month in the Pashtun calendar) Revolution. Started in the afternoon of April 27, PDPA-loyal army units took complete control of the country from a few forces and presidential guards loyal to Daoud. The presidential palace was attacked by aerial rocket strikes. After midnight of April 28, armed forces surrounded the palace and asked all to surrender. Daoud and his brother Naim, instead of surrendering, came out with pistols in hand and charged at the soldiers. They were shot and killed. Subsequently, most of his family members and many of his associates were executed in the palace. Instead of announcing his death, the new government declared that President Daoud had 'resigned for health reasons'.

His body, along with those of sixteen members of his family, was excavated after three decades in June 2008 from an Afghan army compound in two separate mass graves in the Pul-e-Charkhi area by a specially appointed commission for the purpose. His body was positively identified from his dental mould, and there was a small golden Quran along with his remains. The Quran had been a gift by the king of Saudi Arabia. On 17 March 2009, Daoud was given a state funeral attended by Afghan president Hamid Karzhai, some of his associates, family members, and army officers. The Taliban offered no attack on the area during the ceremony to mark respect for him. Immediately following the coup, the army leader of the coup took control of the country for the next three days, followed by formation of the new rule under Nur Muhammad Taraki. They renamed the country Democratic Republic of Afghanistan (DRA).

Taraki and his successive Marxist PDPA governments started implementing a variety of socialist, pro-poor radical reforms. Taraki's government initiated a land reform on 1 January 1979 which attempted to limit the amount of land a family could own. The rest above the limit was taken by the government without compensation and distributed to landless people. They abolished the traditional usury by local landlords who used to lend money at exorbitant interest rates to poor farmers. But it had been the backbone of countryside agriculture. The Afghan leadership believed all these reforms would gain popular support and weaken feudalism. But the reforms were met with stiff resistance. Contrary to expectation, agricultural production reduced substantially and traditional farming became difficult. So the reforms were put on hold in the middle for a while. More than these economic reforms, many radical social reforms started, including equal rights for women, encouraging women in politics, a drive for universal education, and abolition of forced marriage of women. All these were perceived as anti-Islamic. It had been a conservative society for centuries with deeply entrenched local power structures which were unaffected by any central government. Laws overtly people-friendly, including the usury law—though usury is forbidden in Islam too—were perceived as anti-Islamic acts of communists. Social unrest spread in the country, and a large part of country became outside the grip of government, heralding the beginning of civil war. Afghanistan was a landlocked country with a strong traditional tribal culture of a feudal background. About 4 %per cent of rich people owned most of the land in large parcels, and the rest worked under them as laborers. The feudal landlords not only owned farmlands and wealth but also maintained arms and small armed groups for maintaining control over the locals and settling feuds with other landlords.

From the era of Russian tsars, Afghanistan had maintained a long relationship with Russia, which became more reinforced after the formation of the Soviet Union. The Soviet Union spent billions of dollars equivalents in economic and military aid to Afghanistan between 1955 and 1978. Soviet influence was far-reaching in Afghanistan, with most people in Afghanistan knowing the Russian language by 1978. The Soviets maintained good relations with all sections of ruling class, including King, Daoud and the communists. They heavily invested in Afghan infrastructure, including roads, power plants, hospitals, schools, and civil structures. There were substantial investments in the education system in Afghanistan. Many Afghan universities and technical institutions were built and maintained by Russians, including Kabul University. A large number of Russian faculties taught in these institutes, and many Soviet experts advised Afghanistan at various levels. A treaty signed in December 1978 by Taraki with Russia allowed the PDPA to call upon the Soviet Union for military support for the next twenty years. During the unrest, Taraki sent several requests for overt Soviet military assistance, which Russians denied, especially Alexei Kosygin, the chairman of the USSR Council of Ministers. He feared it would be a tactical blunder to overtly send Russian soldiers to Afghanistan. Following Kosygin's refusal, Taraki contacted Brezhnev, head of the Soviet state, who warned Taraki that a full Soviet intervention 'would only play into the hands of our enemies—both yours and ours' and asked him to go slow on reforms and ease tensions. Taraki met Brezhnev again in March 1979 following a massive rebel uprising in Herat under Ismail Khan, resulting in death of three thousand to five thousand people. About one hundred Soviet citizens and their family members were also killed. This time, he secured assistance of deployment of two armed divisions along the Afghan–Soviet border, sending five hundred military and civil advisers and an arm shipment at reduced price. Soviets continued to maintain a distance from Afghan affairs in spite of a series of requests.

Though initially all the major communist factions were united and shared government responsibility, relations soured soon. Taraki, who maintained posts of both president and party general secretary, marginalized all other leaders. Most senior PDPA leaders other than Hafizullah Amin were living abroad, fearing for their lives at the hands of Taraki. In the initial months after the revolution, Hafizullah Amin and Taraki had a very close relationship. Taraki used to remark, 'Amin and I are like nail and flesh, not separable,' and Amin tried to create a personality cult centred on Taraki, calling him openly the Great Leader or the Star of the East, while Amin was given such titles as the True Disciple and Student. Amin would later come to realize he had created a monster out of Taraki who became overconfident and believed in his own brilliance. Taraki began avoiding the suggestions of Amin, who was controlling the Afghan army, which had many PDPA members and supporters and about half of its officers were trained in Soviet academies. As their relationship turned increasingly sour, a power struggle developed between them for the control of the Afghan Army. Their relations worsened later that year when Taraki accused Amin of nepotism after Amin had appointed several family members to high-ranking positions. Taraki tried to consolidate his power, giving wide powers and influence to a group of four power-hungry army officers, including Assadullah Sarwari, known as the Gang of Four. While Taraki was on a foreign trip to Cuba the Gang of Four falsely informed him of an intelligence report that Amin was planning to arrest or kill him. In retaliation, he ordered to execute Amin. They selected Sarwari's nephew to assassinate Amin. But not realizing the plot and its secret nature, Sarwari informed the Russian embassy. Due to timely information from the Russian embassy, Amin saved his life.

On his arrival from the foreign visit Taraki's flight was purposefully delayed from landing to show the influence of Amin. On arrival, Taraki tried to neutralize Amin and advised Amin to take an ambassador post abroad. Amin refused and told him, 'You are the one who should quit! Because of alcohol and old age you lost your senses.' Taraki invited Amin to have a lunch the next day along with his Gang of Four.

Amin refused and told them he would like to have their resignation, not have lunch with them. Then the Soviet ambassador, who was close to Taraki and was against the influence of Amin, managed to persuade him to visit the presidential palace along with his two confidants, Sayed Daoud Tarun, the chief of police, and Nawab Ali, an intelligence officer. Upon his arrival at the palace, unknown gunmen from the building opened fire on them, killing Tarun. Ali sustained an injury but escaped with an unharmed Amin. Shortly afterwards, Amin returned to the palace with a contingent of army officers and placed Taraki under arrest. After Taraki's arrest, Amin discussed the incident with Leonid Brezhnev and asked what to do with Taraki. Brezhnev replied that it was his choice. Amin, realizing the support of the Soviets, ordered the death of Taraki. Taraki was subsequently suffocated with pillows by two army officers. The Afghan media reported that an ailing Taraki had died with no mention of his murder. That marked the beginning of the 104 days of Amin's rule.

Amin tried initially to project himself as moderate and claimed the end of Taraki's one-man government. He tried to pacify the agitated population and blamed Taraki for high-handedness. He released a list of about 18,000 people who had been executed before by the Taraki regime. But detention and torture of agitated people continued. It is believed that 10,000–27,000 people were executed during PDPA regime till the end of Amin's rule, mostly at the Pul-e-Charkhi prison. This included about four hundred army officers. Amin's rule was widely unpopular, and most of Afghanistan became outside his control. Mass desertion of Afghan army men caused an army reduced to about fifty thousand to seventy thousand at the end of his rule from one hundred thousand at the beginning of PDPA rule. His political opponents went into exile and demanded his removal. By this time, PDPA was heavily infiltrated by Russian intelligence, KGB. A special politburo on Afghanistan argued to end the impression that the Soviet government supported Amin's rule and policies. Brezhnev was convinced by his colleagues that Amin's policies had destroyed the military and government's capability to handle the crisis. Also, a small force had to be deployed to expel Amin from power and replace him with Babrak Karmal, a senior PDPA leader. The Soviet Union declared their plan to intervene in Afghanistan on 12 December 1979 and initiated Operation Storm-333. Amin was informed of the Soviet invasion, and on his behalf, his brother discussed the plan and route of invasion with senior Russian military officers. Amin was confident that Russia would only support his rule, but for Russians, he was a probable CIA agent. Soviet forces quickly invaded the Afghan capital starting on December 25, taking control of all key installations by December 27. Amin was killed by Soviet forces on 27 December 1979 at his presidential palace as part of the pre-planned operation.

On 27 December, Kabul radio-broadcasted Karmal's pre-recorded speech in which he said, 'Today the torture machine of Amin has been smashed, his accomplices—the primitive executioners, usurpers and murderers of tens of thousands of our fellow countrymen—fathers, mothers, sisters, brothers, sons and daughters, children and old people . . .'' At the same time, Soviet military command announced on Radio Kabul that Afghanistan had been liberated from Amin's rule. Soviet Politburo claimed that they were complying with the 1978 Treaty of Friendship, Cooperation, and Good Neighborliness and that Amin had been 'executed by a tribunal for his crimes' by the Afghan Revolutionary Central Committee. That committee then elected Deputy Prime Minister Babrak Karmal as the head. On January 1, Leonid Brezhnev and his senior party colleagues congratulated Karmal on his 'election' as leader. It was before any Afghan state or party organ elected him to any such post. When Karmal came to power, he promised an end of executions and the establishment of democratic institutions. He also promised a free election, a new constitution respecting individual and personal property. But most Afghans did not trust his government. The Soviet invasion, rather than quell the agitation, made it more widespread. Unrest spread to twenty-six of twenty-eight provinces of Afghanistan eventually forcing Russians to deploy heavily throughout Afghanistan with a troop level of two hundred thousand. Most of the Afghan army soldiers and officers left the army, and many joined the rebels.

Contrary to the expectation of communists and Russians, the presence of Soviet troops did not reduce the unrest. In fact, it exacerbated nationalistic feelings, causing the rebellion to spread further. The new Soviet proxy Afghanistan president, Babrak Karmal, blamed the Soviets for causing an increase in the unrest. He demanded that the 40th Army step in and quell the rebellion, as his own army had proved unreliable. Gradually, Soviet troops were dragged into fighting against urban rebel uprisings, engaging with tribal armies, and even mutinying Afghan army units. Initially these forces fought openly, forming easy targets for Soviet artillery and air power. But soon the conflict turned into a prolonged guerrilla war by small groups of fighters who called themselves mujahideen. Soviet troops controlled major urban centres and tactical locations. Thus a prolonged war against the ruling communist government and supporting Soviet forces ensued, which lasted about a decade.

In 1987, the rule of Karmal was replaced by former KHAD (Afghan secret police) chief and then PDPA general secretary Mohammed Najibullah, who ruled Afghanistan till 1992. In 1991, with the dissolution of the Soviet Union all his external support from Russia stopped. Soon his government collapsed. He took refuge in UN headquarters in Kabul during the takeover of Kabul by mujahideen in 1992 till 1996. He was offered asylum by India many times, but he refused, even during the Taliban advance, as he expected leniency from them, being a Pashtun himself. In 1996, the invading Taliban brutally executed him and hanged his body on a light post for public view, causing worldwide condemnation. Najibullah initiated a series of measures to end the civil war and introduced a new constitution in 1990 declaring Afghanistan an Islamic state. All references to communism were removed. He changed the name of PDPA to al-Watan party (Homeland party). But none of these measures really stalled the ongoing civil war. Even after the Russians left Afghanistan in 1989, they supported the Najibullah regime financially and militarily. At the same time, the USA was continuing to support mujahideen.

Mujahideen casualties were very heavy, but thousands of new recruits joined every day. KHAD forces tried tactics to spread rivalry among groups, often resulting in infighting between mujahideen groups rather than fighting with the Afghan army. But mujahideen soldiers also got recruited in the Afghan army and KHAD militias. They gained training, weapons, and information about forthcoming attacks and then used to desert their groups. With the massive supply of stinger missiles by the USA, the tide against Russian air power came to a halt, resulting in heavy Russian Air Force casualties. Russia lost more than five hundred aircrafts and thousands of their soldiers. After a heavy loss and no visible improvement in the Afghan situation, a worldwide condemnation against the war mounted. Also, there was loss of interest among the Russian population for a war in a foreign land. The last Soviet leader, Mikhail Gorbachev, ordered the Russian troops' withdrawal. It started on 15 May 1988 and ended on 15 February 1989 under a mutually agreed deal between Russia and mujahideen fighters, ensuring the safety of withdrawing army men along the route.

Americans tried to get involved in the bloody game of Afghanistan to bleed their Cold War rival, USSR. US relations with Russians and the Afghan government soured after the death of the US ambassador to Afghanistan. On 14 February 1979, a group of four men belonged to the Maoist group called the Settam-e-Melli group, which was previously part of PDPA, kidnapped Adolph Dubs, the United States ambassador to Afghanistan, and he was killed in crossfire when Afghan police, under guidance from Russian agents, stormed the hotel room where he was kept as a hostage waiting for a negotiation. After his death, the USA removed most of the non-essential staff from the US embassy, and no new ambassador was appointed. After the occupation of Afghanistan, the USA swung into action with the CIA in the forefront. The result was a supply of billions of dollars in arms to the Afghan mujahideen, one of the CIA's most expensive and longest covert operations ever, named Operation Cyclone.

This idea of recruiting and arming a large number of fighters and worldwide campaigns to gather volunteers for fighting in a foreign land was a new concept. Inflating religious passion against purported atheists and disregarding and misjudging the impact of massive mobilization of a large number of people with a perverted idea of religious war by agencies not anywhere related to the cause was one of the biggest political blunders of modern times. The impacts of which crippled the world far more than all those countries involved in the conflict. The ensuing war ruined Afghanistan, bled USSR, and might have significantly contributed to its demise in 1991. All the countries who supported the war with over enthusiasm also suffered heavily. A new wave of terrorism gained root in those countries, including the USA, Saudi Arabia, Pakistan, Egypt, China, and to an extent, the UK and other European countries. It also spread wide to many parts of Asia, including India, Indonesia, the Philippines, and most countries of north-west Africa.

All essential ingredients for breeding terrorism, like an area of lawlessness, the lack of economic opportunities with poverty and unemployment, a perceived sense of persecution, an ideological renaissance, and a constant support base with money and weapons were amply available in Afghanistan that time. For religious terrorism, this means a feeling of religious persecution and groups or ideas promoting religious awakening with an element of animosity for another sect, another religion, or another secular establishment. After the Soviet occupation and their withdrawal, Afghanistan was such a perfect medium with all these ingredients. Almost all areas of Afghanistan were lawless, with no effective government, police, national army, or judiciary. All normal economic activities stopped. Most of the farmlands became arid and dangerous with millions of mines planted all around, estimated to be about ten to fifteen million, which needed thousands of years to dig out all. Virtually all were unemployed, ready for any job. Abject poverty reined everywhere. There was constant indoctrination of the population about atheist communists destined to destroy Islam. There was an Islamic awakening everywhere in the world calling for unity and strength and to fight in the cause of Islam. Mushrooming madrasas replaced traditional schools all across Pakistan and Afghanistan, teaching narrow, perverted versions of Islam and imparting training on weapons and ammunitions. Countries were ready to pay salaries to anyone willing to fight, and there was an ample supply of weapons from competing donors. The USA and Saudi Arabia pumped billions of dollars worth of money and arms. Pakistan's ISI (Inter Services Intelligence) provided recruitment and training of volunteers. A host of other countries, like China, Britain, Egypt, and Iran, provided a variety of services with open hands. A newfound respect spread in the society for willing fighters, who had been neglected and unimportant before. All these contributed a constant supply of mujahideen ready to fight and die, more than enough to replace the large number of dying or injured fighters in the battlegrounds. Pakistan was overwhelmed by the huge supply of money by donors, a substantial amount of which they could siphon off, driving their economy, making the war a profitable business.

For United States president Carter, who initiated the efforts, Soviet aggression was not an isolated geographical event but a potential threat to US influence in the Persian Gulf region. The USA was also afraid that the USSR would gain access to the Indian Ocean by forging an arrangement with Pakistan. For Pakistan, it was an opportunity to gain control in Afghanistan and punish USSR for their support of their arch-enemy, India. The USA did not want any direct involvement to expose them as what had happened in Guatemala. Also, a potential war with USSR, which had reached its zenith of world power by then, was unimaginable. So the CIA channelled the activities through Pakistan's ISI. Shortly after the Russian involvement, Pakistan's military ruler, General Muhammad Zia-ul-Haq, who was facing stiff resistance from world powers following his military coup and the assassination of popular prime minister Zulfikar Ali Bhutto, called for a meeting of senior military members and technocrats. The director-general of the ISI at that time, Lieutenant-General Akhtar Abdur Rahman, advocated for a covert operation in Afghanistan by arming the Islamic extremists. The idea was widely accepted. Many in the meeting shouted, 'Kabul must burn! Kabul must burn!' Pakistan started accepting financial aid from the Western powers, Saudi Arabia, and other Muslim countries. Following the 1981 election of US president Ronald Reagan, who was a stronger advocate of Cold War politics, aid for the mujahideen through Zia's Pakistan significantly increased. That was the beginning of migration of Islamists from all parts of the world to Afghanistan to participate in the so-called Afghan jihad, the mother of all modern pan-national jihadi movements. Pakistan organized Sunni mujahideen groups, which were collectively called Peshawar Seven, an alliance of seven large factions with a multitude of small groups supporting them. The USA and Saudi Arabia supported them; Pakistan and China provided them training in their territories and other assistance. Shia groups were organized and supported by Iran, which was called Tehran Eight. Both groups were initially united by a single cause but later started fighting against each other after the withdrawal of Soviet forces.

The war, though, helped Pakistan economically to an extent; it also imparted lasting changes in its geopolitics. Pakistan received the majority of refugees. Though they tried to contain them in Baluchistan, the largest and least populated province neighbouring Afghanistan, it spilled all across Pakistan, mainly in the urban areas. This refugee influx affected Pakistan with many sectarian violence and terrorist incidents in their urban areas. Many border clashes with Russian and Afghan fighters affected Pakistani border areas. Hundreds of incidents caused several hundred deaths in Pakistan. KHAD organized attacks in Pakistani territories in retaliation for many direct Pakistan actions in Afghanistan. An ammunition depot fire in Islamabad in 1988 which killed about 100 people was possibly perpetrated by KHAD. During and following the Afghan war, Pakistan faced religious extremism, rise of religious politics, sectarian violence, and sprouting up of a large number of terrorist groups. ISI gained more importance in Pakistan's politics. All this later became a large security threat sufficient enough to cause an existential threat to the nuclear-armed Pakistan, which is home to more than 180 million people. China, though a communist country, faced border clashes with Russia and gained support from the USA to defend itself against the Russians. They found the war an opportunity to retaliate against the Russians. Iranian border villages also faced attacks in crossfire, border clashes, and refugee flow.

For Islamists all across the world, the Afghan jihad was a great inspiration, an optimism that defeated a superpower by a group of poorly armed mujahideen united by the spirit of Islam. An Afghan veteran became a direct entrant to leadership of any Islamist group in the world. Unfortunately, there were plenty of them in almost all major Muslim landscapes. In those mountains and deserts of Afghanistan mushroomed some of the most notorious terrorist organizations, including Al-Qaeda and dozens of their affiliates. After the Soviet withdrawal, Afghanistan became an almost completely lawless country dotted with dozens of militant training camps. Thousands of Islamists came to Afghanistan to be trained in the camps there. There were around twenty training camps by Gulbuddin Hekmatyar alone. Most of the aspiring students were trained with a fee in those camps. The fee was often paid by their sponsoring organizations in their countries. These arms-trained extremists, upon return to their homelands, started leading terrorist groups which affected all major nations. But many were beneficiaries of the war and lawlessness, creating a strong war economy capable of sabotaging any future governments. The poor population of Afghanistan turned to drug cultivation and became the major opium producer in the world. The militia and, later, the Taliban controlled all drug trade and profited from the business, gaining them money and weapons.

In spite of Soviet withdrawal and the ongoing civil war in Afghanistan, the major backer of mujahideen, Pakistan was looking for a powerful friendly government in Afghanistan. That was behind the creation of the Taliban directly under support from ISI. With training, guidance, and tactical support from the Pakistan army and ISI, the Taliban could quickly establish their rule in Afghanistan. Their primitive interpretation of Islam and a ruthless imposition of sharia of their own version caused the suffering of millions of Afghans who were just recovering from decades of war, poverty, and migration. The Taliban was also a refuge for ultra-religious organizations like Al-Qaeda, which used Afghanistan as a base for training and supporting a worldwide jihad. This ultimately led to the US invasion of Afghanistan in 2001 and the beginning of another set of jihadi activism the world over, spilling to many other conflicts. The same story was repeated in Iraq with the US invasion in 2004. Duplication of another bout of jihadi activism occurred when Syrian civil war started in 2011. Involvement of foreign countries in other conflicts like Libya left a country of immense oil wealth to turn into a lawless country easily harvested by Islamist radicals. Fortunately, people in Egypt were cleverer, not entertaining any overt foreign support and deciding their destiny was in their own hands, saving the most populous and volatile Arab nation from going into a state of lawlessness as what had happened in Afghanistan, Syria, Libya, and Iraq. That was due to the conviction of people against violent means with a long history of violent extremism in the country in spite of luring from many sponsors of armed extremism.

There was one country—better called people—who closely shared the character of Afghanistan and its similar fate: Chechens. Many of the dreaded death squads of Al-Qaeda were Chechens who were small but part of elite fighting groups in Afghanistan, Iraq, and Syria, originally with Al-Qaeda central and now with ISIS and related groups. A Chechen group fought for Taliban during the US invasion. There were several suicide bombing campaigns in Russia and massive hostage-taking in large hospitals, schools, and theatres, resulting in brutal killings which were unheard of in history. There was a prolonged guerilla war by Chechens against a strong army of Russia with bombings and suicide squads in the 1990s. Chechens ruled as an independent state but fought amongst themselves and tried to invade neighbouring territories, causing two major wars with Russia. Chechen terrorism reached far-off areas outside conflict zone, such as in the USA with the Boston Marathon bombing in 2013. In a largely prosperous and mostly democratic world of Europe, how did the Chechens of Chechnya make an altogether different nationality and difficult people?

Chechnya, a small country in the mountain region of Caucasus, had been under Russian control for a century. But the central rule was practically a namesake with little relevance or importance in the traditional life of Chechens. They were the most difficult people to be integrated into the Russian community of USSR. In 1944, Stalin forcefully relocated almost all Chechens to Siberia and Kazakhstan, suspecting them of collaborating with invading Germans. Chechen people were allowed to return to their land by Nikita Khrushchev in 1957 after the formation of the autonomous Chechen–Ingush Republic under USSR. An independent parliament and president ruled the country till the end of USSR. In October 1991, when the Soviet Union was in the waning stage, militants of the recently formed All-National Congress of the Chechen People (NCChP) party, created by the former Soviet Air Force general Dzhokhar Dudayev, stormed a session of the Chechen–Ingush ASSR Supreme Soviet with the aim of capturing the regime and asserting independence. It resulted in the death of the head of Grozny's branch of the Communist Party of the Soviet Union. Russian president Yeltsin dispatched internal troops to Grozny in November 1991. But they were forced to withdraw when Dudayev's forces surrounded them at the airport to avoid a major casualty. In the following election, Dudayev was elected as the president of Chechnya by a large margin. He unilaterally declared a sovereign republic and secession from USSR and later from Russia. He introduced a new constitution in March 1992. In June 1992, Chechen–Ingush Autonomous Republic split into two, with Ingushetia forming a separate republic and joining the Russian Federation. Chechnya reinforced full independence from Moscow and renamed the country as Chechen Republic of Ichkeria (ChRI). At least there were two coups by the opposition to remove him from power.

Though Chechens mostly favoured independence, his rule was not so popular. Opposition groups created a provisional council as an alternative government for Chechnya and called for Moscow's assistance. To consolidate power, Dudayev declared direct presidential rule and dissolved the parliament to prevent any non-confidence motion against him. Religious extremism started ground in Chechnya. Non-Chechen citizens faced discrimination and violence, and thousands fled Chechnya. With the forced migration of engineers, teachers, and other Russian technical staff from Chechnya, the economy went into collapse, the economic situation worsened and crime increased.

Kidnapping for ransom and oppression of non-Chechens became commonplace. By February 1994, all the eighty-seven states out of eighty-eight who were part of the Russian Federation under Boris Yeltsin signed a treaty with the federal government. The last to sign was Tartaristan with reluctance. The situation in Chechnya worsened in later 1994. Reluctantly, Russians decided to intervene. In October and November 1994, Russia supported the Chechnyan opposition in a clandestine operation to take control but failed. Russian soldiers and recruits were captured by the Chechnyan forces, causing major embarrassment for Yeltsin. On 29 November 1994, Yeltsin ordered an ultimatum for all fighting groups in Chechnya to disarm and surrender, to which Dudayev and his government refused. Massive Russian air strikes began in Grozny, followed by a land invasion that had started on December 11, anticipating a quick surgical strike. But the initial Russian ground troops were poorly trained, disorderly new conscripts. Almost all were killed or captured by rebels, causing about two thousand Russian casualties. That was the beginning of a prolonged and fierce fight lasting the next twenty months, with heavy civilian and Russian military casualties causing widespread opposition including in Russia.

Many of the civilian casualties were Russians who had been left in the city amid crossfiring. But most of the Chechen people, especially young adults, escaped to mountains and strategic battlefields. Only the elderly and children were left in cities, putting Russia in a quagmire of prolonged and brutal war. Most of the areas of Grozny were destroyed in heavy artillery and aerial bombing. The necessity of brutal force and invasion of villages and mountains created many stories of human rights abuse; loss of Russian soldiers, equipments, and morale; and portrayal of brutality turning public opinion against Yeltsin in Russia. Russia lost more tanks in Chechnya than in any other war front (over 1,997 tanks).

In April 1996, the commander of Chechen rebels, Dzhokhar Dudayev, was killed by laser-guided missiles fired from a warplane. Following the death of Dudayev, his deputy, Zelimkhan Yandarbiyev, became the acting president of Chechnya. In later May, he signed a peace agreement with Yeltsin which lasted for few months. Yanderbiyev was shadowed by more powerful separatist leaders like General Aslan Maskhadov and Shamil Basayev. With the threat of a massive attack with ballistic missiles and strategic bombers by Russian forces, a peace treaty was reached in August 1996 with Mashkadov and Yeltsin ending the war formally. About 100,000 civilians were killed, of which approximately 35,000 were ethnic Russians as per Russian newspaper, *Gazeta*. More than 5,000 Russian soldiers and about 4,000 rebel fighters died. Russian troops formally withdrew from Chechnya by December 1996. Following the war in January 1997, Mashkadov, a moderate among Chechen leaders, who was more pro-peace, was elected as president of Chechnya. Basayev came second and Yanderbiyev a distant third. Russia approved a general amnesty in February 1997 for Russian soldiers and Chechen separatists alike who had committed illegal acts in connection with the war in Chechnya between December 1994 and September 1996. Newly elected Chechen president Aslan Maskhadov travelled to Moscow on 12 May 1997 signed a formal treaty with Yeltsin 'on peace and the principles of Russian-Chechen relations'. Maskhadov predicted the treaty would demolish 'any basis to create ill-feelings between Moscow and Grozny'. But history proved otherwise.

In that era of crumbling USSR and defeat of Soviets in Afghanistan, there was a worldwide Islamic activism. About five thousand Chechens served as foreign volunteers there mostly by religious motivations. In 1994, several hundreds of Chechens were arms-trained in Afghanistan, mostly in Al-Qaeda camps. Ibn Khattab, a young Saudi jihadist, came to Afghanistan in 1989 to participate in the war against Russians at the age of eighteen years. He became involved with Chechen militants. Ibn Khattab was known among Al-Qaeda circles there and met Osama Bin Laden. He was a little known jihadist but had participated in the Bosnia, Azerbaijan, and Tajikistan conflicts. Posing as a television videographer, Ibn Khattab entered Chechnya in 1995. Later, he made many war videos of rebels and used them in promotions for donations and demoralizing Russians. He was involved in some of the heavy ambushes of Russian soldiers, including his first attack in October 1995 on a Russian convoy, which killed forty-seven soldiers. During the course of the war, he became close friends with more radical rebels like Shamil Basayev and Zelimkhan Yandarbiyev. Ibn Khattab was declared as a terrorist and wanted by Interpol. At the end of the war, ibn Khattab became an independent warlord. He formed Arab mujahideen in Chechnya with many Arab, Turkish, and other Islamist fighters trained in his training camps. He received funds from Arab countries and Al-Qaeda sources, a large part of which had been acquired during the war, acting as conduits between donors and Chechen fighters. On 22 December 1997, his Arab mujahideen fighters and a group of Dagestani rebels raided the base of 58th Army of the Russian Army at Buinaksk, Dagestan, causing heavy Russian casualties and material loss. Ibn Khattab and Shamil Basayev formed the Islamic International Peacekeeping Brigade (IIPB) group in 1998. In August 1999, they invaded Dagestan in support of independence declared by Shura Dagestan, causing the death of several hundred people. During the same time, militants under ibn Khattab organized the Russian apartment bombings. They bombed four apartment blocks in the Russian cities of Buinaksk, Moscow, and Volgodonsk from 4–6 September 1999, killing 293 people and injuring 651. Almost all were civilians. Most of them died when they were sleeping at night. These events of terrorists led to worldwide condemnation. Khattab openly denied his role. Several other bombs were successfully defused in Moscow at that time. These two events eventually lead to the Second Chechen War in October 1999.

During the course of Chechen conflicts, militants were able to polarize the society. Chechens became more militant and radicalized. Wahhabi ideology gained roots. Akhmad Kadyrov, the chief mufti of the Chechen Republic during the wake of the First Chechen War, cried that Chechnya was waging a jihad against Russia. His call received response from jihadis from other regions and even outside Russia. He advocated, 'Russians outnumber Chechens many times, thus every Chechen would have to kill 150 Russians.' Later, towards the beginning of the Second Chechen War, he changed his attitude.

It may have been to gain position or he was worried about destruction or spreading Wahhabism in the country which he was against. He had his own militia. Later, he became the president of Chechnya with Russian support and tried to integrate former militants into the army or militia. He faced several assassination attempts by Islamist militants. Finally, he was killed in 2004 during a Soviet Day victory parade along with thirty others in a powerful bomb blast. Shamil Basayev later claimed that he paid $50,000 for the attack. Later, his son Ramzan Kadyrov took over his militia. In 2007, he became the president of Chechnya.

Chechen rebels fought a pitched battle with Russian soldiers during the initial period of the First Chechen War, when they had an edge over Russians with about 12,000 fighters. Later it became a guerrilla war with ambushes, IED attacks, extensive use of mines, and human shields. Many of the refugee camps were infested with rebels who chose it as safe hideouts against attacks. A large number of child soldiers were recruited, including girls of even 11 years, as reported by the UN. Later, this changed into several terrorist plots deep within Russian territories and other countries, including hijacking of aircrafts and ships. In June 1995, a group of rebels led by Shamil Basayev took hostage of more than 1,500 patients, staff, and relatives in a hospital in Budyonnovsk. This led to the death of 120 Russian civilians before a ceasefire was signed, releasing the rest of the hostages and temporary halting military operations in Chechnya. It allowed the militants to regroup and renew their attack with new recruits and more arms. These events made Russians more reluctant about peace settlements with militants in future hostage-takings and kidnappings.

After the First Chechen War, many people expected peace to prevail. But by this time, militants became large enough in number to challenge the weak government. The country's economy was shattered with plenty of jobless armed militants. Chechnya witnessed a wave of kidnapping, which became a major economic activity, collecting about $200 million from about 1,300 kidnappings. Most of the initial victims were released with ransom money. But later, the ransom money went up, depending on the victims' financial status. They started killing victims if the bargain failed. Some of the captives were sold as slaves and were called slaves openly and endured all forms of torture. Most of those victims were non-Chechens who were sold to Chechen families. In 1998, about 176 people were kidnapped, of which 90 were released during the year. When the new president, Maskhadov, took over the country, it was facing severe poverty. Businesses and industries were in ruins to provide any worthy economic activity. About 40 per cent of Chechen out of a total population of 1.2 million were living in overcrowded refugee camps. Maskhadov managed to get large funds from Russia to rebuild the country and to pay salaries and pensions for schools and hospitals. But most of these funds were taken by Chechen authorities. They were divided among favoured warlords who maintained their militias further, worsening the security and marginalizing people. The country became almost completely lawless. In central Grozny, there was a large arms market where all weapons were openly sold for any buyers. Machine guns were sold for about $200–300 and a grenade was as cheap as equivalent to $1. The top anti-kidnapping official of the country was killed by militants. 'Political violence and rising Wahhabism' caused authorities to declare a state of emergency. Islamist fundamentalist radicals defied the order. Many warlords like Basayev controlled more power than the Chechen national government. Another source of income for rebels and militants was looting the oil from oil wells and pipelines. The Special Purpose Islamic Regiment (SPIR), also known as the al-Jihad-Fisi-Sabililah Special Islamic Regiment, a loosely formed organization by Chechen warlord Arbi Barayev, was one of the main hostage-taking, kidnapping, and oil-smuggling groups operating in Chechnya during the lawless interwar period of 1994–1996. To appease the fundamentalists, Maskhadov introduced Islamic sharia law in February 1999, though he was against it. People were sentenced to death, flogged, and executed for crimes such as adultery by the sharia court.

A US Department of State enquiry revealed that during the wake of the Second Chechen War with Russians to expel militants from

Chechnya who were continuing to plot terror attacks and making incursions to Dagestan, representatives of ibn Khattab and Basayev met Osama Bin Laden in Kandhahar and pledged substantial military and financial assistance and made arrangements to send several hundred fighters to Chechnya. Later in 1999, bin Laden sent substantial amounts of money to Basayev and Khattab for training, supplies, and salaries. During this time, many Chechen fighters attended Afghan training camps. Some of them stayed and later joined al-Qaeda's elite 055 Brigade, fighting against the Northern Alliance. During the US invasion of Afghanistan in 2001 against Taliban, ibn Khattab sent his fighters to Afghanistan.

In the Second Chechen War, Russians were more prepared. The population was convinced of the dangers of terrorism and Chechnya going lawless in the hands of fundamentalist terrorists, criminals, and separatist nationalists. Maskhadov was the Chechen president and army commander. He declared *gazavat* (holy war) to confront the approaching Russian army and personally involved himself in attacks. A more planned and prepared Russian army quickly invaded Chechnya following a massive air raid and a hunt for militants who hid in the mountains began. Ibn Khattab, who had already lost his right hand from explosives in Afghanistan, was wounded with a heavy-calibre bullet wound in his stomach and landmine explosion but still survived. Russians devised a new strategy to kill him rather than attack his mountain hideouts and risk soldiers. With the help of his courier, a Dagestani double agent of FSB (Federal Security Service), Khattab was poisoned by a letter sent by his mother from Saudi Arabia coated with a fast-acting nerve agent. It took about six months for the Russian intelligence agency to recruit the courier and plan the attack. The courier was later tracked and killed by Basayev's orders. Ibn Khattab was succeeded by Abu al-Walid as amir.

After the war, pro-Russian Akhmad Kadyrov became president of Chechnya. He tried to rebuild the country and rehabilitate militants and free the country from Wahhabism. Maskhadov continued to assert himself as the leader and went into hiding. He blamed Russia on high-handedness in Chechnya but was soft on terrorist plots by

Chechen militants. Investigators revealed Maskhadov's complicity in the infamous 2002 Moscow theatre hostage crisis, in which 40 to 50 armed Chechen Islamist militants took 850 hostages in a crowded theatre and demanded the withdrawal of Russian forces from Chechnya and an end to the Second Chechen War. It was led by Movsar Barayev. His connection with Maskhadov was later revealed. After a two-and-a-half-day siege, Russian Alpha Group forces pumped an undisclosed chemical agent and raided it; all 40 militants and 130 hostages were killed in the event. Maskhadov publicly accepted the responsibility for the July 2004 Nazran raid, in which 98 police officers/troops were killed. He threatened similar attacks in the following months. He claimed that the winner of Chechnya's upcoming presidential election would be illegitimate and would be attacked if necessary.

Maskhadov and Basayev were declared terrorists by Russia and were on a $10 million reward for their capture. The death of Maskhadov was announced by Russian FSB on March 2005. On ballistic evidence and further interrogation, it was found that he had been shot by Hadzhimuradov, his nephew and bodyguard, who claimed that he had been instructed by Maskhadov to shoot him in case he was injured or captured. Russia wanted to capture him alive. Four of his close associates were captured alive in the operation. He was buried in an undisclosed location due to his alleged terrorist activities as per Russian rules. Another separatist leader and vocal supporter of Chechen terrorist activities, Zelimkhan Yandarbiyev, escaped to Afghanistan and then to other Arab countries. He was living in exile in Qatar with his family in spite of being labelled as a terrorist. Russia formally asked for his extradition, and he was wanted by Interpol on Al-Qaeda–linked terrorist activity. Yandarbiyev was a key player in directing funding from foundations in Gulf Arab countries in order to support a radical Chechen faction, dubbed the Special Purpose Islamic Regiment, a militant group responsible for the Moscow theatre hostage crisis of 2002. While living in Qatar, Yanderbiyev was killed by Russian agents and his son seriously injured when his car was exploded by bombs planted on it. The Russian agents were arrested and later put on life imprisonment. Strong diplomatic efforts by Russia secured them, and they were extradited and later released in Russia.

Most notorious among Chechen militants, Basayev was killed in July 2006 in Ingushetia, a republic bordering Chechnya. Russia claimed it had been a planned work of FSB, while rebels claimed that he was killed in accidental explosion. He was killed by a powerful blast triggered by a mine exploding a truck full of explosives, scattering his body parts over a mile. His body was positively identified from his retrieved prosthetic leg among the debris.

In spite of the several changes in the culture and social practices of the population of USSR and Russia, the Chechens maintained their identity. Though they were Muslims, traditional rules, called adats (customs), ruled most of their life. They were a kind of warrior tribe who had survived many invaders for centuries, with their inaccessible mountain hideouts where they could live for many weeks without any support and could launch attacks on invaders. Traditional concepts of Chechen honour emphasize courage in life. Fear of shame was for self, for the family, and for the coming generations. Also the strong motivation for revenge and blood feud made them unique in Europe. They were never under a proper federal rule or king and not subjected to any proper rulers but dictated by simple rules in the small village, or *teip*. So they were altogether different people to adapt a federal system and vulnerable to fight because of inherent courage, honour and blood feud. Even women became suicide bombers; wife and sisters of martyred men formed the infamous Black Widows. The status of women in Chechen society is very low, and honour killing of women is very common and acceptable among Chechens. With consistent efforts and international coalition against terrorism, Chechnya is gradually returning to normalcy. Now few people talk about separation and more for peace and stability. Still, a small group of terrorists are there in Chechnya and in other countries in the Caucasus Mountains, some of whom declared the so-called Caucasus Emirate with not much of a political or geographical base. But the members of the Caucasus Emirate are closely related to Al-Qaeda and still pose a formidable threat. Chechen terror reached

America on 15 April 2013 during the Boston Marathon, which paralyzed the city for two days and reminded them of the horror of terrorism as had happened on 9/11. In the 2014 Winter Olympics at Sochi, Russia, these terrorists threatened to disrupt the event, which necessitated unprecedented security arrangements for the event and throughout Russia. Immediately following the Winter Olympics in Sochi, the Caucasus Emirate announced the death of its leader, Doku Omerov, who had organized three suicide attacks in Volgograd, former Stalingrad, and threatened more attacks during the Sochi Olympics. Its members are currently fighting along with Al-Nusra Front and its rival, ISIL, in Syria or Iraq.

The stories of Afghanistan and Chechnya are probably basic in understanding the evolution of terrorism and terror-linked nationalist ideology. Several tactics evolved in the war in these areas were used elsewhere. Kidnapping, hostage-taking, and looting of oil wells and pipelines were tactics that had evolved in Chechnya which were used by Al-Qaeda–linked terrorists in Iraq, Syria, and Libya. Portrayal of a strong oppressive force was common in Afghan and Chechen fights, which was duplicated in Iraq during the American invasion. Many areas of lawlessness accessible to Islamists became dens of terrorists. That was the story of Pakistan, Sudan, Somalia, Maghreb, Mali, Yemen, remote lawless parts of Indonesia, and the Philippines, apart from typical examples in Afghanistan, Chechnya, and now Iraq, Syria and Libya. The key to preventing the spread of terrorism is preventing lawlessness in volatile areas with whatever conflicts. Countries should realize their past mistakes in meddling with the internal politics of other countries, deposing rulers, and spreading anarchy and chaos, which eventually bite back with brutal force in peaceful societies. It is not what any prosperous modern society expects from its rulers.

CHAPTER 10

The Tale of Two Cities—Karachi and Tripoli

There's nothing in here worth taking, so please just leave it alone.

Notice on front door of a house whose residents fled following unrest in an area under the control of Misrata militants in Tripoli

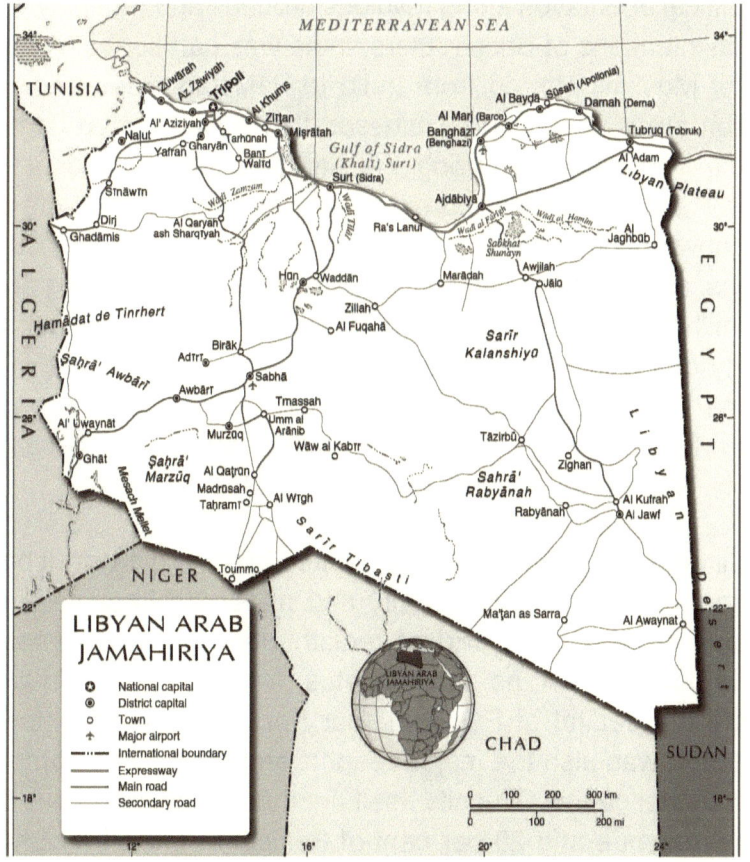

Libya—Country Map

Welcome to Karachi! The first capital city of the modern Islamic country made for the Muslims of the Indian subcontinent, created by political activism in 1947. Probably the only other similar country created for a dispersed population in a large part of a region is Israel. The areas of British India which later became a new country called Pakistan, though mostly inhabited by Muslims, were not very enthusiastic about a new nation for Muslims alone. Most of its proponents were Muslim leaders from other parts of British India, which later became India, and who were the vocal proponents of partition and a new homeland for Muslims. They dreamed of a homeland for Muslims which would become the model for the entire world in terms of peace, harmony, stability, ideological unity, and prosperity. In the background of a growing Hindu–Muslim conflict and political orientation along religious grounds and probably with the imperial intentions of British rulers, India was partitioned. A massive influx of Muslims started from India to Pakistan areas and Hindus to Indian areas. The world witnessed the most dreaded communal violence in the history during the partition, killing about a million people. Karachi, the most vibrant city in Pakistan, became the capital of the new country. A vast city, truly a melting pot of many cultures, religions, and traditions, was a real metropolis and a bustling port city. Karachi, home to about a population of about 400,000 with a marginal majority of them (51 per cent) Hindus, received a massive influx of Muslims from India called *muhajir*. It changed the demography of Karachi forever out of favour for native Sindhis, who became the minority. At least 75 per cent of Hindus left the city.

Karachi went ahead. Its population soared to many millions. It became a symbol of Pakistan's prosperity and pride and became a model for many countries. As part of redistribution of development and political power, it lost the capital status. A newly created Islamabad became the capital of Pakistan. But Karachi was the gateway to Pakistan. It was also the major seaport and airport and commercial and industrial capital. The city itself contributed about 25 per cent of national revenue and 20 per cent of Pakistan's GDP. Its institutions generated and controlled about 50 per cent of Pakistan's wealth. It was the city of Muhammad Ali Jinnah, father of the nation, and home town of Benazir Bhutto, Pervez Musharraf, Altaf Hussain, and about 23.5 million people at present. It was one of the largest megacities of the world and the largest city in the Muslim world. It was a city with all religious, ethnic, regional, and linguistic groups of Pakistan, aptly called mini Pakistan.

On 8 June 2014, the major international airport of Pakistan and hub of all its international airlines, the Karachi airport was laid siege to by about a dozen militants belonging to the Pakistani Taliban, Tehrik-e Taliban Pakistan (TTP). The siege continued for hours, and airport functions were disrupted. Events were telecast live on many TV channels, exposing the security scenario of Karachi and Pakistan. Heavy gunfights and explosions ripped the busy airport, causing fire in many aircrafts. In the end, thirty-six people lost their lives, including the ten terrorists, and a heavy catch of arms, including rocket launchers and suicide vests, was recovered from them. Militants dressed in the uniforms of airport security guards split into two groups. They started attacking using heavy machine guns, rockets, and grenades and tried to hijack some flights. But airport security officers killed eight of the terrorists within the two hours of attack, and the other two exploded their suicide vests and died when they were cornered. Within two days, in spite of heavy security, another attack on the airport security office was made, which was promptly repelled. The attackers involved were foreigners of Uzbek origin belonging to the Islamic Movement of Uzbekistan (IMU), an Al Qaeda –affiliated militant organization that works closely with TTP, as confirmed by TTP. TTP claimed the attack as retaliation for killing of TTP chief Hakimullah Mehsud in November 2013 by US drone strikes. This TTP attack was not sporadic.

The situation in Karachi became so fluid. A vast area of Karachi was no-go zone for law enforcement agencies which are Pashtun majority areas and strongholds of TTP. Karachi airport is one of the heavily protected areas in Karachi, considering the risk of many past terrorist attacks in the city. On 22 May 2011, following the assassination of Osama Bin Laden by US forces, a sophisticated attack occurred at PNS Mehran, the heavily guarded headquarters of the Pakistan

Navy's Naval Air Arm division. It caused heavy material loss to the Pakistan Navy and the death of eighteen military personnel and fifteen attackers. Pakistan navy assets were targeted many times before, with bombings of naval buses on three occasions in April causing the death of seven personnel and injury of about one hundred people. The naval base attack, though, was claimed to have been done by TTP in retaliation for killing of Osama Bin Laden. The previous attacks even before Bin Laden's death and the necessity of long planning and training pointed to another agenda. The attackers were also mainly Uzbeks. A Pakistan daily, *Asia Times*, reported online that the navy had cracked an infiltration of its cadres by members of TTP and Al-Qaeda. They had formed a cell working in many naval bases, and the captured officers were undergoing a court martial. Al-Qaeda asked the navy to release them and threatened to attack the naval base if they were not released. Shortly, the investigation team found their secret detention centre of naval intelligence was already known to Al-Qaeda. They then shifted them to a highly secured centre to which only top-level officers had access. To their horror, they found Al-Qaeda knew about all these details, exposing a Pandora's box of high-level Al-Qaeda infiltration of naval command. With the history of Al-Qaeda's strong interest in naval missions, this possibility was more likely. Later investigations suggested that the mission was directed by Ilyas Kashmiri. He was a dreaded terrorist known for his many plots with experience working with many terrorist organizations targeting Indian, Pakistani, and US interests during his terror career. He was finally patronized by the Al-Qaeda core and Pakistani Taliban. He was killed shortly later in a drone strike in North Waziristan in June 2011.

On 9 January 2014, Karachi and the entire Pakistan were shocked by the news of the death of the head of the anti-insurgency wing of Karachi police, SP CID Chaudhary Aslam Khan. He had been fighting a popular battle against the Taliban and criminal elements in Karachi. He was killed in a powerful suicide bombing, jamming a barrel with over one hundred kilograms of explosives in his convoy of vehicles. TTP's Mohamand Agency chapter claimed responsibility for the attack. There had been several such attacks on his life before.

After a powerful bomb by Taliban ripped off the front of his house in September 2011, he told the reporters, 'I will give my life but I won't bow to terrorists.' He kept his promise after a brave fight widely accepted all over Pakistan. All these attacks indicate the power of Pakistani Taliban and Al-Qaeda that any site, however protected, any dignitary with even the highest level of protection can be targeted successfully by TTP. Also, all these attacks exposed the complicity with internal info from a higher establishment.

After Aslam Khan's death, Karachi law-enforcement agencies went for a crackdown on terrorists and arrested about twenty-nine terrorists, mainly from Taliban strongholds. In less than two weeks, a reprisal attack by the Taliban killed eleven police officers. It was not only against the establishment Taliban militants were fighting. Just three days before Aslam Khan's death, Taliban killed six devotees of a Sufi saint in a shrine on the outskirts of Karachi. All victims' throats were slit, and some of them were decapitated by a dagger. A note on the scene claimed TTP responsibility and threatened a similar fate to anyone praying at a Sufi shrine. Taliban followers of the Deobandi tradition of Sunni Islam proclaimed Sufi traditions of worshipping at a dargah (tomb of Sufis) heresy.

A large number of Pakistanis are followers of the Sufi tradition, supported by another Sunni sect called Barelvis. The clashes between these two sects are very common throughout Pakistan. There were about eighty terrorism-related deaths in the first two months of 2014 in Karachi alone. Two polio vaccination teams were attacked on January 2014 during the polio vaccination drive to children in Karachi, killing three people, including two women. Polio vaccination teams were also attacked in the provinces of Khyber-Pakhtunkhwa and Baluchistan, both Taliban strongholds. After these attacks, polio vaccination drives halted in Karachi and in these two provinces. The Taliban spread the rumour that polio vaccines made the children infertile, and hence, they were against the drive. Polio, a dreaded disease which caused crippling disabilities for millions of children throughout the world, is practically eradicated in almost all countries by the vaccination drive. By 2013, only three countries had endemic polio: Pakistan, Afghanistan (thanks to the Taliban), and Nigeria, due to Islamic extremists spreading similar rumours and attacks on vaccination teams. Unfortunately a single endemic area can be a threat to the entire world. Polio re-emerged in 2014 in war-torn Syria and in Somalia and Somali populations in neighbouring Africa. Now many parts of Africa, the Middle East, and South East Asia are under threat of polio. From here, it can spread everywhere. Many Western countries eradicated polio long back and are not pursuing polio vaccination and, hence, are at high risk from non-eradicated endemic areas. Thus militants are not just a threat to their society but also to the security and health of the world.

All forms of organized crimes are rampant in Karachi, including targeted killing, sectarian violence, religious riots, political violence, drug violence, and armed robberies. Karachi every day faces 2–10 violent deaths apart from major violence. The Human Rights Commission of Pakistan reported 10,693 civilian deaths in Karachi from 2008 to 2012. In Karachi, 2,350 people were killed in 2013 and more than 2,000 in 2012, making Karachi the most dangerous megacity in the world. Not only are these numbers are alarming but the grip of administration is also loosening on criminals, and large areas of Karachi have already become no-go zones for law-enforcement agencies. There criminal gangs are mostly in Pashtun areas controlled by the Taliban. Their primitive rules and laws are applicable there with rampant land-grabbing, extortion, bank robberies, drug trades, and arms sales. Karachi has been the biggest trading centre for opium and heroin for the last two decades and now for methamphetamine also. It is coming mainly from its largest producer, Iran, carried by almost the same drug smugglers of opium.

Karachi, once a stronghold of Altaf Hussain's MQM (Mutahida Qaumi Movement), which controlled almost everything happening in Karachi, is loosening its grip due to political infighting and loss of support and also due to a large influx of Pashtun population from Afghanistan and war-torn FATA and Khyber-Pakhtunkhwa. In the last decade (from 2000 to 2010) alone, Karachi's population increased by an unbelievable 80 per cent of its population, an addition more than the entire population of New York City. It is difficult to accept for long-time natives of the city. Many of the new settlers brought their Taliban ideology, their tactics and weapons. If somebody says Mullah Omer lives in Karachi, not many will disbelieve it. Terrorist groups might have established their bases in urban areas of Karachi from their old vulnerable mountain terrains. If one is in Karachi, life can be lost for political reasons, for being of another religion or sect, for resisting an armed robbery, for not paying protection money, and even for just being in the wrong spot at the wrong time when two gangs or groups are fighting. Police lose hundreds of their cadres every year in Karachi. Violent deaths became a common event in Karachi. Deaths are not much of news value here. Criminals can escape through a crowd after firing at someone. Not many are bothered about what is happening in their surroundings if none of their relatives or friends are involved. Violence is not only the story of Karachi, but also, as a 'mini Pakistan'; it is a mirror of Pakistan. Karachi is failing every day to maintain the law and order. Many security experts believe it needs urgent correction—if not now, never. Karachi's lawlessness and sense of irresponsibility make it just a few steps away from a complete breakdown to a failed state. The city of many millions cannot afford to be a failed place in a country descending to failure in almost all other parts.

People familiar with Karachi acknowledge the fact that Karachi was a politically violent city. But the gun culture was not there before 1979. After the Soviet invasion, a large number of Afghan refugees reached Pakistan. A good number reached Karachi too with legally allowed arms at their disposal as part of the Islamization process of the then-ruling military dictator Zia-ul-Haq. Over a period of years, some of the poor neighbourhoods of Karachi became strongholds of Pashtun and Afghans, who shortly became a challenge to the already-dominant muhajirs and Bengalis. In April 1985, ethnic violence following a single traffic accident precipitated a violent response against the strengthening Pathan community that dominated in transportation and construction businesses by Bengali and muhajir activists. The next day, Pathans organized a counterattack by burning houses and police vehicles. Violence spread all over Karachi, marking the beginning of a series of future Pathan–muhajir conflicts. The newly formed (in 1984) MQM (originally Muhajir Qaumi Movement, later changed to Mutahida Qaumi Movement) was having militant elements in the party which orchestrated the conflict from their side.

Some of the Afghan refugees became involved in the arms and drug traffic. Karachi, being the biggest port in the country, naturally became the important transit place for arms and drugs. Pakistan witnessed a huge inflow of arms meant for the Afghan mujahideen supplied by a host of countries. Also, a concomitant outflow of drugs like opium and heroin was used to finance the purchase of arms through Karachi, making it the centre of arms trade. Since it was officially a clandestine operation, some of the army, naval officers, and intelligence agencies controlled most of the arms dealings. Many arms shipments were diverted and sold illegally due to poor record-keeping and monitoring of distribution by the donor countries. The flow of drugs for export through Karachi for arms purchase for mujahideen did not initially bother the authorities much. Soon, both became well-established war economies with a series of gangs entering into the lucrative business. At the end of the war, Pakistan became the major consumer of both commodities: arms and drugs. Pakistanis became one of the most addicted societies in the world, with about 6.7 million drug addicts forming 6 per cent of the total population in 2013. It is estimated that 20 million illegal arms are circulated in Pakistan. After the war, a huge number of arms came to the open market for sale. In both cases, in Karachi, with already-established criminal-official-political-religious networks and gangs, the trade flourished. Many of the religious and political groups started acquiring arms and started hiring arms-trained people. A series of violence started all across the society—in colleges, universities, and streets and during religious functions. With changing scenes in world terrorism, extremist tactics were also changed. From mass violence to executions, target killing, random firing at crowds, IED explosions, and suicide bombings, al-Qaeda became a role model for all terrorist activities.

By 1985–86, Sohrab Goth, a locality at the periphery of Karachi, predominantly populated by Pathans from NWFP and Afghan refugees, became the main place for drugs and arms dealing in Karachi. On 13 October 1986, a bus full of MQM activists coming to Karachi was fired at by Pathans, resulting in six deaths. Violence spread in Karachi, resulting in the death of forty people. The army was determined to end the violence. Following a military operation in a MQM stronghold of Orangi town, capturing arms and bombs, the army went for a 'clean-up' operation in Sohrab Goth. They destroyed illegal constructions supporting heroin manufacturing and a distribution centre. The next day, hundreds of Pathans and Afghans wielding AK-47 machine guns attacked muhajir and Bengali neighbourhoods in Aligarh, Qasba, areas, killing hundreds of muhajirs. Also, there was widespread burning and looting of their houses and properties. It was later known as the Aligarh massacre. That was a show of strength of the 'drug and Kalashnikov culture' in the city. The violence resulted in forty-nine deaths officially and more than four hundred unofficially. The violence was forcefully suppressed by the army, but small-scale violence continued.

For most of the current problems in Pakistan, if one wants to blame a single individual, his name is General Zia-ul-Haq. He started his draconian Islamization process, the result of which was far-reaching. He took control of the government in 1977 as the army general, deposing the democratically elected Prime Minister Zulfikar Ali Bhutto. Bhutto, at his convenience, chose a relative junior but acclaimed army officer Zia as army chief in 1976, ignoring seniors' thinking that he would side with him. Following a civil unrest in Pakistan, Zia expelled Bhutto and declared martial law. In 1978, he became the president of Pakistan and was in the post serving more than a decade until he was killed in an aircraft crash proven to be sabotage. Zia orchestrated the killing of Bhutto. After a hurried court hearing of a case involving Bhutto, he authorized the execution of Bhutto. Zia became isolated in the international community but regained his importance with the Russian invasion of Afghanistan. Zia was the architect of the Afghan war against the Russians. He started a process called Islamization in Pakistan. The Pakistan army became increasingly religious. Many militant ideologues became its officers and army men. Its intelligence agency, ISI, was more radicalized. Mullahs, till then neglected and often wretched by modernizing Pakistani society, were given a hearing and eminence during his reign. But they were regularly consulted by Zia on all religious and administrative matters. Schools were ignored, and madrasas (Muslim religious schools) were promoted; their number became severalfold over a decade. Many madrasas started giving arms training, at least one hundred of them as per the records of the Human Rights Commission of Pakistan. Islamist parties and militant groups started training grounds and were given support by the army, intelligence, and political circles.

Most Afghan refugees carried their weapons, which was a norm in Afghan societies. They were freely allowed entry and spread to Pakistani territories, altering the demography of many cities and territories already suffering from ethnic, sectarian, and religions conflicts. The war in Afghanistan against Russia ended. Afghanistan was ruined. A civil war in Afghanistan started. Still no favourable Pakistani government could be installed in Afghanistan. They started supporting friendly mujahideen and ultimately selected Taliban. With overt Pakistani support, training and a large number of radical arms-trained madrasa students joined (about 20–40 per cent of soldiers were Pakistanis) the Taliban. Ultimately, Pakistan won the Afghan war with the Taliban, taking rule of Afghanistan. The barbaric rule of Taliban was beyond the sense of ordinary Muslims. Their narrow views, brutal punishments, alienation of women, and collapse of economy, social order, and dignity of a large number of Afghans provoked revolts against the Taliban. Several countries became sympathetic to their cause.

In a conglomeration of seven tribal territories, called FATA (Federally Administered Tribal Area), in the north-western part of Pakistan adjoining Afghanistan, tribal rules had been the norm since independence. It was not governed by Pakistan rules and was completely outside the grip of Islamabad. After the US invasion of Afghanistan to expel the Taliban, many of the Taliban and Al-Qaeda fighters entered the FATA area and launched their attacks in Afghanistan from time to time. This necessitated Pakistani army operations in FATA after hard negotiations with tribal leaders.

But the hitherto-unexpected army presence in their territories and, later, beginning of US drone strikes against Al-Qaeda and Taliban leaders living in FATA alienated the tribals. They later organized under a banner of Pakistani Taliban, which later emerged as TTP (Tehrik-e Taliban Pakistan). TTP, in contrast to Afghan Taliban which maintained good relation with Pakistan, considered the Pakistan Army their main target. Attacking US interests and the support of the Taliban in Afghanistan were also on their agenda. TTP was a loose organization of several leaders with no central command. Its initial leader was Baitullah Mehsud. After his death, his driver and one of his young confidants, Hakimullah Mehsud, took charge. He was more aggressive than his mentor. He coordinated many attacks against the Pakistani Army and its civilians, mostly Shia, Ahmedi, and Sufi targets, with IED blasts and suicide bombings. Adjustments with Pakistani army and intelligence agencies and insider information were behind the success of many TTP organizations. Many Arab, Uzbek, and Chechen fighters of Al-Qaeda also supported TTP in their missions. After the death of Hakimullah in November 2013 in a US drone strike, Maulana Fazilullah, or the so-called Radio Mullah, a former SWAT Taliban commander, became the leader of TTP. With the military actions in FATA and SWAT, a large number of people from these areas became refugees. Many of them reached Karachi, causing a sudden rise in population of Karachi and demographic changes.

The spiralling violence in Karachi by Pathans and members of TTP in recent times is mostly neglected by the once-pervasive MQM in Karachi. Once the vocal opponents of Pathan influence and TTP aggression, MQM is becoming more silent. Their silence can be equated with the infighting in Iraqi Parliament for new government formation when the country itself was threatened by imminent swallowing by a marauding militant Islamic army of Islamic State. If the political class, the army, and the Pakistan establishment will not rise to quell the growing mistrust in the population, this largest city of the Muslim world may soon lay siege to a rapidly growing militant population of TTP and criminal gangs. Unplanned war, militarization of ordinary citizens, neglect of raising fanaticism and militancy—all may ultimately destroy even prosperous countries. But unlike small nations of the Middle East, a serious militant takeover of nuclear-armed Pakistan would be a catastrophe. Its sprawling cities, huge military, industrial infrastructure, and a country which is home to about 186 million people is not a matter the world can afford to happen.

Pakistan, which became a promoter, later turned into a victim of terrorism after promoting the neighbour's war. They were trying to protect their geopolitical interest and importance in the world. But Libya lost peace almost completely after a revolution which was meant to give its people dignity, freedom, choice, and democracy. A strong popular revolution uprooted the long autocratic and kleptocratic rule of Muammar Gaddafi for more than forty years following the unexpected political tsunami of the Arab Spring, which started in 2011, in Tunisia, their neighbour country. But Gaddafi had very few friends outside his country, which made his oust easy, unlike that of Bashar al-Assad, who had strong allies which kept his rule alive. But he made long-lasting social changes in the country, improving education, healthcare, and the status of women, more than anywhere else in the Arab world. Tripoli, a vibrant city during Gaddafi's regime, turned into its ghost after his violent death. Gaddafi also developed a loyal force in army, police, and intelligence. They almost became completely uncooperative with post-war government, leaving the law and order and security In the hands of newly formed militias which spontaneously sprouted up during the revolution. Many of them whose only motive was freedom of their country dismantled their militia or joined the mainstream army or police. But some, due to their political, religious, or criminal intentions refused to dissolve but promoted their militia. With the money and arms they got during the revolution and later from looting, donation, extortion, and other criminal activities, they flourished. By July 2014, in the biggest city and capital of Libya, Tripoli, all hell broke loose.

Libya was governed under a parliament with disputable power. Though they had some control over the sale of large oil wealth the country wielded, they did not have any proper national army or police at their disposal. Instead, numerous militias maintained law and order; many large militias were on the government's payroll. Ironically, the government writ was not applicable to even the capital, Tripoli. Arguably even inside the parliament; which came under attack several times by the militia. The previous prime minister, Zeidan, was kidnapped and later released by the militia. That was the state of affairs of the government. If the government wanted to talk to the militia, they have been able to do so, but the onus was on the militia to obey or not, though they may be on the government's payroll. When a large part of the country became completely lawless, militias, many with terrorist connections, started gaining control of major cities, including Tripoli and Benghazi, and also many oilfields.

At this point, a former general, Khalifa Haftar, who had defected from the former Gaddafi regime and gone into exile in the USA, returned. He started a military unit called Libya National Army (LNA) with support from many former army and air force officers, soldiers, and militia to fight against the terrorists. Sensing a coup and unwilling to recognize it, the national government declared his group as not authorized. Haftar could repel many militant attacks and expel them from many parts of cities, mainly Benghazi. He vowed to extend his control into Tripoli in May 2014. This precipitated many military attacks, which eventually worsened the law and order situation in the country. Kidnapping of opponents and political leaders became common. Extortion, looting, and armed conflicts made the life of a Tripolian difficult.

Since the 2011 revolution, the main international airport of Libya, Tripoli airport, was controlled by the Qaqa militia of men from Zintan, a mountain town close to Tripoli. A large part of Tripoli city was under control by armed militiamen from Misrata, the third largest city in Libya that had the largest militia in Libya with heavy weapons. Both groups were under the payroll of the Libyan Ministry of Defence. The Zintan group was allied with Haftar. Misrata militia aligned with

Libyan Revolutionary Operations Room (LROR), with many extremist elements among them and with backup from the Muslim Brotherhood of Libya. LROR was behind the kidnapping of former Libyan prime minister Ali Zeidan. During the 2014 *Ramzan*, when most of the men of Zintan militia went to their home towns, the Misrata group attacked the Tripoli international airport to capture the airport with missiles, rocket-propelled grenades, and anti-aircraft machine guns, causing a heavy retaliatory fight from the Zintan militia controlling the airport. The fighting resulted in many aircrafts bursting into flames, damaged the airport infrastructure and put the whole area under security threat. Thus the only major international entrance–exit for the country was closed indefinitely. The attack prompted most Western countries to evacuate all their citizens from the country, including those who manned the embassies and key installations. The fighting resulted in massive fire in the nearby oil storage facility. About six million litres of oil went into flames. The city was engulfed in a thick smoke in the summer sky. Not only did it cause an enormous loss to the Libyan National Oil Company but it also cut the city's fuel supply for an uncertain future. Most of the petrol pumps were closed due to lack of security and absence of fuel. A select few petrol stations were selling fuel at the end of hours or even days of waiting in queue. Most of the banks and ATM stopped operations due to lack of security and money as many banks were looted. The central bank stopped distribution of money as their money trucks were regularly looted and they were unable to secure their safety.

Many gun battles and heavy fighting with missiles landed up in residential areas. Inmates fled their homes, taking few of their valuables. Leftover homes were systematically looted of all possible valuables. Citizens fled to nearby towns which faced less trouble. Other major cities like Benghazi face similar situations. For people in Tripoli and stranded foreigners, the only exit route was the Tunisian border. Tunisian border crossings faced unprecedented traffic, causing long waiting at the border. This eventually caused a major clash between the Tunisian officials and fleeing foreign nationals, mainly Egyptians and Libyan citizens, on 31 July 2014. These incidents forced the Tunisian authorities to close their border, practically the only exit route outside Libya for people from Tripoli. Thus worsening humanitarian situation turned into an out-of-proportion tragedy. The Egyptian border was already in trouble as Benghazi was under severe turmoil, and the areas were very remote, more than 1,000 km away from Tripoli and unsafe. In later July 2014, the Philippines asked all their about 13,000 nationals to leave Libya urgently following one of their nationals being beheaded and a nurse gang-raped. They had been the backbone of the Libyan hospital and service industry. The UN evacuated all their staff. Most of the foreigners had to depend on the Tunisian border as the Tripoli airport was closed. Hundreds of people died in the clashes, mainly in crossfire between militia, reaching a toll of 214 dead and 980 injured by the first week of August 2014 as per the health ministry.

Looking into the root of sudden spurt in violence, it can be traced to political development in the country. For the militants, the fights were part of their survival and controlling the territories just part of their importance. Not much ideology governed them, so they could go into any political or military alliance at their convenience. Most of the Tripoli clashes in the past can be traced to the political developments in the government. The Libyan parliament came under attack several times by the militia when a new president, prime minister, or speaker emerged as a winner; in order to sabotage or postpone the elections. This time, a newly elected team of House of Representatives which would replace the National Congress was about to hold their first post-election meeting. The elections were postponed many times by their namesake, National Congress, where Islamists have control. They tried everything possible to delay the declaration of results. The elections were held with members contested independently so as to avoid more division along political lines. People punished Islamists, including the Muslim Brotherhood, severely in the election. Having lost in the election, the proxy war started to extract power, creating lawlessness and anarchy in the already mostly lawless country, thanks to their support and arming militias. Each group accused the other as being a remnant of the old Gaddafi regime and portrayed the fight as legitimate. Muhammed Sawan-the Muslim Brotherhood leader, leader of its political wing, the Justice and Development Party, and a member of the Misrata Shura Council- claimed the new war legitimate. The conflicts put the troubled country on the list of failed states in the group of Somalia.

But unlike many failing states, Libya was very rich with huge oil reserves. If it happened to be in militants' hands, could sustain a prolonged war, plunging this nation of six million people; once boasted as the most welfare country in Africa into anarchy. As in any turmoil, the law-abiding, peaceful people have to take the brunt of suffering. Criminal elements and bloodthirsty extremists are trying to build their delusional paradise of the ideological caliphate. The Muslim Brotherhood, the closely linked Ansar al-Sharia, and many militant groups are all in the picture. But all will try to put a secret presence so as to prevent their full exposure. So the groups try to avoid showing much of their banners. Instead, they focus on a proxy war with who is leading and for whom they are fighting left to speculation. In any case, the most populous city of Libya and one of the most developed cities in Africa and the Arab world is slowly drifting into darkness, with no power, no water, no medical supply, few doctors and nurses to attend the hospitals, and few beds for their ailing people. Any revolution has its own price, but is this price worthy enough? Any international force that tries to intervene in this highly fractured nation will be engulfed in a bloody and prolonged war which they don't want to meddle with. It remains to be seen what those countries like Qatar that supplied the rebels and Muslim Brotherhood–aligned militants with weapons including anti-aircraft machine guns will do in the new conflicts. Will they still be flying sorties to supply militants, or are they just watching for suitable opportunities to make the trouble deeper, or have they learned their lessons from world history?

The fall of a major city is synonymous with the fall of a country, as the cities are the last stronghold of a central government. The second decade of the twenty-first century has stories of many falling cities, so also countries, most of them victims of rising Islamic extremism tearing apart people and creating deep religious, ethnic, and sectarian conflicts which may take many decades to heal. Aleppo, Mosul, Tripoli, Benghazi—and the names go on to cities with still a string of control attached to them like Karachi, Damascus, Peshawar, Sana'a, Baghdad, and Lagos. Small countries with a failing security situation cannot hold their cities. They need foreign support, at least freedom from undue meddling to topple the existing order. The support of rival groups with arms and money has been part of the bloody history of conflicts in the late last century and the early part of this century, leaving the countries in ruins rather than giving political and intellectual support.

CHAPTER 11

Justice and Taming of Terrorists—
Some Thoughts

My brother Osama, how much blood has been spilt? How many innocent people, children, elderly, and women have been killed in the name of al-Qaeda? Will you be happy to meet God almighty carrying the burden of these hundreds of thousands or millions (of victims) on your back?

Sheikh Salman al-Ouda, a prominent Saudi religious leader, previously a noted Islamist and later critic of militancy, in a video addressing Bin Laden.

If jailing can be regarded as a punishment, it has seldom worked against terrorists, especially radicalized Islamic terrorists like those in Al-Qaeda. Many senior Al-Qaeda leaders and most associated terrorist leaders have had ample jail experience and have spent a sufficiently long time for enough thinking on their past, activism, and validity of their deviant ideology. The list includes Ayman al-Zawahiri, Abu Musab al-Zarqawi, Nasir al-Wuhayshi, Omar Abdel Rahman, Anwar al-Awlaki, Sayyid Qutb, and a host of other militant ideologists like Muhammed Sawan, Maulana Masood Azhar (chief of Jaish e-Muhammed, an Al-Qaeda ally), Ahmed Omar Saeed Sheikh (associated with the kidnapping of Western tourists in Kashmir and the killing of Daniel Perl), Abu Muhammad al-Maqdisi, David Headley, and several Taliban leaders. Most of them, in fact, became more radicalized after their incarceration.

The reasons could be many. Jail and jihad are two major medals for any militant. It signifies his authority, that he is worthy of attention and stature on a militant group, making him an enviable leader compared to others. Another aspect is human psychology of the ego—a man who has killed dozens or hundreds of people cannot live peacefully if his consciousness does not accept his deed as justifiable or enjoyable, as it is for hard-core criminals. The inner psyche of such an individual will compel such an individual to accept and rationalize his deeds as legitimate or rewarding. Otherwise, bearing the guilt of killing several people whom he didn't even know is not easy. Many of the victims are innocent even in his own belief, as they just happened to be collateral damage. *Takfiris* go a little further in their mindset, making everyone around (except those from their group) infidels and legitimate to kill as per the wish of God. Further, there is no distinction between an enemy and innocent non-target, thus making them mentally strong and more ruthless. Al-Qaeda has an element of Takfiri basis, especially Ayman al-Zawahiri and his groups from the Egyptian Islamic Jihad and Takfir Wal-Hijra.

On the other hand, it is more likely that a long history of incarceration and learning of today's history of terrorism can change ideological supporters of terrorism. Those whose hands are not stained with the blood of innocents may not have much difficulty evolving themselves from the horror of terrorism or their vehement support for such cause, as their egos will be rewarded for selecting the right path. One such individual was Sayyed Imam al-Sharif or Dr Fadl, who was a founding member of Al-Qaeda and an ideological figurehead of Egyptian Islamic Jihad. After witnessing for a long time the events in the current world and Al-Qaeda activity, he denounced the current form of Islamic jihad and blatant violence against innocents without putting clear guidelines for religious jihad. Though he was a leader of the group, he was apparently not directly involved in violent activities though a proponent of such acts before. In his book *Rationalizing Jihad in Egypt and the World*, he claimed, 'We are prohibited from committing aggression, even if the enemies of Islam do that.' He is currently serving a life sentence in Egypt after having been extradited from Yemen, where he had been working as a doctor.

Jailing is the common form of punishment as more and more countries are coming out of the death penalty. But most of the countries where terrorism is rampant are going through volatile situations where the safety of many jails is always threatened. So honouring a life sentence or a life in prison is very risky. Many of those countries may have the habit of releasing political prisoners without much review based on favouritism or even threats. Zarqawi was a prisoner once jailed for being part of a terrorist group and possessing military weapons. But he was released when a new king took over in Jordan as part of amnesty for prisoners. Shortly, he became a dreaded self-made terrorist responsible for the murder of thousands of people. Within a few months of his release, he organized a major terrorist plot in Jordan. Many of the extremist political leaders with a violent history in the past were released by the governments following revolutions in Egypt, Libya, and Tunisia. Many of them later formed terrorist groups. During the initial months of the Syrian civil war, many dangerous terrorists were released by the Syrian regime. They later fought along with Al-Qaeda–linked groups and became trouble for the regime and civilians alike. During the Egyptian revolution, thousands of prisoners were released by Muslim Brotherhood activists with support from terrorists from the high-security Wadi el-Natroun prison complex. Many of them were associated with Islamic jihad, Al-Qaeda, and militant groups in Sinai. It included Ramzy Mowafy, who was an Al-Qaeda leader and personal physician to Osama Bin Laden, and he spent a long time in Afghanistan. Later, he concentrated on extremism in Sinai, which became a national security threat for the Egyptian army and its people. During the revolution, about twenty thousand prisoners escaped from Egyptian prisons, about eleven thousand from Wadi el-Natroun prison, along with Mohammed Morsi. Morsi was charged later for the jail break, after the ousting of President Zine El-Abidine Ben Ali in Tunisia during the Arab Spring. A number of prisoners and convicted terrorists were freed in a pardon by Tunisia's transitional government in March 2011. One of them was Sayfallah bin Hussayn (also known as Abu Iyyadh al-Tunisi). He was the co-founder of the Tunisian Combatant Group in Afghanistan, which conducted the assassination of Ahmad Shah Massoud just two days prior to the September 11 attacks to weaken Taliban opposition on the orders of Osama Bin Laden. Immediately after being released from prison, Abu Iyyadh organized the first annual conference for Ansar al-Sharia in Tunisia (AST) in April 2011. Abu Sufyan bin Qumu, a former Guantanamo Bay inmate, after his release, started Ansar al-Sharia in Derna in Libya.

Keeping a senior militant leader in prison involves enormous risk and cost to the country especially for a poor country. On 24 December 1999, Indian Airlines Flight 814 was hijacked from Nepal. It was taken to Kandahar Airport under protection of the Taliban against any possible Indian commando operation. Three terrorists spending time in Indian jail were released in exchange for the release of passengers and aircraft. The three Jaish-e-Muhammed (JEM) terrorists Masood Azhar, Omar Sheikh, and others immediately escaped to Pakistan where they lived as free citizens. They received a heroic welcome. Omar Sheikh was later rearrested following Daniel Perl's murder case and was convicted for death penalty, which is still pending. Omar and JEM had close connections with Taliban, Al-Qaeda top leadership, and the Pakistani establishment.

In spite of being implicated in several terrorism plots and his intentions revealed during a sting operation, Omer Abdel Rahman is still being portrayed as an innocent Islamist persecuted in the USA. His release was part of many future negotiations with Egypt when Morsi was in power. In the modern era, imprisoned dreaded terrorists are better supported by human rights activist groups and legal safeguards than legitimate law-abiding citizens who become the prey of terrorists. Keeping a long jail term for dreaded terrorists is a costly affair in terms of money, political or activist support, risk of security, and risk of being freed in the future. In Afghanistan, aid workers and Western citizens are systematically kidnapped for ransom deals to swap against the release of imprisoned terrorists from US prisons.

In May 2014, five top Taliban leaders were released from their captivity in Guantanamo Bay, Cuba, after spending a decade in secluded jail there in a swap deal against US army sergeant Bowe Bergdahl, who had been in Taliban captivity under the Haqqani network for five years. Though others might have been relatively moderate, a senior

Taliban leader, Mohammed Fazl, was also part of the deal. He was chief of staff of the Taliban army. He was accused of commanding the forces that massacred hundreds of civilians in the final years of Taliban rule before the 2001 US-led invasion of Afghanistan under Taliban. Arrested in November 2001 after surrendering to US allied warlords in northern Afghanistan, he was shifted to Guantanamo Bay. As expected, they were shifted to the most Taliban-friendly country, Qatar, where they are expected to spend one year before they were freed. The released Taliban leaders were received warmly in Qatar, where they were supposed to stay away from politics. Encouraging such swap deals encourages terrorists to kidnap other people. In April 2014, the Jordanian ambassador to Syria was abducted by armed men. Jordan pulled out their embassy staff and offered the release of Mohamed Dersi, a Libyan terrorist in a Jordanian jail. He had been sentenced for life in jail for his plot to blow up the major airport in Jordan.

The perception of a terrorist in another country may be totally different. Some may be extradited for crime in the country but with a secret intention to protect the criminal. Depending on the prevailing political scenario, the opinion in a foreign country may change. Though Egyptians widely perceive Omar Abdel-Rahman as a terrorist or terror ideologue for his Muslim Brotherhood—oriented groups, he is their spiritual leader. On 29 June 2011, newly elected Egyptian president Mohamed Morsi pledged to free Omar Abdel-Rahman, whom he described as a political prisoner, and on August 2, Egypt formally requested that the United States release Abdel-Rahman. Al-Gama'a al-Islamiyya and Islamic Jihad called for a protest at the US embassy in Cairo on September 11 to demand the release of Abdel Rahman. An online campaign started a few days before urged 'sons of Egypt' to pressure America to release Abdel-Rahman 'even if it requires burning the embassy down with everyone in it'.

Some countries, even though they have friendly relations with the country with whom they have an extradition treaty, may have poor political will, corruption among law enforcement agencies, or widespread acceptance of terrorism in the society. Pakistan tried to extradite many terrorists but had a poor history of those under trial going into hiding or terrorists left off with reasons of lack of evidence. In countries like Saudi Arabia, on the other hand, though the support for terrorists is high, there are active programmes to monitor terrorists during their rehabilitation. One such active Al-Qaeda operative was Juma al-Dosari, a Saudi and Bahrain citizen involved in many Al-Qaeda–linked activities including wars in Chechnya and Bosnia, and the USS *Cole* attack. He was captured from Tora Bora in Afghanistan during the US invasion in 2001 and was imprisoned at Guantanamo Bay. He was not charged in the US. Following several suicide attempts, he was released in 2007. After reaching Saudi Arabia, he was enrolled in a government rehabilitation programme for those involved in terrorism charges, known as a soft approach, designed to prevent them from relapsing into violent extremism. He was given psychological support, a car, a monthly allowance, help in finding a job, and assistance to get married. After one year, reporters of *Los Angeles Times* found him settled, married, and doing a new job. He said to reporters, 'Osama Bin Laden used my religion and destroyed its reputation.' Such success stories of terrorist transformation are there, but it needs strong will from the government and society.

Any suspect released after a jail stay may be viewed with suspicion, constantly monitored, or even harassed by the authorities. He may be lured by extremist groups and new aspirants looking for experienced leaders and inspiration. So all those released terrorists or those accused of terrorism need constant support from society. Cultivating such real victims of terrorism may be part of the most successful antiterrorist strategy. Jamal al-Fadl, who defected from Al-Qaeda, faced severe psychological distress feeling a traitor to his once fellow activists. He needed constant support who later became an invaluable asset in the trial of Al-Qaeda leaders.

Saudi Arabia dedicated programmes to commendable monitoring of all extradited terrorists and defected suspects. But a 2010 June AFP report cited that 25 (20 per cent) out of the 120 former detainees transferred to Saudi custody had returned to radical activities and joined Al-Qaeda. Out of these, 10–11 persons disappeared and the rest were either killed or caught again in antiterrorism operations. One such example was Said al-Shiri, who was transferred to Saudi Arabia in 2007. He became a senior leader of Al-Qaeda in the Arabian Peninsula and orchestrated a bombing outside the US embassy in Sana and attempted a Christmas Day bombing of Northwest Airlines Flight 253 in 2009. Abdul Hafiz (a.k.a. Abdul Qawi) and Abdul Qayum Zakir are other notable examples of Guantanamo Bay prisoners returning to Taliban militancy. Both returned to their high positions in Quetta Shura. Zakir was transferred to Afghan custody in 2007 and was released in 2008. He quickly joined a militant group and became second in command of Taliban leadership, the Quetta Shura. At the time of release, he was assessed as a moderate risk. But in fact, he was one of the most successful Taliban commanders, and after rejoining his team, he inspired his supporters to fight until death. The release of such high-risk leaders will invigorate the weakening insurgent leadership. Of course, the motive of the major war, continues hunt, detention in spite of opposition from various quarters was not meant to release terrorists time to time when the number of terrorists on the field shrunk. The release of terrorist needs to be based on a single criterion: that there is enough evidence that the terrorist has changed his mindset and there is enough conviction that he will not return to the militancy. Any bargain based on political, humanitarian, or social pressure or a swap deal is a basic tactical failure and should be resisted. Otherwise, there will be no difference between the terrorist sympathizers and those fighting against them. Several terrorists were released on false humanitarian grounds. A Lockerbie bomber was released on humanitarian grounds, as he was suffering from terminal cancer. But upon his arrival in his native country of Libya, he got a heroic welcome under Gaddafi. The grounds of release may be accurate. But a criminal who did not show any mercy for hundreds of his captives does not deserve veneration as a national hero. Unfortunately, after events in USA and Afghanistan, there are strong sentiments in favour of releasing terrorists to reduce the burden on the government in terms of cost and opposition. Critics allege that it is because they forget the history of why they were caught in the first place.

Many jailed Al-Qaeda leaders gave valuable keys to their future activity and other emerging terrorists, including Khalid Sheik Muhammed. A captured German militant named Ahmed Siddiqui in Afghanistan in July 2010 apparently told the Abbottabad location of Osama Bin Laden, which became a crucial turn to capture Bin Laden. It was when almost all hope had been lost about his whereabouts. After the revelation, US intelligence tracked the Bin Laden's courier Ibrahim Saeed Ahmed to his compound in Abbottabad, eventually leading to the US raid. The USA also made sure that it was a killing mission, not one to capture Bin Laden with all possible legal, political, and economic risks of capture like kidnappings or hijackings. They did not leave any trace of his body on earth, and he was buried from the deck of USS *Carl Vinson* in the Arabian Sea following Islamic rites, obviating any future veneration of his burial site. After having fought for decades against terrorism, US agencies appear to have some grip on the situation. But for its allies, this conviction is not so great. In Pakistan, which used to be the gateway to terrorism and, later, the gateway to antiterrorist operations, including the War on Terror, ironically, both operations existed almost at the same time. Initially, the former activities were in full swing; later, the focus of establishment shifted to the latter operations with a mix of both activities in between. Similar kinds of convictions and motivation issues exist for Western government agencies. The apathy or inherent weakness to detect and prevent terror-breeding grounds eventually led to proliferation of terrorism to great extent.

The strength of terrorists is their small group spread out in a large geographic area with no identification tag with them or on their trail make them difficult to detect or track. So a fight against terrorists necessitates constant focus, vision, and commitment. In this regard, terrorists are more successful than governments as they rarely lose focus. No matter if a terror network is exposed or terrorists are jailed or tortured; they would come back with more strength and vigour. Even a small aggression by government agencies may attract severe criticism from political opponents, civil society, and most virulently, from human rights groups. In case of terrorist atrocities, they are either silent or put blame on the government for their inaction. Modern terrorists thrive on this social psychology. They want to project those protecting the law-abiding persons and fighting against criminals as oppressors of human rights, religion and, freedom, thus gaining sympathy from certain corners. On top of that, there are attacks on the government and law enforcement agencies by the overzealous media, commentators, and social media. Terrorists seldom need to face these attacks, and their focus is usually clearer.

In all societies where terrorism is a problem, there is widespread social support. Terrorists may enjoy more loyalties than the security forces, and they may have support from the wide spectrum of society and establishment. This keeps the terrorists alive when they are about to be crushed or eliminated. This happens more often in Pakistan. After many past major military operations with heavy losses to the militants, an official ceasefire would be announced on the pretext of saving lives and giving deviated minds a chance to change. This is usually from pressure from within the army, its ISI, and political and religious groups with covert support to the militant cause. Such groups regularly oppose armed action against militants, mainly Pakistani Taliban (TTP), and vehemently oppose US drone strikes, since they are proven to be very effective against high-value militants. They are otherwise untouchable due to tough terrain and impenetrability of the army in remote tribal areas.

The public may need brutal attacks by militants which terrorize consciousness to mobilize their opinion against terrorists. Only during those waves of strong anti-militant public sentiment, even the traditional sympathizers have to change their opinion to avoid public outrage. One such incident was the unprecedented attack by TTP militants on a Karachi airport, Pakistan's main international airport. Even the alleged supporters of the Taliban, like ex-cricketer-turned-politician Imran Khan, were forced to support military action, at least before the media. Following the attack on 8 June 2014, the Pakistan military launched a multi-step attack on terror hideouts in North Waziristan on June 15, nicknamed Operation Zarb-e-Azb, which means 'sharp and cutting strike', with combined Air Force and army offensive killing several high-ranking militants, including the commander of operations who coordinated the Karachi airport attack. Several foreign militants, many of them Al-Qaeda affiliates, were also killed. The USA also renewed their drone strikes on high-value terrorists on difficult mountain terrains with much success. Till that time, there had been strong protests against US drone strikes against Al-Qaeda and Taliban militants from Pakistani society, Islamic parties, and certain political groups. But unfortunately, strong public opinion against terrorists comes only after massive devastating militant attacks. A similar thing happened in Iraq. Even after almost half of the country became under the control of militants of Islamic State, the political leaders were fighting on who should lead the government. Ultimately, when they were united against militants, massive destruction had already happened and half of their country which they were fighting for rule had gone to the militants. Public opinion also follows a similar pattern.

Modern terrorists are not only masters of tactical military victory but they also possess a good intelligence network. Also, they try all methods to gain control, including bribery, luring and the usual standard weapon of threat. It is also interesting that terrorist threats have more strength as they are not bound to any principle and are not challengeable in contrast to government rules. So people are generally forced to follow them. Almost in all terrorized areas, when the terrorists initially conquer an area, they first try to gain local support. When they spread their wings on a terrain properly, they then start their agenda of terror and primitive rules with their narrow interpretation of sharia and its forceful implication. When people realize the horror, they usually cry foul and blame the government or the international community. This happened when Taliban started their rule, with Al-Qaeda in Iraq and Al-Qaeda–related groups in Syria, Somalia, Chechnya, Mali, and Yemen.

On almost all occasions, talks and compromises with militants are counterproductive. They use the ceasefire opportunity to regroup, acquire more arms, spread to more areas, and increase their demands from time to time. Just before the Karachi attacks in 2014, the Pakistan government was seriously holding talks with Taliban militants. Many were not optimistic of the talks, as on several past occasions, militants had used those talks to their advantage, helping them spread. During the course of talks, the Taliban unilaterally withdrew from ceasefire with the killing of twenty-three Pakistani soldiers in their captivity and renewed attacks including those on Karachi, their largest city. War with a state has to be taken as an irrevocable crime and has to be tackled even at a small conflict level, not wait for a conflict to reach catastrophic levels, necessitating heavy casualties for state and militants. In practical terms, any human or material loss is a loss to the state. When terror spreads like wildfire, it may need massive, often brutal, efforts to suppress it when it reaches out of control. Prevention at all levels needs to be the key. Preventing youngsters from becoming rebels of family and society is of great importance. Terrorism may offer great attraction with mutually supporting and caring ambience which youngsters lack at home and society. Sensing the budding of hatred; no matter whether religious, sectarian, or ethnic as any of which can lead a human to become a militant. In a new world with Internet, social media, fast connectivity, and flowing money and weapons for the cause of terrorists, the threat that one can become a terrorist is real, pervasive, and omnipresent.

For those fighting terrorism, two models of the antiterrorist success story stand out: the history of the Irish Republican Army (IRA) and that of LTTE in Sri Lanka. In the Irish scenario, IRA rebels were increasingly frustrated when they finally realised the futility of the violent struggle that was alienating even the people they were fighting for. They went for peace talks, and its leaders were released from prison, and both parties struggled together to forgo differences and settled the grievances finally by the Good Friday Agreement of 1998. Sri Lanka struggled with an organized insurgency and militancy from LTTE (Liberation Tigers of Tamil Eelam) for more than two decades, which controlled a major part of the country, constantly threatened central leadership, and terrorized the people with suicide bombings, assassinations, and piracy. It was eventually crushed with massive force with all their leaders eliminated and all sympathizers captured and isolated. Both worked well, but ruthless force attracts more condemnation. But for an organized militant group equipped with fighter planes, hundreds of suicide bombers, and warriors with cyanide capsules tied on their neck and able to strike any part of the country, whether it is a hospital, school, or religious place, the price of war and brutal force becomes a necessity. Unfortunately, a large part of society who failed to make a choice or were apathetic became victims of brutal state force. Essentially, that is the biggest threat of terrorism. To crush a few militants, the state needs to exert massive force, causing severe collateral damage. But no country should be under ransom by a few ruthless, misguided, or self-praising terrorists. Each situation needs careful assessment and wider support than just the hue and cry of state ruthlessness when the media portrays human suffering against befitting actions against terrorists. State agencies fall prey to the attack by society on protecting their society rather than getting sympathy which they deserve!

CHAPTER 12

Supporters and Missing Links

We were among them and the numbers of Qataris on the ground were hundreds in every region. Training and communications had been in Qatari hands. Qatar supervised the rebels' plans because they are civilians and did not have enough military experience . . . We acted as the link between the rebels and NATO forces.

Qatari chief of staff, Major-General Hamad bin Ali al-Atiya, on their involvement in the Libyan Revolution to remove Gaddafi and arming opposition long before other countries responded

In medieval wars, where soldiers and severed body parts were abandoned on war fields, vultures were plenty, and they flocked to the war zones from far-off places. Modern conflicts are also similar, but in a world where vultures are becoming endangered species, certain humans have taken their role. They come as supporters of democracy, protectors of Islam, custodians of a particular sect, and supporters of justice. They may come as advisers, religious leaders, mujahideen fighters, donors, arm smugglers, drug dealers, and professional helpers seeking hands-on experience in war fields. An established conflict may attract money, weapons, and even volunteers ready for advice or to fight or even just die as cannon fodder. Several countries and their intelligence agencies are looking for conflicts, not to solve a problem but to be a part of the problem. This is to take fame, dignity, importance, and most importantly, to fool their citizens about their regime's support of the institution of justice and restoration of religion even if it is a far-off country. Modern history is full of such examples. Now the Western world is almost convinced that supporting terror anywhere in the world may backfire some day.

246

But many oil-rich Middle Eastern countries that have still not become bitter victims of terrorism in their soil continue to meddle in armed conflicts, tearing down countries and their infrastructure until ultimate destruction, making them failed states and eventually a threat to the whole world. Terrorism, even those restricted to a small geographical area, may become a concern, even for an unrelated far-off country. Militant networks and the use of territories as recruiting grounds and sanctuaries can drag countries to many unpredicted conflicts. There is a risk of hijacking of flights or people during a conflict with another country, and there are dangers of fighting against such extremists and their retaliation. But in spite of such history, terrorist support in the world is still high. The US War on Terror concentrated on a select few countries, and designation of sponsors of terrorism was not as effective. Friendly countries or allies against terrorism turned out to be the biggest sponsors of terrorism. The world has evolved through many revolutions. But in a modern world with many peaceful modes of protests and local and international support for such cause, military struggles are seldom needed. Tactically, an armed conflict against a strong ruler or government force is a blunder in the era of modern warfare. Any powerful attack provokes a more powerful counterattack, eventually leading to mutual destruction rather than a clear one-sided victory. Moreover violent attacks distort public and international opinion and allow both groups to gain wider support, eventually making the conflicts more bloody and destructive. A largely peaceful protest in a large volatile country like Egypt brought an end to the decade-long dictatorial regime of Hosni Mubarak. On the other hand, a violent military attack with a host of supporters with an endless arms supply in Syria against the brutal regime of Bashar al-Assad polarized the country. Moreover, the brutal dictator's regime gained political and military support from other countries like Russia, China, and Iran with ruthless suppression of violent revolution. In spite of an almost complete destruction of the country, either side could not reach a decisive victory. On the other hand, in Egypt, when the peaceful revolution started with an overwhelming response from the public in spite of brutal suppression, they maintained calm. This is remarkable for a country with several armed groups and a history of many militant attacks. It caused even the guardian of the regime, the army, to switch over their loyalty to the people's favour, eventually replacing the regime with little bloodshed. In Egypt, there was an easy regime change with an intact country, people, and morale, but in Syria, an entire country was ruined. Several militants and sectarian forces are fighting for their piece of land and looting wealth, leaving millions poor and homeless, begging the mercy of other countries. It is leaving deep wounds in society which may need many decades to heal. The crucial thing which separates both these conflicts was that Egyptians were fed up with violence, extremism, and terrorism and chose not to follow its past and not to take any arms support from other countries, but unfortunately, Syrians became victims of donors with plenty of weapons and a little money only meant to maintain the fight. A glimpse into the foreign assistance in those conflicts may reveal shocking truths. The current political stand of many old supporters of extremism were mostly evolved in the last two decades of terrorism's history. Before these decades, many Western countries were bases and even international headquarters for several terrorist organizations.

In one of the early Al-Qaeda operations, Al-Qaeda and their Egyptian Jihad cell plotted an assassination attempt on Hosni Mubarak in Kenya. Mubarak narrowly escaped the attack, and his bodyguards were killed. The attack resulted in a heavy crackdown on EIJ, and Egypt extradited many of the involved terrorists. But the mastermind of the attack, Anas bin-Libi, was given political asylum in Britain with patronage from MI6. Libi, a tall man who looked similar to Bin Laden, was used as a decoy to Bin Laden when he travelled. Libi was also involved in the 1998 African embassy bombings. Egypt tried to extradite him, but the request was declined on the grounds that he would not receive a fair trial. In 1996, MI6 allegedly send Libi to Libya to assist in a plot by the Al-Qaeda cell to kill Gaddafi, which was believed to have been paid for by MI6. The plot was unsuccessful. Following this, Scotland Yard arrested him, only to release him shortly as he had already deleted his hard drive, leaving no evidence to implicate him. He became untraceable later. When the police searched his flat in Manchester, they recovered a handwritten manual for Al-Qaeda, which later became known as the Manchester manual. Libi was nabbed by US forces in a risky covert raid following the Libyan revolution. His arrest created uproar by the Libyan government and Al-Qaeda, notably Ansar al-Sharia. In 1999, Egypt released a list of fourteen most wanted terrorists, most of them associated with Al-Qaeda, Islamic Jihad, or Gama'a Islamiyya. After 9/11, British newspaper the *Guardian* reported on 28 September 2001, that seven of them lived in Britain. Two of them were given asylum in Britain and two others in Germany and Austria. None of them was reported to be arrested after the report. Many of them were exposed later after 9/11, and there was reduced support on growing antiterrorist sentiment across the world. Bin Laden himself tried to get British asylum in 1996 when he was facing deportation from Sudan. Islamic Jihad maintained their London office at least till the late 1990s.

A radical imam of a London mosque, Abu Hamza al-Masri was a leading supporter of GIA (Groupe Islamique Armé), an Al-Qaeda–linked militant organization in Algeria which conducted hundreds of attacks on civilians and security forces. They became so notorious than even Al-Qaeda could not accept their brutality. He was editing the GIA newsletter *Al-Ansar*. In 1997, due to protests from angry worshippers at the mosque where he preached, he was forced to stop editing and severe ties with GIA. He was an informer to British intelligence. Terrorist groups worked in Britain prior to 9/11 without much resistance, preaching and raising funds for many jihadi fronts in Afghanistan, Egypt, Chechnya, Bosnia, Algeria, Kashmir, Yemen, etc. After 9/11, crackdown on these groups revealed many secret plots. Apart from collecting money from donors, they had extracted money from government welfare schemes for jihad finance. The arrest of two cell leaders of terrorist fundraising among Leicester police recovered skimming machines used to steal details from credit cards and several boxes of unembossed cards from Visa and MasterCard used to make duplicate cards. The cards were used to purchase goods in other countries like Spain, and the group was estimated to have raised more than a million dollars. The group also created forged visas for those travelling to Afghan terrorist camps. Criminal money from fraud and racketeering was critical for terror funding from Europe involving fraudsters and shoplifting gangs. After 9/11 and several incidents of terrorist plots in British soil, Britain started a heavy crackdown on most terrorist cells.

Initially during the years of Afghan war against Soviets, there was widespread enthusiasm in supporting jihadists. On a meeting of visiting delegates of the Afghan mujahideen in the White House, then president Ronald Reagan said, 'To watch the courageous Afghan freedom fighters battle modern arsenals with simple hand-held weapons is an inspiration to those who love freedom.' Two decades after his comment, America sent its forces to Afghanistan to expel the same mujahideen from power. During that era, mujahideen fighters and their leaders had been given open access to US and European countries for treatment, fundraising, and recruitment. That was then the highest national security priority for the USA. A host of terrorists, including Omar Abdel-Rahman took asylum in the USA with active support from national security apparatus in spite of being charged for terrorism and existing entry restrictions in the USA. In other Western countries also, terrorist cells were seldom monitored. The 9/11 hijackers, including Mohamed Atta, preached, recruited, and prepared their team in an apartment adjacent to a mosque in Hamburg, Germany.

If the USA was desperately looking for an opportunity to punish USSR in the Cold War era with active participation of their security apparatus in the Afghan war against Russians; in Pakistan, authorities under Zia ul-Haq were preparing an entire nation and its population for the Islamist or jihadi cause. By 1979 Pakistan society became radicalized with Islamist organizations, and madrasas became a major focus for support by the government. The Pakistan army, which maintained a mostly secular character, was turned into a more religious character. Religious extremists in the army and ISI were promoted and given support for many clandestine terrorist organizations. So even after the future ruling governments wished to support the terrorist cause, a large part of establishment, a wide section of society and the education system became radicalized. It became difficult to revert, and they were even ready to fight back against the government. Thus, once preferred radical elements turned against the government. Two major incidents provoked the rise of the Pakistani Taliban, the Lal Masjid siege in Islamabad and military presence in tribal areas of FATA following the US invasion of Afghanistan and War on Terror. It was to flush out Taliban and Al-Qaeda terrorists to re-establish in the Pakistani territory close to Afghanistan after having been expelled from there. Though both actions were necessary for the existence of Pakistan, widespread public opinion against government action on its own people encouraged more militancy in a highly religiously charged atmosphere that existed in Pakistan at that time. Also, problems were worsened by the growing polarization in society, anti-US sentiments, Pakistani support for US, and the secularization process within Pakistani establishment. Extremist elements in establishments, including ISI, tried to whip up religious and practically anti-national sentiments, which became a substantial force enough to threaten the very existence of the Muslim nation of Pakistan. The events in Pakistan reminded all history students that when an idealism based on hatred is created, it is difficult to eradicate it without much bloodshed. Terrorism often behaves like a snake which bites back the creator and supporters when it matures.

Many societies, political parties, movements, government agencies, and even governments support terrorists with the aim of using them as proxies, to gain control or access to a different country or even to destroy another society or country. Terrorism has risen to such alarming levels due to constant support for them from various quarters. But once they establish themselves, they became self-existing, and self-financed and seldom need any further support. In that regard, terror support is like giving initial training and a loan to establish a business; once established, they no longer need advice from their guide or banker. Two countries from the beginning of Al-Qaeda–related terrorism maintained their forefront in terror support, Pakistan and Saudi Arabia. Both now project as mere victims of terrorism as there are more and more attacks, and constant vigilance is needed in these countries against their very own militants once they are supported at state level or, at least, society level. Fifteen of the 9/11 hijackers were from Saudi Arabia. This was not mere coincidence. Its society has traditional puritanical Wahhabi-oriented Islam with lots of political importance in the ideology and practically no political activism in the country per se. People and the state have to look for other avenues for their extra religious zeal, an opportunity to let out. The Saudi establishment must be convinced that too much Islamic extremism and terrorism in the country is an existential threat to the monarchy supported by a sponsored clergy. But such experiments and support are still possible in foreign lands like Iraq and Syria, especially for ISIS and all their past and emerging avatars. Saudi support was crucial at state level through its intelligence agencies and direct participation of a large number of volunteers. Saudis have proved to be much more welcome jihadis than those from any other society due to their strong willingness as suicide bombers and enormous money they brought along with them into terror camps. It is almost impossible that Saudi authorities were not aware that their citizens went out for jihad, and society contributed generously to the jihadi cause. They may vouch that one of their terrorists killed in a foreign jihad mission was one less on the execution list in the home country for terrorism with an additional bonus of freedom from their mischief in their home terrain. In the era of Arab Spring, too much alienation of clergy might have thought as a risk by preventing them from contributing or collecting donations in mosques and social gatherings. But in any case, ordinary Saudi citizens are facing discrimination in foreign lands for being citizens of Saudi, which is being among the list of radical- and terrorist-sponsoring countries. For jihadis, that may be a medal, but for peace-loving citizens hoping for freedom, choice, and peace among all people in the society, that is a great discredit.

Pakistan coordinated all activities of the mujahideen war against Russians in Afghanistan. Finally they chose to make Taliban the rulers of Afghanistan, even at the cost of near-total destruction of Kabul and other cities and villages. It was clear that Taliban was a formidable fighting force with clear tactics, experience, and goals, not just a procession of madrasa students (Taliban). A substantial number of the Taliban fighting force was composed of Pakistan army men. So naturally, when the US started the war against Taliban in Afghanistan, the Pakistan establishment was reluctant and confused. They allowed almost all top Taliban leaders to escape to Pakistan and develop sanctuary there. Many of the Taliban and Al-Qaeda fighters reached the border tribal area of Pakistan, called FATA (federally administered tribal area), where all rules and administration were done by tribal bodies. The Pakistan army never went there for any activity nor established any base. On compulsion from the USA during the War on Terror after 9 September 2001; after many negotiations with tribal leaders, the Pakistan army went to FATA with the intention to nab Al-Qaeda fighters who were setting their bases there. But quickly, tribes felt the army presence was an infiltration into their territory and assault on their authority. They tried to fight against the army and, later, against the wide section of Pakistani state and society. That was the beginning of Pakistani Taliban. Many tribal militias formed a loose coalition, which later came to be known as TTP (Tehrik-e Taliban Pakistan). The tribal warlords who had supported Pakistan all along its history including during the era of Afghan jihad and civil war, now became enemies of Pakistan. They had initial support from a section of the Pakistan establishment, mainly intelligence agencies, the army, and certain politicians. With the portrayal of the conflict as sectarian—as most of their members were ethnic Pashtun—the conflicts became more and more bloody. Al-Qaeda and affiliated groups gave them support, training, and fighters. Pashtun dominated areas and parties became their sympathizers. In spite of hundreds of deadly terrorist attacks across Pakistan, their former masters in ISI still supported them at various levels, as in frequent negotiations, avoiding actions against top leaders, covertly encouraging resistance against drone strikes, and anti-militant operations.

A wide section of the Pakistan army and intelligence agents harbours extremist ideas that support militants. Unlike politicians who can change overnight and move along the wave in tune with public opinion, international compulsion, or pure vested interests, these men in the army and intelligence who work at grass-roots level cannot change overnight. Once creators, custodians, and allies of those extremist elements; they cannot change altogether on a new political will. But now the militants in Pakistan, especially TTP, have grown beyond what their former masters wanted. They neither take orders from Pakistan anymore nor get significant financial or military support from government. They have reached a level which can threaten even the Pakistan army, one of the major military powers stretched so big in the world while trying to rival their bigger neighbour, India. Also for the state of Pakistan, a nation of more than 185 million people alarming rise of TTP will be a shame. So in establishment, TTP and other militants are losing support as they become destructive almost to the very existence of their masters. It remains to be seen how the government, army, and intelligence of Pakistan tackle the terrorist monsters they created to fight against India, Russia, and Afghanistan by raising political and sectarian movements.

Insider help was clearly evident in frequent attacks on NATO conveys on the way from Karachi to Afghanistan. Also was crucial in the attacks on PNS Mehran naval base in Karachi in 2011, one of the heavily protected military establishments in Pakistan. Without detailed knowledge which is accessible only to top naval officers, militants cannot wield surgical destruction of high-value military equipment, including a P3C-Orion aircraft. TTP alone could not handle such sophisticated attacks and they got Al-Qaeda groups' help. The attack per se was retaliation against cracking an Al-Qaeda cell inside naval officers. The depth of penetration of Al-Qaeda among naval officers baffled the investigators who unearthed the plot. ISI was believed to be supportive of the 1999 hijacking of Air India flight IC-894. Al-Qaeda help was suspected in this hijacking, which was primarily organized by Jaish-e-Muhammed. It was eventually resolved after eight days at Taliban-controlled Kandahar after releasing three terrorists from Indian jail. In a later interview with CNN, the captain of the flight, Devi Sharan, whose experience and tactics were crucial in maintaining the safety of passengers, commented that the hijackers of the flight used a similar technique and modus operandi as used by 9/11 hijackers. Hijackers praised Bin Laden and used a knife to slit the throat of a passenger, and one of the hijackers told him that he had been trained on a simulator.

A former ISI chief and one of the major architects of the Afghan mujahideen war, General Hamid Gul was a vocal supporter of almost all major terrorist groups in Pakistan, including Lashkar-e-Taiba, TTP, and Taliban. He openly campaigned against NATO air strikes in Afghanistan and drone strikes inside Pakistan. In his many interviews following 9/11, he claimed that Osama Bin Laden was not responsible for 9/11 attacks. Israel and their intelligence agency, Mossad, and some renegade US Air Force officers were alleged to be behind the attack. He commented that Osama Bin Laden had no such means to carry out such an attack. He was not any ordinary mullah but a former army general and ISI chief, a man with wide knowledge of all terrorist movements in the Af-Pak region. He was a darling of the Taliban, similar groups, and almost all Pakistani militant groups, including TTP and Lashkar-e-Taiba. Many Pakistan observers believe him to be the 'Grandfather of Terrorism'. Following the US drones' strike, which killed the biggest anti-Pakistan terrorist of that time, Hakimullah Mehsud (who had a bounty of 5 million dollars from the USA and 50 million rupees from the Pakistani government), Gul along with many Islamic parties and terrorist organizations like JUD under Hafiz Saeed organized a multiparty rally on 1 December 2013 at Lahore under the banner of Difa--Pakistan Council, or Defence of Pakistan Council (DPC). Surprisingly, even before the religiously hardcore elements organized protests, cricketer-turned-politician Imran Khan and his party organized massive rallies in late November 2013 against US drone strikes and called for a blockage of the NATO supply route through Pakistan. He threatened to disrupt NATO convoys if the drone strikes were not stopped. His newly formed party, widely regarded as an aspiration of youths of Pakistan compared to other traditional feudal-based parties, was then ruling the crucial Khyber Pakhtunkhwa Province, which is the gateway to Afghanistan and FATA. They wasted no time organizing protests when the top Pakistani Taliban (TTP) leader was killed in US drone strikes. Some can argue that it was just a political move to gain votes at a time when the national elections were nearby. But as a politician viewed as modernist and secular, people expected more from him, though these tactics may have given him some local votes. But his involvement with TTP was revealed later. TTP though initially publicly opposed his anti-drone rally entering FATA, later declared protection for his rally. When the newly formed government at the centre in 2014 started a peace dialogue with TTP, they selected Imran Khan as their representative, along with others. Sensing trouble of labelling him as Taliban spokesman, Imran Khan declined the offer not to popularize his already known nickname of 'Taliban Khan'. His allegation was that drones strikes are unpopular in Pakistani tribal area and are killing innocents. Another reason was that killing Mehsud would further provoke Taliban attacks. Most of the public sentiments were due to TTP propaganda and their covert supporters. But practically, it was a spontaneous reaction of frustration to the killing of the head of TTP by Americans. All those people realised that unlike in the past, the drone strikes became more precise, targeting only high-value Taliban and Al-Qaeda militants, and their central leadership might be eliminated if allowed at that pace.

Support (direct or more often indirect) for terrorist groups in Pakistan from its army, ISI or political parties are their major lifeline to grow and exist in Pakistani territories. Many groups are in fact on the government payroll. The notorious anti-India militant group which was responsible for the Indian parliament attack and Mumbai attack in 2008, Lashkar-e-Taiba and its amir Hafiz Saeed received multi-level protection from Pakistani security agencies and his personal security. Their headquarters is in a sprawling campus in Muridke, called Markaz-e-Taiba, near Lahore. There are many schools and colleges with thousands of students learning and living there along with new recruits to the militant cause. Following the Mumbai attack in 2008, in which 164 people were killed, including six US citizens and 308 people injured, the USA declared a bounty of ten million against Saeed. The UN designated him as a global terrorist and his organization Jama'at-ud-Dawah (JUD) a terrorist group. There is an Interpol red-corner warrant against him.

Pakistan per se banned LeT, but it was allowed to operate under the banner of Jama'at-ud-Dawah (JUD), which is not yet banned. In spite of all this, Saeed moves around freely with dual protection by the police and his bodyguards. His institution receives huge financial assistance from the government, especially from the Punjab state government. This is apart from the ample support from Saudi Arabia, as they are followers of the Ahle-Hadith sect, the Pakistani version of Wahhabism. All successive budgets of the state government from 2009 allocated large sums in budget for the Muridke campus. It is the de facto headquarters of LeT and JUD. The gates of the same institution the lone survived Mumbai-attack terrorist Ajmal Kasab and hundreds of other aspiring militants went through during their recruitment and training on their journey to become a terrorist. To give a cover-up, this terror headquarters have many educational institutions and hospitals. A perfect model for a modern terrorist headquarters, effectively safeguarding from any possible attack from an enemy nation! It may get enough sentiments if someone attacks the area, including attacks by any future Pakistan government. The reason for funding the institution was cited by a minister: since the US and other governments asked them not to allow fundraising for JUD. Central government banned them and closed all their offices in principle. Then government itself came forward, took control, and funded them from the public fund! The JUD chief and their leaders came and went there as ever and ran the centre with not much botheration for finance, as they were sponsored by the government itself, thanks to an international ban. That is the state of affairs of government support for terrorists in Pakistan. Many terrorist groups, including TTP, are just like rogue sons of the big father state. When they misbehave with too much terrorist strikes inside Pakistan or do not heed their orders, they scold or slap the son but never kill or crush them completely!

Mullah Omer, much of his Afghan Taliban leadership council (Quetta Shura), and many members of Al-Qaeda like Ayman al-Zawahiri lived in Pakistan, some of them in urban centres. People were expecting one day some drone strikes in remote tribal areas of Waziristan would kill Osama Bin Laden if at all that was possible. At the end he was found living in a sprawling safe house which had been custom-made for him. About two dozen people worked or lived in that house which was located less than a mile away from the Pakistan military academy at the city of Abbottabad. Support for terror in Pakistan is still at the highest level of establishment. The kinship between terrorist groups and Pakistani establishment has not yet broken amidst growing pressure within Pakistan itself against terrorists. It has lost a prime minister (Benazir Bhutto) and thousands of lives of fellow citizens (more than 53,500, including 18,400-plus civilians, 5578-plus security personnel, and 28,362-plus militants) since 2003 from terrorism. In contrast, Pakistan has lost a total of 15,000 security personnel from their four major wars it fought against India from 1948!

Many Middle Eastern countries support terrorism on many levels. At least a small but significant section of society promote, venerate, and finance the terrorist cause; as they are believed to be part of protecting religion. The fact that these terrorists are killing mostly people from the same religion has not yet become a deterrent for these finances. It is as widespread as evidenced by rising terrorism in Syria, Iraq, and Maghreb. A suicide bombing on a police recruitment centre killed 127 people in al-Hillah in Iraq on 28 February 2005 when the country was struggling from lawlessness, looting, and robberies following the crash of Saddam regime. The family of the suicide bomber, Raed Mansour al-Banna, in Jordan gave him a heroic funeral which was reported in the media. This angered the Iraqi people, and thousands of people protested outside the Jordanian embassy in Baghdad, finally leading to recalling of ambassadors from both countries. In an interview, Hudhayfah Abdullah Azzam, son of Abdulla Azzam, recalled that money was never a problem for jihad. There were several people in the Middle East who donated earnestly for the jihadi cause in the earlier days of Islamic jihad. He personally collected more than million dollars in a day from donors. Some were ready to donate a substantial sum of their wealth, though they were not so rich. Later, though these became synonymous with bloodshed of their fellow Muslims elsewhere, the popular funding did not dry out. Al-Qaeda collected money from most Middle Eastern countries through a host of Islamic charities and private donors. This was from countries including Kuwait, UAE, and Bahrain, apart from the two major donors, Saudi Arabia and Qatar. Often, charity funds were diverted for militant causes.

Al-Qaeda had support at higher levels of regimes in the Middle East, almost throughout its history. In February 1999, a planned cruise missile attack on Bin Laden in the Afghan desert was cancelled at the last moment. Intelligence inputs, including satellite pictures of aircraft revealed that UAE (United Arab Emirate) crown prince Sheik Maktoum and members of the royal family were camping in the same area on a bird-hunting expedition hosted by Bin Laden. Similar incidents of royal family members of UAE and Saudi Arabia spending time with Bin Laden were reported. Several senior Al-Qaeda leaders like Khalid Sheik Mohammed and Ramzi Yousef had extensive high-level connections with the ruling class in Middle Eastern countries.

In 1998, a long-time Al-Qaeda operative in Yemen, Nasrallah decided to defect and told in detail about the location of Ayman al-Zawahiri and also the strength, tactics, and future plans of Al-Qaeda. He offered to spy more. But two radical members in the Political Security Organization (Yemen's bureau of crime) with militant ties handed him to Al-Qaeda, who planned to kill him. But he succeeded in escaping to Egypt and apparently told the agencies what he knows. Similarly, Islamic State and all Al-Qaeda affiliated groups maintained a good intelligence network and enjoyed insider help, which was key to their territorial success.

Iran had a complex relation with Al-Qaeda. Per se, they were against Al-Qaeda for being a Sunni terror outfit, and Al-Qaeda and affiliated groups often targeted Shias in Iran and elsewhere. During the initial years, Bin Laden and Al-Qaeda had contacts with Iranian agencies, and the concept of suicide bombing of Al-Qaeda might have evolved from Iranian influence. After the US invasion of Afghanistan in 2001, many of the Al-Qaeda operatives, including twenty to twenty-five people in leadership positions, reached Iran, including many in the top leadership like Saif al-Adel and two sons of Bin Laden. They were officially put on house arrest but were freed with watchful eyes on them. They were probably hoping to use them as bargain chips with the USA. But they were also turning over many of them to other Arab countries, notably to Egypt. But after January 2002 President Bush's speech on the 'Axis of Evil' criticizing Iran which he repeated many times thereafter; they stopped officially recognizing their presence and their whereabouts. It became difficult to trace terrorists in Iran, causing a major blow to antiterrorism efforts.

In relatively lawless Yemen, where Al-Qaeda had many sympathizers within the establishment and later carved out a geographical area under their rule, the Al-Qaeda presence is pervasive, even in capital Sana'a. Even during their Afghan era, Al-Qaeda had their major communications hub in Sana'a. As they headquartered in difficult terrains in Afghanistan, they needed a place with regular telephone services and major air links. In this regard, the Yemeni capital Sana'a was an ideal choice. With local supporters, they maintained the Al-Qaeda switchboard at a Sana'a house to receive and divert calls among various Al-Qaeda operatives worldwide, including Bin Laden, other members of central leadership in Afghanistan, and operatives in USA.

Among all the Muslim and Middle Eastern countries, the most neglected but crucial supporter of Al-Qaeda and related terrorism is Qatar. Qatar with enormous gas and oil reserves and a burgeoning economy, now seldom faces any bitterness of terrorism in their soil except a few small stray incidences. It dominates the current terror sponsorship, maybe far ahead of other established rivals like Saudi Arabia. As a close ally of US in the region and a trusted colleague in their War on Terror, its importance is generally kept as a secret or caution. It is the country with deep-rooted involvement in Libya, Tunisia, Syria, and Iraq. Taliban, Hamas in Palestine, and almost all Muslim Brotherhood branches in the world were supported one time or always by Qatar.

If any Islamic terrorist needs an asylum or any Islamist terrorist group want a foreign office, Qatar, in theory, is the ideal choice. The only reason of disinterest posed may be just due to foreign alienation. Qataris are carefully trying to avoid these allegations by emphasizing more on maintaining friendly think tanks and strong favourable media houses like Al Jazeera and also by projecting themselves as the mediator or champion of peace. But careful assessment of each Qatari involvement reveals a story which no one against terrorism can ignore. The early Al-Qaeda and Taliban-related news and videos were exclusively released by Qatar-based Al Jazeera TV, which baffled many. But most people dismissed it as mere coincidence and it just being a major Arab language channel. When the world was looking for alternative news media outside the grip of media tycoon in US, the spreading popularity of Al Jazeera was a pleasant welcome. But questions were raised on the focus on Al-Qaeda and the Taliban and armed struggle around the world where Islamic extremism was intertwined. It is a simple fact that terrorism thrives on publicity of any sort, and it was free and ample for Al-Qaeda and Taliban with frequent coverage of their activities and claims. After the expulsion of the Muhammed Morsi government by the army, following widespread public outcry and violent agitation by Brotherhood leaders, many journalists of Al Jazeera were arrested in Egypt and charged for anti-national activities. Questions were raised whether the army-backed regime was simply targeting the freedom of the media. The past history of the channel complicates the picture, where it is accused as a mere publicity outlet of terror groups and that the channel was used as a proxy or cover-up for Qatar's involvement in conflicts, misusing the freedom of media.

Even after a long period of the Karzhai government rule in Afghanistan and a massive hunt for its leaders, the Taliban surprisingly resisted disintegration, and almost all of its top leaders escaped unharmed. The US and Afghan governments became convinced that it is difficult to eradicate the menace of the Taliban and it will continue to remain a threat. They decided to talk to Taliban leadership through mediators. Pakistan, Saudi Arabia, and UAE are the traditional allies of Taliban;

but instead, Qatar was chosen. How is Qatar connected to Taliban? Taliban officially opened its Qatar office at Doha in 2012, and it acted as a base for all international negotiation. Few people have realised what the role of Qatar was in Afghan affairs. Qatar was crucial in the negotiation on the release of detained US soldier Bowe Bergdahl in exchange for five senior Taliban leaders held at Guantanamo Bay. Qatar bargained hard with the USA in favour of Taliban, for which they were successful. All five leaders were handed over to Qatar to remain in their custody for an year. In Qatar, they received a warm welcome. It remains to be seen how they are going to play in the new Afghan scenario where Taliban is increasing their attack on Afghanistan when the USA and their allies are pulling out from the field. The newly formed central government in Afghanistan may be weak and face strong political opposition. It is to be remembered that a weak, unpopular, and corrupt government in Iraq was the crucial background for the victory of Islamic State conquering about half of the land of Iraq.

The Muslim Brotherhood was a banned organization in Egypt during most of the years after its formation. But Brotherhood ideologues enjoyed the support of Qatar throughout these years. Prominent Egyptian brotherhood scholars like Yusuf al-Qaradawi are working with their base at Doha. When Brotherhood leader Morsi was elected as Egyptian president, Qatar greeted his government with a 7.5-billion US-dollar aid. There were many incidents of political and terror-linked violence following the removal of Morsi by its associates. Qatar still supported the Brotherhood and its leaders. The support of the Brotherhood was the major reason its allies in the Gulf Cooperation Council (GCC), Saudi Arabia, UAE, and Bahrain withdrew their envoys from Qatar in March 2014. These countries do not want Islamist parties like the Brotherhood to get roots and inspiration in their kingdoms.

Saudi Arabia was the main financier of many Islamic movements in the world, notably Al-Qaeda. But for a few years, Qatar started giving it a strong competition. Qatar and Saudi Arabia are Sunni-majority countries, and both follow the same conservative Wahhabi Sunni

Islam. Both supported the war in Chechnya and Bosnia to an extent. Chechen rebel leader Zelimkhan Yandarbiyev, who supported and might have coordinated many terrorist attacks in Russia, including the invasion of Dagestan along with Caucasus militants and the October 2002 Moscow theatre hostage crisis was on the run, looking for asylum. Finally he landed up in Qatar. He was under government protection in spite of an Interpol warrant against him on behalf of Russia. They denied his extradition to Russia. Following frustration, Russian authorities orchestrated an assassination attempt on him. Yanderbiyev was killed in Doha in February 2004 after living there for three years and organising support for Chechen militants from Arab countries. Even his former revolutionary colleague Maskhadov denounced him for importing Wahhabi Islamic radicalism in Chechnya, anti-state activities, and working with illegal armed groups.

When the rebels started fighting against the long dictatorial regime of Muammar Gaddafi, Qatar started financing and supplying arms even before any other country supported the armed struggle. Many of those arms reached the extremists. Even after the victory and execution of Gaddafi, they resisted disarmament and formed many militant groups controlling various parts of the country including ports and oilfields. The elected government after Gaddafi avoided open fights with such gangs in order to avoid bloodshed and due to their support from many groups, including Qatar. Qatar continued to finance and arm Islamist groups, including those associated with the Muslim Brotherhood in Libya like the 17 February Martyrs Brigade and other Islamist militia. After the regime change, Qatar corrected their previous position in Libya that they only supported NATO forces. The Qatari chief of staff, Major-General Hamad bin Ali al-Atiya, revealed in a public forum that hundreds of Qatari forces were there in Libya during the revolution, giving guidance and training, being actively involved in fighting, and maintaining military communication. Their military and air force support was crucial in the war. Mustafa Abdel-Jalil, chairman of the National Transitional Council (NTC) of Libya and de facto head of state from 5 March 2011 until its dissolution on 8 August 2012, commented that Qataris planned the war and led to victory. During the crucial final assault of the Libyan war on Gaddafi's Bab al-Aziziya compound in Tripoli in August 2011, Qatari Special Forces took the lead role.

Qatar's contribution in Libyan war was acknowledged by Libyans, as Qatar's flag was widely seen flying during and after the revolution in Libya. The old Algeria Square in central Tripoli was renamed Qatar Square. But the Qatar is itself a monarchy, with almost all powers vested with the amir. They supporting a democratic revolution in another Muslim country may appear strange. Their policy was to support democracy elsewhere to gain international importance; but any power dilution in the Gulf region has to be suppressed. They want to be projected as the champion of human right and freedom. But in their country, foreign workers work close to the level of slavery, as revealed by a former Nepalese ambassador. But for Libya, the Qatar support was helpful in the revolution to topple the regime, and also it became a long-lasting problem which ruined the country.

Qatar almost selectively supported rebels with an Islamist background. Due to their strength and arms power, they could become major players. Qatar's support for the 17 February Martyrs Brigade led by Abdel-Hakim Belhaj, who was close to the Qatar emirate and that made it the largest formation. This militia became the dominant militia in Libya, and they allied with Ansar al-Sharia and contributed many fighters to it. Ali al-Sallabi, an influential Islamist cleric who lived in Doha for four years, acted as a key conduit for weapons, vehicles, and funds from Qatar to the Libyan rebels during the conflict. He was a Salafist and close friend of Yusuf al-Qaradawi, the international spiritual leader of Muslim Brotherhood. Apparently to galvanize the Qatar's influence in post-war Libya, Sallabi started his own political party, the al-Watan (Homeland) party, but failed to make even a single seat in the next general election. During the time of transition Council (NTC), rebel commanders outside their circle were devoid of weapons and medical supplies. The head of NTC government, Mahmoud Jibril sent a delegate to Doha to lobby for weapons and supplies sent through them. Later, Qatar sent eighteen plane loads of supplies, but only five went through the NTC channel, and the rest were delivered to

Islamist rebels. With this, NTC and foreign observers realised the true intention of Qatar was to support the Islamist rebels at the expense of NTC, though it was the only internationally recognized governing body of Libya. The Muslim Brotherhood in Libya also started their political party, the Freedom and Justice Party (FDP). The Brotherhood was an existing party in Libya, but it was banned, and most of their leaders were in exile. It had strong support from expatriates. As a long-existing organization with a Salafist background, it had support from Qatar and other Gulf countries. In Libya, a country with no political activism allowed under Gaddafi for decades, the FDP made second position in the first general election after the revolution and later effectively controlled the government. There were several attacks on Sufi Muslim sites in Libya after the revolution by Salafists. Many tombs were destroyed, and some were converted to Salafi schools.

Many people expected a democratically elected government in Iraq after Saddam Hussein would bring peace, stability, and happiness. But unfortunately for its Arab neighbours with dictactors and kings, a prosperous democratic government in their neighbourhood was intolerable. So they started supporting all sectarian groups and rebels. Saudi Arabia and Qatar naturally supported Sunni groups, and to counter it, Syria and Iran funded Shia groups. The result was chaos, anarchy, suicide bombings, bomb blasts, and bloodshed. Former Iraqi prime minister Nuri al-Maliki overtly criticized Qatar and Saudi for 'waging an undeclared war' in his country.

Along with the Arab Spring, in other parts, Syrian rebels started organising against the brutal regime of Bashar al-Assad from March 2011. They started mobilizing people against the government, and many foreign nations became sympathetic to their cause and started supporting them. Turkey, Saudi Arabia, and Qatar became bigger players in this game. At one point, it was almost sure that the Assad regime was about to collapse. Western governments also started to supply aid to the fighting rebels. Suddenly the fight turned more violent and ugly. Al-Qaeda groups started to dominate the picture; fights became more ruthless and destructive. Ordinary citizens were massacred and tortured by Al-Qaeda. Many of the arms supplied by Qatar reached the Al-Qaeda affiliated groups, notably Jabhat al-Nusra, and they became a dominant opposition force. Saudi Arabia also started to compete with Qatar, encouraging the other rebel fractions of Islamist fighters, notably Al-Qaeda–linked Islamic State of Iraq and the Levant (ISIL). Both started fighting against each other. The liberal and secular nationalist Syrian opposition forces became marginalized. A peaceful revolution started along the model of Egyptian revolution and started getting momentum when a large part of the army defected for the cause, along with people from all strata of society. But it was hijacked by foreign countries' flooding with weapons to civilians. This led to violent counterattacks heralding an endless bloodshed and destruction of the country. Here also the existing Muslim Brotherhood in Syria attracted prompt arms support from Qatar and acted as a base for recruitments for various militants, eventually spoiling the revolution.

US warned Qatar about arming the Islamist groups. But they did not press hard for it since the USA recognized that Qatar deserved to have more to do with Syria and that it was a crucial partner with the base for many of their military operations. But Qatar on the other hand was smarter, not restricting themselves to Western allies. It acquired arms and assistance from all possible sources, including China and Russia. Now the Qatar oil money is believed to be financing much of the bloodshed in the Arab world, as in Iraq, Syria, Libya, and to an extent, in Egypt. Qatar openly supported freedom fighters, but at the same time, they preferentially armed extremist groups which were often rival to each other, undermining the cause.

When the issue of arming the rebels in Syria came, the USA vehemently banned the supply of shoulder-fired missiles, which if they reached terrorists' hands could be used against any civilian aircraft. But Qatar defied that order and supplied large shipments of those weapons to the Islamist fighters in Syria. Most of those missiles were acquired from China. Weapons from Qatar were so large that its affiliated group suddenly became a major armed fraction. When about thirteen Christian nuns and three maids were released from captivity from Al-Nusra fighters, one of the nuns who was representing the group openly thanked the Qatar amir for mediating and securing their release. Both Qatar and Syria publicly denied any link with Qatar's negotiation as part of the understanding not to expose their Al-Qaeda link.

Qatar is a country supporting the USA in its war on terror. But many former Al-Qaeda–affiliated banks, like the Bank-al-Taqwa had connections with Qatar. A Wikileaks cable revealed that Qatar, though a strong US ally of the US military for many years, was reported as 'the worst country in the region' in counterterrorism efforts and that it purposefully avoided acting against many known Al-Qaeda activists. Many shadow arms supplies in the Middle East and Islamic states can be traced to Qatar. Qatar was the first country in the Middle East to acquire large long-range military carrier aircraft, Boeing C-17, enabling them to carry heavy arms shipments to far-off areas. Many Al-Qaeda and Taliban leaders were given support in Qatar. Khalid Sheik Muhammed, 9/11 mastermind, was believed to have been briefly sheltered in Qatar. He was given a tip off when the CIA and FBI planned to arrest him in Qatar in 1996 under auspice of Sheik Abdullah Bin Khalid al-Thani, then religious affairs minister and later interior minister. Al-Thani also was believed to have hosted Bin Laden two times in his farm. Abu Musab al-Zarqawi was believed to have provided a safe house by Qatar.

Numerous charitable institutions based in the Middle Eastern countries were involved in the funding of Al-Qaeda and other Islamic terrorist groups. They usually use the pretext of supporting the welfare scheme and religious institutions. Some are genuinely involved in charitable operations, while some are mere front agencies for extremist support. Among the many groups, many of them were banned following 9/11. In spite of worldwide alert, some still survived and continued to work under many names and pretexts. One notable such Qatari charity by the name Qatar Charitable Society, was consistent in terror links. As per evidence submitted on a terrorism trial in US, the group was used by Bin Laden in funding Al-Qaeda's overseas operations as early as 1993. In 1995, the group's funds were used in an assassination plot of Egyptian leader Hosni Mubarak. During the Syrian war, the entity supplied shipments to Syrian Islamic Front (SIF). These groups formed networks of groups. But the Qatar charities were believed to have played the major role when Salafist Islamic militants known by the name Ansar Dine occupied Northern Mali and imposed discriminatory sharia law in 2014. These groups were not only well armed but well funded. They were able to spend on welfare schemes to lure the inhabitants to their cause during their early infiltration. The same strategies were used when militants started their presence in Syria, Tunisia, and Libya.

It is now more obvious that they all are supporting insurgents and terrorists but difficult to pinpoint the origin of funds and arms, as terrorists and their funders use innovative networks. But the support—or at least, silence—of certain countries and groups is clearer than before. Even if there is a reason to fight, one needs enough motivation and assistance to be part of an armed group. There are several organizations to fund, supply, and train armed fighters in the name of religion and political ideology. Often the ideologically inclined fighters come to help and liberate people from the oppressors. But the so-called sponsors just finance so as to create anarchy in a foreign country, many times their own neighbour. They promote distrust among people, gain political mileage, and try to avoid popular agitations in their countries by diverting attention from their internal problems. Pakistan has regularly used this tactic to divert people's attention from internal problems. With almost all political storms in Pakistan, authorities would play the card of the Kashmir issue publicly or artificially escalate conflict with India in its border. During his reign, Gaddafi supported Al-Qaeda and many associated armed groups. When the popular revolt started against him, these were the forces supported him, probably more than his own army. The same is true for Assad—when a large part of Syria was taken over by the rebels, Hisbulla mobilized their fighters to fight against the rebels and helped to reclaim many lost territories. Hisbulla has been supported and financed by the Assad regime for a long time. Similarly, though its neighbours are struggling hard in their fight against terrorists, Qatar has hardly experienced any terrorist activity in their soil.

Stories of neighbours supporting insurgency with a free supply of arms for anyone willing to fight are frequent in armed conflicts. Qatar can be increasingly spotted in these situations, especially when Sunni Islamic ideology is a driving factor. An emerging fact is Qatar has become increasingly 'trusted by terrorists' and terrorists are more often funded by Qatar. It is surprising that a tiny nation of just about 250,000 citizens exert a wide influence in the lives of millions of people across several nations, becoming the 'financial capital of terrorism', if not the current political capital too. It has a say in much bloodshed in countries like Iraq, Syria, and Libya. In Syria alone, about 250,000 people have been killed since the uprising began and half of its population displaced from their homes. Through its global sponsorship of terrorists, their actions often pose a great unrecognized security threat to the world!

Terror support is evolving and changing over the years. Many ideologues and supporters are now turning away from terrorism after facing the same trouble in their own lands. Supporting insurgency in other lands was a widely misused strategy during the Cold War era and many border wars. But supporting radicals with heavily indoctrinated religious supremacy and hatred of other religions or ethnic hegemony is becoming a strategic blunder. In a new world of mass media and communication, spreading the venom of religious fanatism with weapons and money can backfire on a country or group. But many countries don't learn from the history of others and they need their own practical experience. That was one of the reasons jihadi terrorism has become so widespread and a pan-national menace. Many countries that fight against the problems once supported such activities themselves for their short gains. So more than labelling and targeting other countries as sponsors of terrorism, more friendly pressure, exposure, and awareness may be better strategies. Those countries ruled by dynasties and autocrats probably will resist themself from supporting the double-edged sword of religious terrorism.

Those donating their hard-earned money to terrorists usually don't think much about where their money ultimately reaches. They may not be aware whether that money kills the people praying to the same God, kills kids in their schools, or makes someone homeless and landless. Money reaching terrorists who buy bullets, guns, bombs, and suicide vests to kill people in markets, shopping malls, mosques, churches, and law-enforcing people who are protecting countries from criminals; is more often not the intention of donors. Also they may not indent to have an utopian kingdoms of religious paradise, where people are whipped, crucified, tortured, enslaved, and killed by masked men. Their rule of law is summary punishment with no lawyers or scientific criminal codes. Doing anything—from torturing, raping, or killing—is lawful, provided they shout God's name. This may not be the paradise modern religious people may be wishing for their sons, daughters, sisters, and mothers! Unfortunately, large parts of the world are controlled by terror gangs. There; children, including girls, cannot go to school. A slight change from the rigidly prescribed dress code is severely punished. Any vocal falsifier can make anyone a criminal, punishable to any extent. Religious freedom is strictly according to the dictate of the ruler. People are forced to fight, kill or be killed. Who was behind all these troubles? Was it the support of some countries, politicians, arm dealers, security agencies, the media, the general public, or the clergy?

Everybody is worried about stopping terrorism.
Well, there is a really easy way: stop participating in it.

Noam Chomsky

SELECTED REFERENCES

ABC News (2007). 'Giuliani's Ties to Qatar Raise Questions for Mr 9/11'.

al-Alam (2013). 'Riyadh Grants $300 m to Finance Syria's Transitional Gov't'.

al-Alam (2013). 'Who Heads al-Nusra Front in the Shadows'.

al-Alam (2014). 'Chechen Terrorist, Saudi Cleric on Front Lines in Syria'.

Al Jazeera (2014). 'US Soldier Freed in Taliban Prison Swap'.

Astill, James (2013). 'Bin Laden's Sudan Years'. *The Guardian.*

BBC News (2014). 'Guide to Key Libyan Militias'.

Blair, Charles P., and Straskulic, Robert (2014). 'Target Sochi: The Threat from the Caucasus Emirate'. *Bulletin of the Atomic Scientists.*

Brumfield, Ben (2012). 'Who Are the Pakistani Taliban?' CNN.

DAWN (2013). 'DPC Leaders Demand End to Drone Attacks in Pakistan'.

Dickinson, Elizabeth (2013). 'Follow the Money: How Syrian Salafis Are Funded from the Gulf'. Carnegie Endowment for International Peace.

Dressler, Jeffrey, and Hock, Issac (2012). Releasing Taliban Detainees: A misguided Path to Peace. Institute for the Study of War.

Garterstein-Ross, Daveed, and Y-Yelin, Aaron (2013), 'Uncharitable Organizations'. *Foreign Policy.*

Grare, Frederic (2014). 'Situation Report: Pakistan'. Carnegie Endowment for International Peace.

Gunaratna, Rohan. *Inside Al-Qaeda: Global Network of Terror.*

Gunaratna, Rohan, and Iqbal, Khuram.. *Pakistan: Terrorism Ground Zero.*

Henderson, Simon (2014). 'The Saudi Problem and the Head of the Snake'. *Foreign Policy*, March 28, 2014.

Khan, Haji Mujtaba (2009). 'Taliban Rename Their Group'. *The Nation.* Retrieved 30 March 2009.

'National Commission on Terrorist Attacks upon the United States 9/11 Commission'. Retrieved 13 August 2010.

Naval Postgraduate School Program for Culture and Conflict Studies. 'Who Is Who in the Pakistani Taliban: A Sampling of Insurgent Personalities in Seven Operational Zones in Pakistan's Federally Administered Tribal Area (FATA) and North Western Frontier Province'.

New York Times, the (2010). 'Leaked Cables Offer Raw Look at US Diplomacy'.

New York Times, the (2013). 'Taking Outsize Role in Syria, Qatar Funnels Arms to Rebels'.

New York Times, the (2013). 'Thousands in Pakistan Protest American Drone Strikes'.

Pall, Zoltan (2014). 'Kuwaiti Salafism and Its Growing Influence in the Levant'. Carnegie Endowment for International Peace.

Reuters (2003). 'Egypt Returns $2 Billion to Qatar in Signs of Growing Tensions'.

Robert-fisk.com (2001). September 14 Hamid Gul interview with Tehelka.com.

Sipah-e-Sahaba Pakistan, Lashkar e-Jhangvi, Bin Laden& Ramzi Yousef. B. Raman South Asia Analysis Group 484; 1-7-2002

Soufan, Ali. *The Black Banners: The Inside Story of 9/11 and the War against al-Qaeda.*

South Asia Terrorism Portal (2014). 'Pakistan Assessment 2014'.

Stein, Jeff (2010). 'The Audacity of Hamid Gul'. *The Washington Post.*

Telegraph, the (2011). 'Libyan Cleric Announces New Party on Lines of "Moderate" Islamic Democracy'.

Turkey News (2013). 'Al-Qusair Battle Marks Saudi Arabia's First Attempt to Lead Fractured Opposition'.

Turkey News (2014). 'Qatar Defends Foreign Policy over Persian Gulf Rift'.

Turkish Weekly (2014). 'Libya Publishes Parliamentary Election Results', Retrieved 1 August 2014.

Wehrey, Frederic (2013). 'What's Next for Saudi Arabia in Syria?' Carnegie Endowment for International Peace.

Washington Post, the (2014). 'Taliban-Held US Soldier Released in Exchange for Afghan Detainees'

Wright, Lawrence (2006). *The Looming Tower: Al-Qaeda and the Road to 9/11.*

INDEX

277

www.ingramcontent.com/pod-product-compliance
Lightning Source LLC
Chambersburg PA
CBHW030420290526
45786CB00001B/70